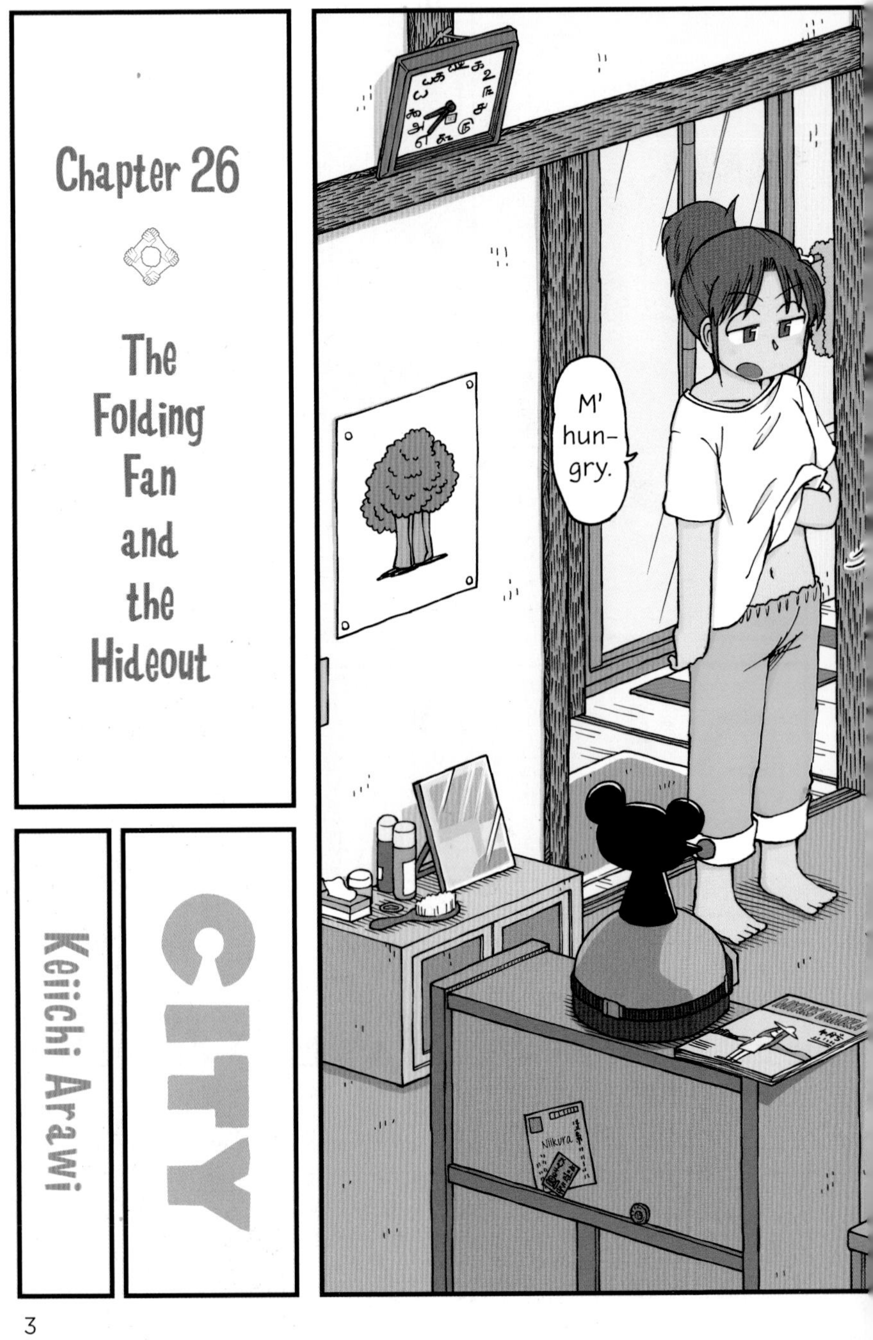
M' hun- gry.
Niikura

Chapter 26

The Folding Fan and the Hideout

CITY

Keiichi Arawi

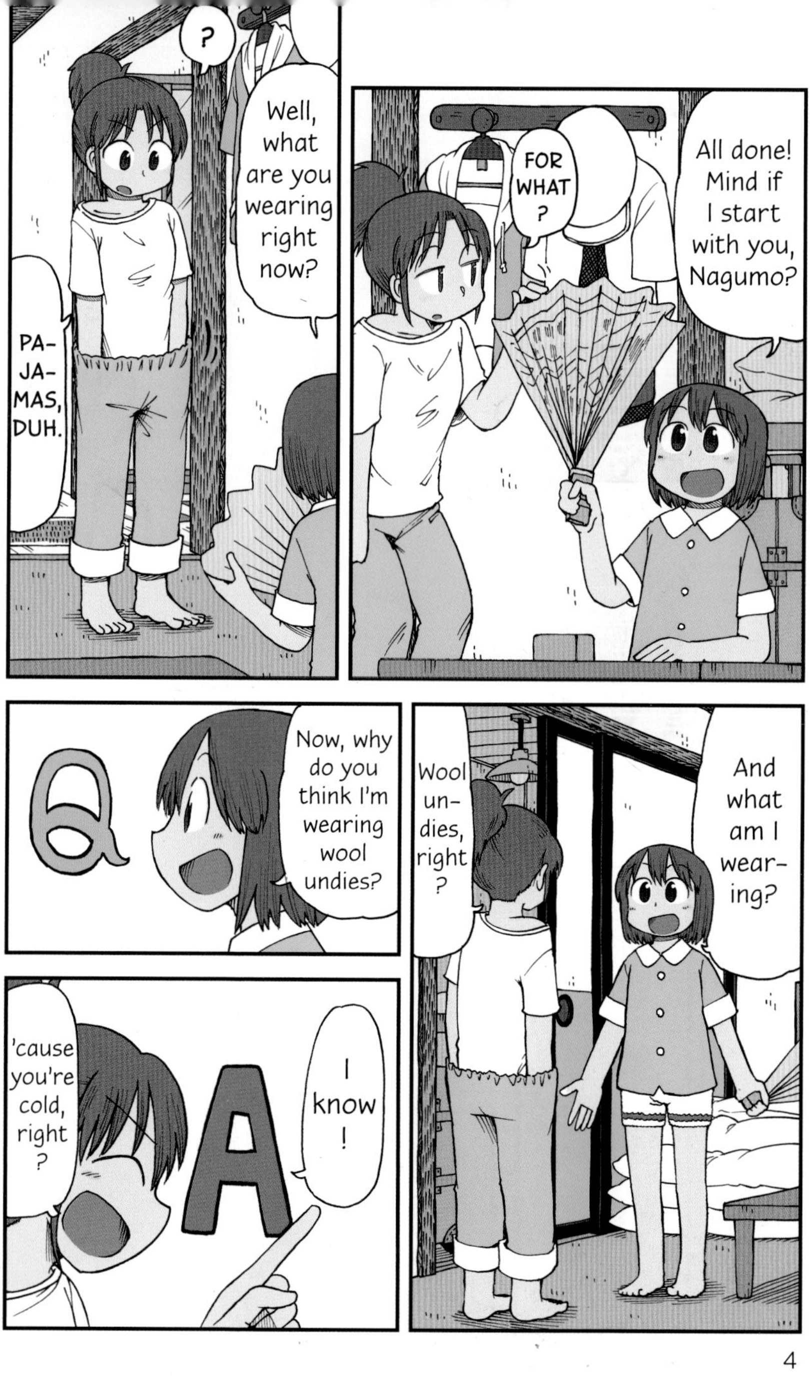
All done! Mind if I start with you, Nagumo?
FOR WHAT ?
?
Well, what are you wearing right now?
PA- JA- MAS, DUH.
And what am I wear- ing?
Wool un- dies, right ?
Now, why do you think I'm wearing wool undies?
Q
I know !
A
'cause you're cold, right ?

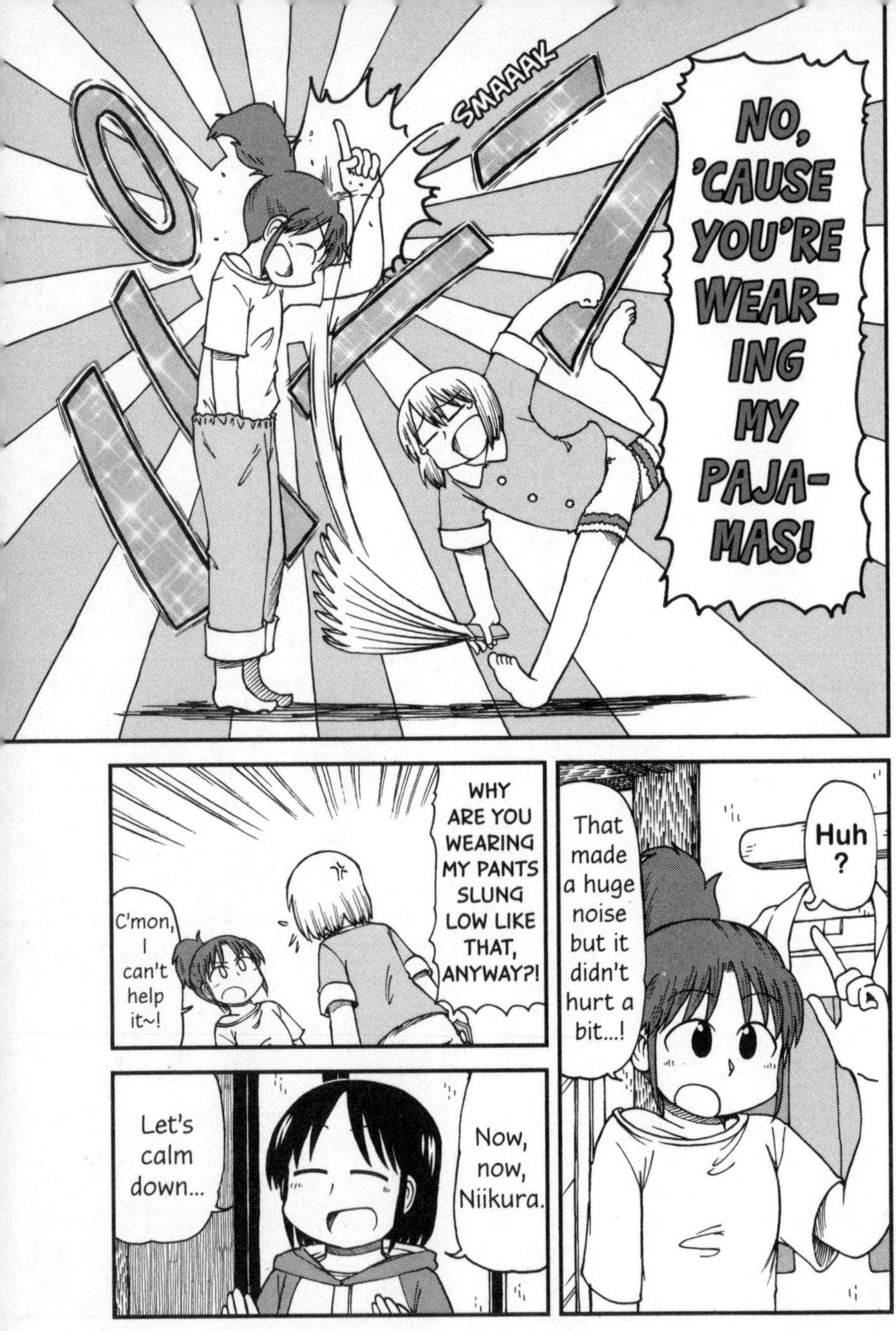
SMAAAK
NO, 'CAUSE YOU'RE WEAR-ING MY PAJA-MAS!
Huh?
That made a huge noise but it didn't hurt a bit...!
WHY ARE YOU WEARING MY PANTS SLUNG LOW LIKE THAT, ANYWAY?!
C'mon, I can't help it~!
Now, now, Niikura.
Let's calm down...

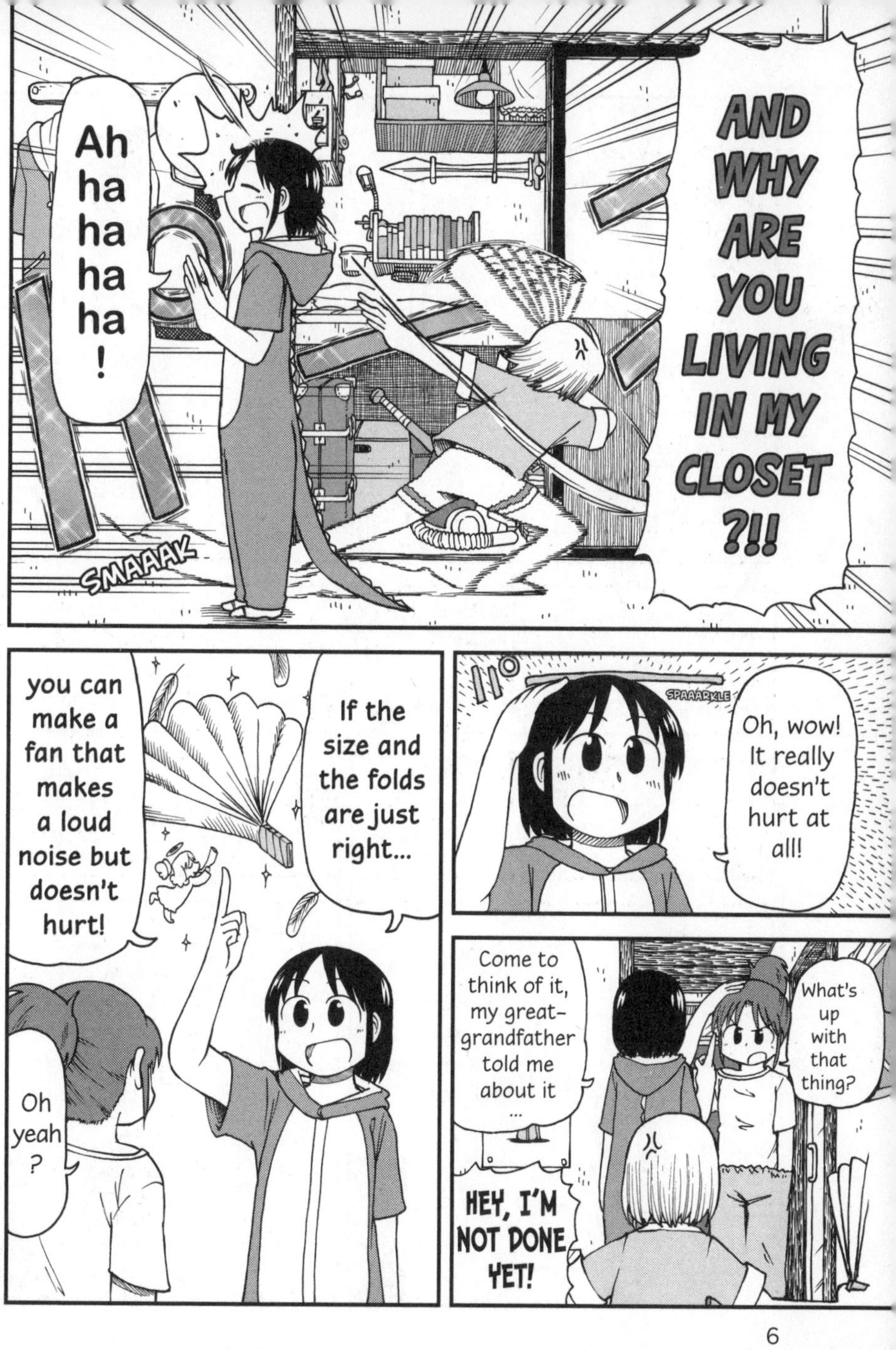
AND WHY ARE YOU LIVING IN MY CLOSET ?!!
Ah ha ha ha ha !
SMAAAK
SPAAARKLE
Oh, wow! It really doesn't hurt at all!
What's up with that thing?
Come to think of it, my great-grandfather told me about it ...
HEY, I'M NOT DONE YET!
If the size and the folds are just right...
you can make a fan that makes a loud noise but doesn't hurt!
Oh yeah ?

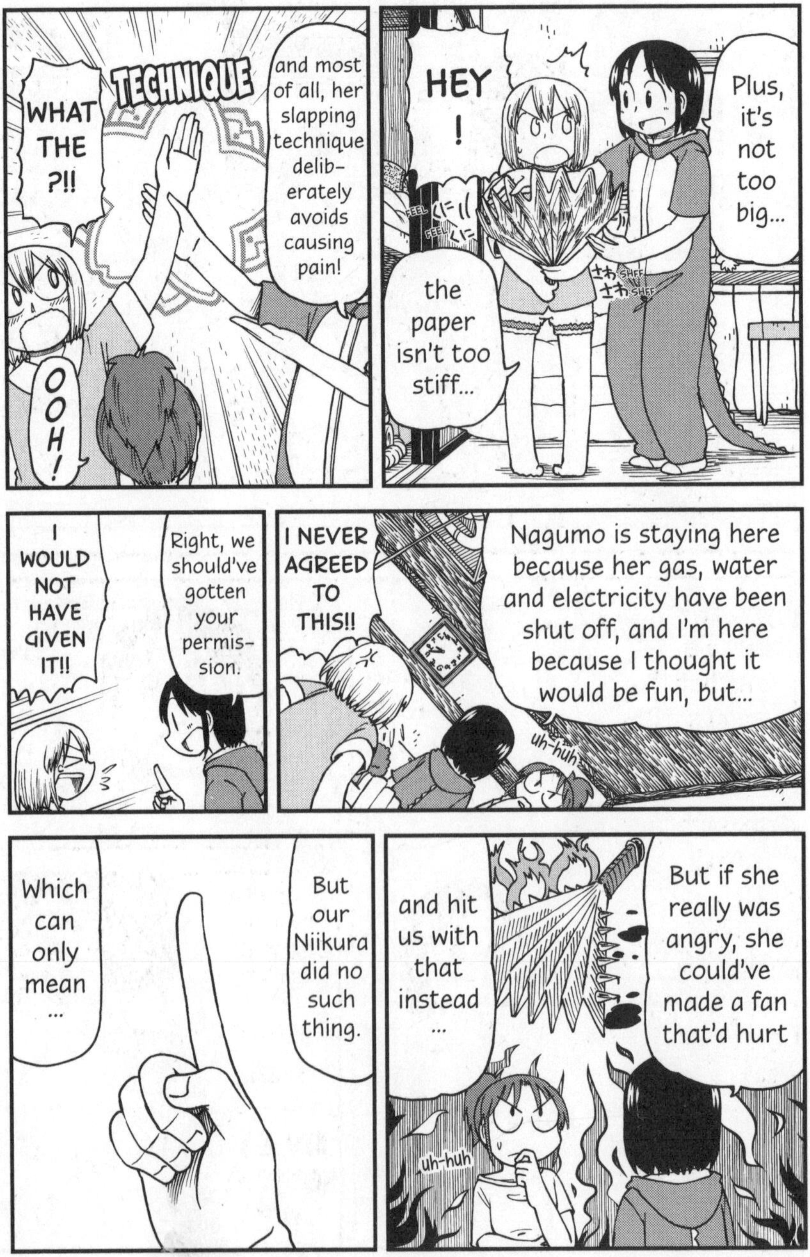

Plus, it's not too big...
HEY !
FEEL
FEEL
SHFF
SHFF
the paper isn't too stiff...
and most of all, her slapping technique delib-erately avoids causing pain!
TECHNIQUE
WHAT THE ?!!
OOH!
Nagumo is staying here because her gas, water and electricity have been shut off, and I'm here because I thought it would be fun, but...
I NEVER AGREED TO THIS!!
uh-huh
Right, we should've gotten your permis-sion.
I WOULD NOT HAVE GIVEN IT!!
But if she really was angry, she could've made a fan that'd hurt
and hit us with that instead ...
uh-huh
But our Niikura did no such thing.
Which can only mean ...

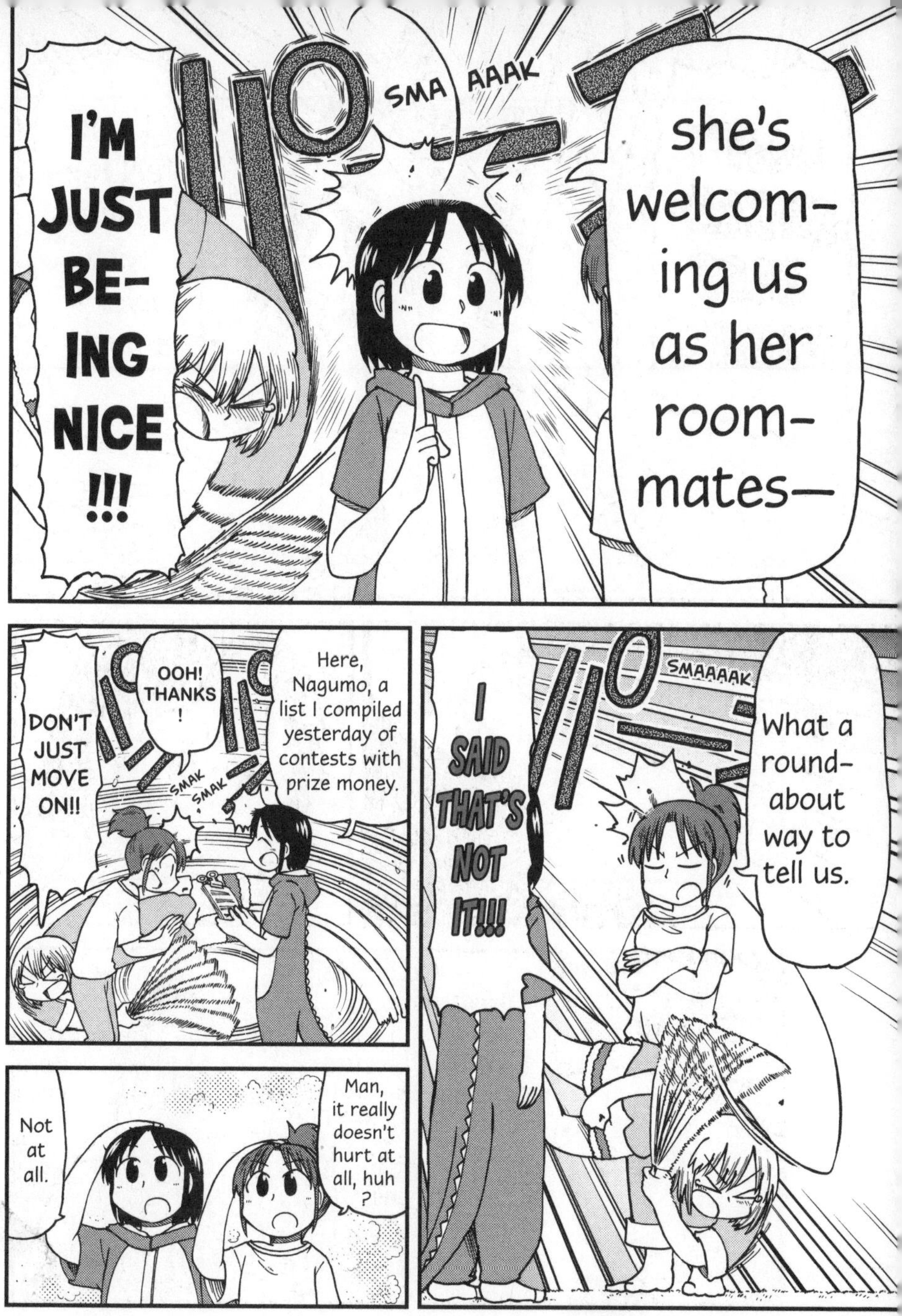
she's welcom-ing us as her room-mates—
SMA AAAK
I'M JUST BE-ING NICE!!!
What a round-about way to tell us.
SMAAAAK
I SAID THAT'S NOT IT!!!
Here, Nagumo, a list I compiled yesterday of contests with prize money.
OOH! THANKS!
SMAK SMAK
DON'T JUST MOVE ON!!
Man, it really doesn't hurt at all, huh?
Not at all.

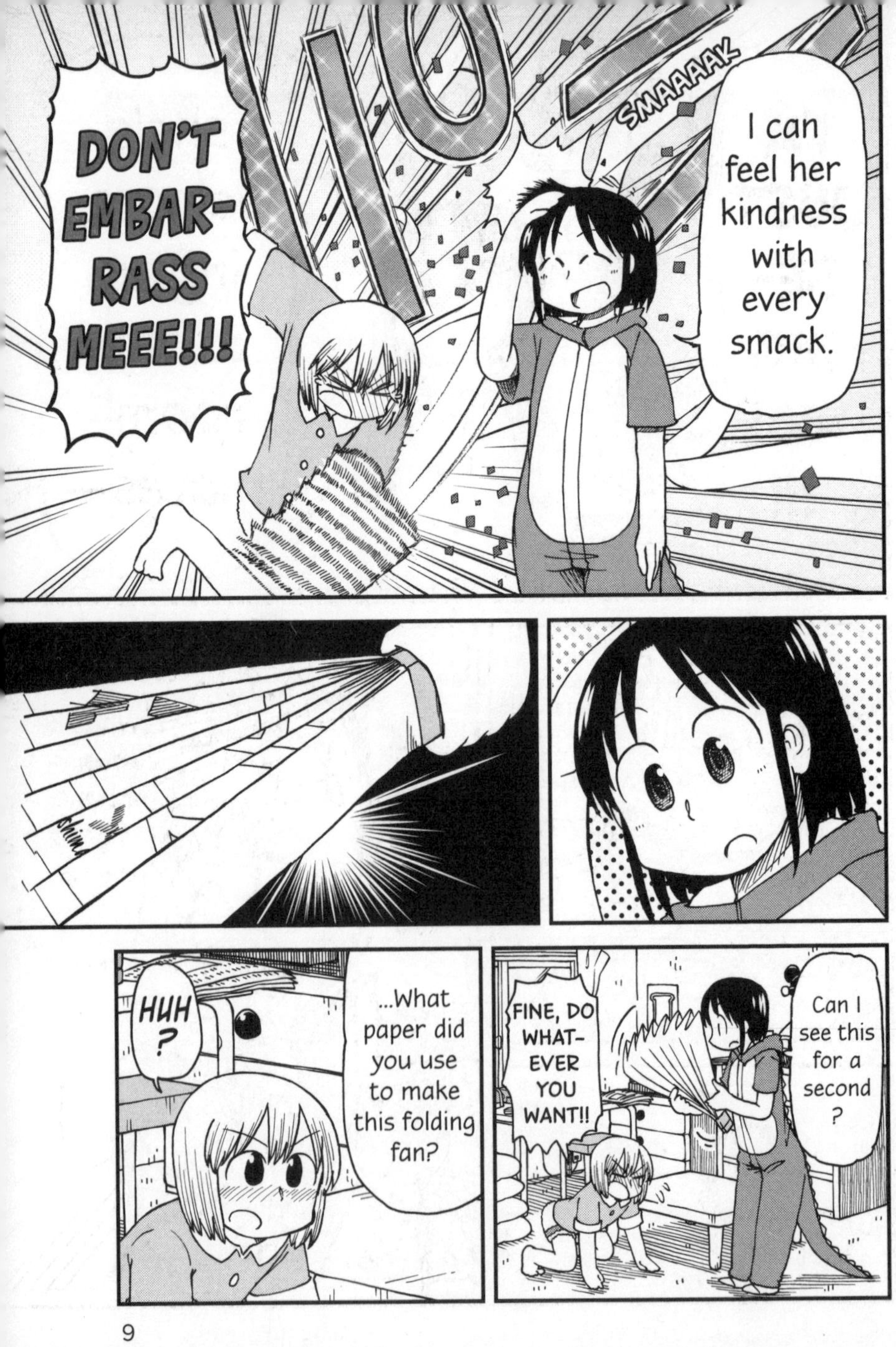
I can feel her kindness with every smack.
SMAAAAK
DON'T EMBARRASS MEEE!!!
Can I see this for a second?
FINE, DO WHATEVER YOU WANT!!
...What paper did you use to make this folding fan?
HUH?

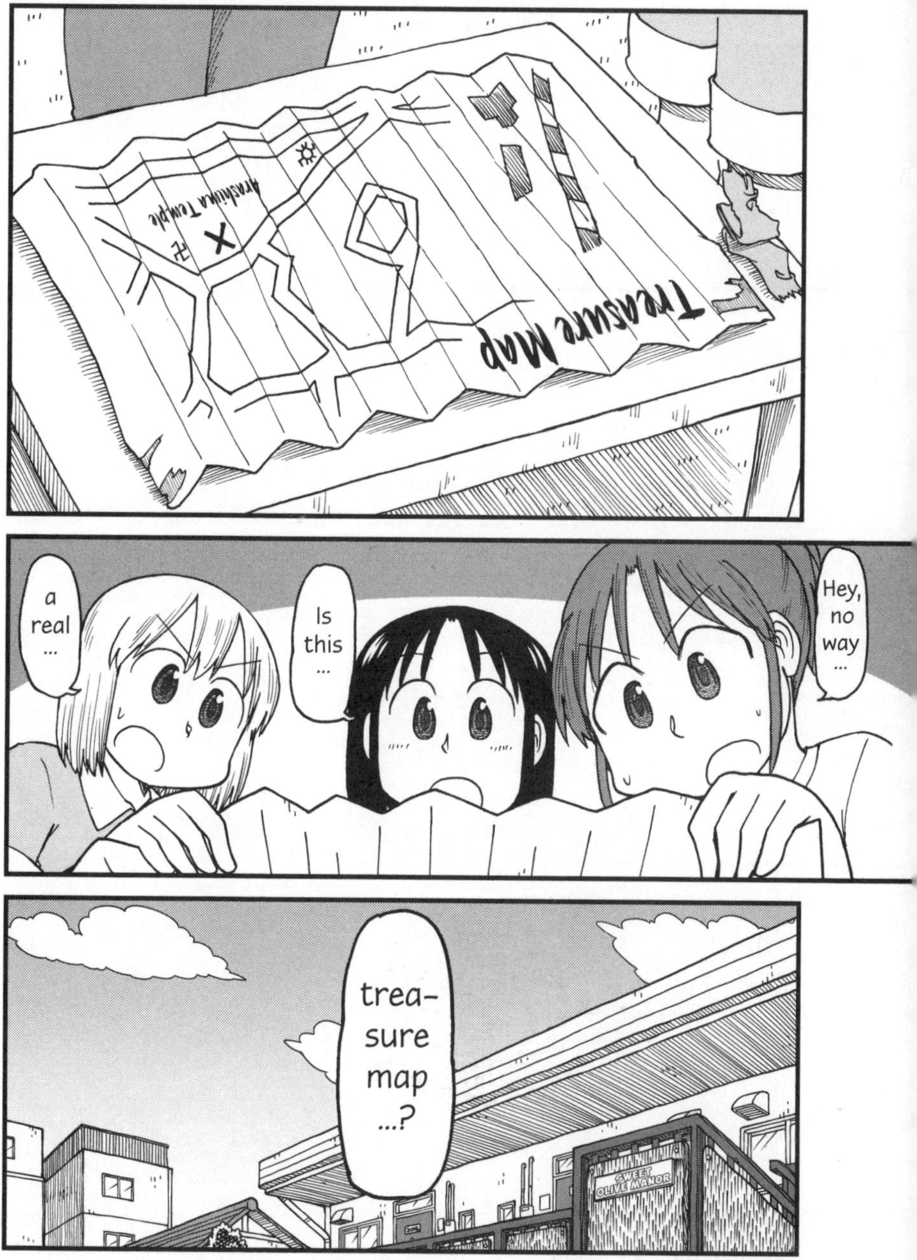
Treasure Map
Arashima Temple
Hey, no way ...
Is this ...
a real ...
trea-sure map ...?
SWEET OLIVE MANOR

CITY

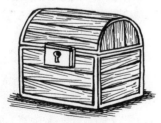

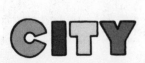

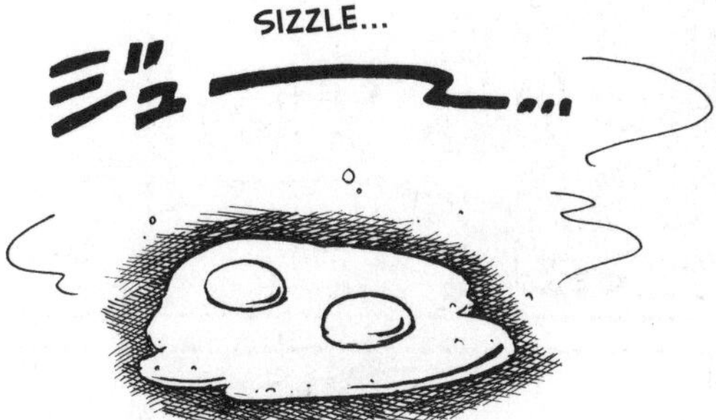
SIZZLE...
ジュー...

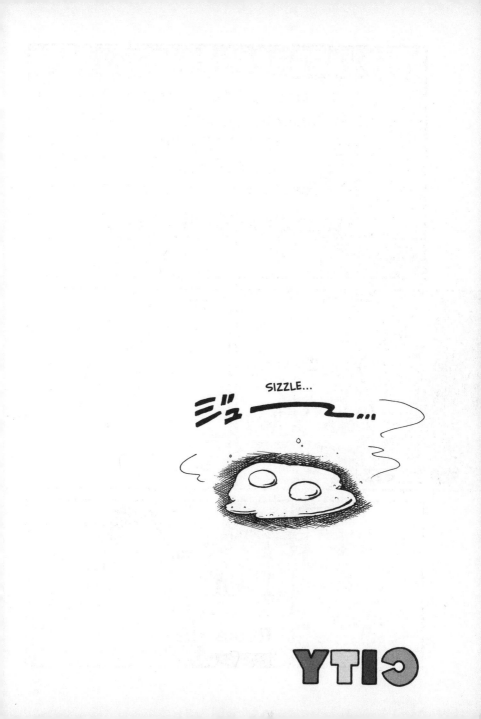

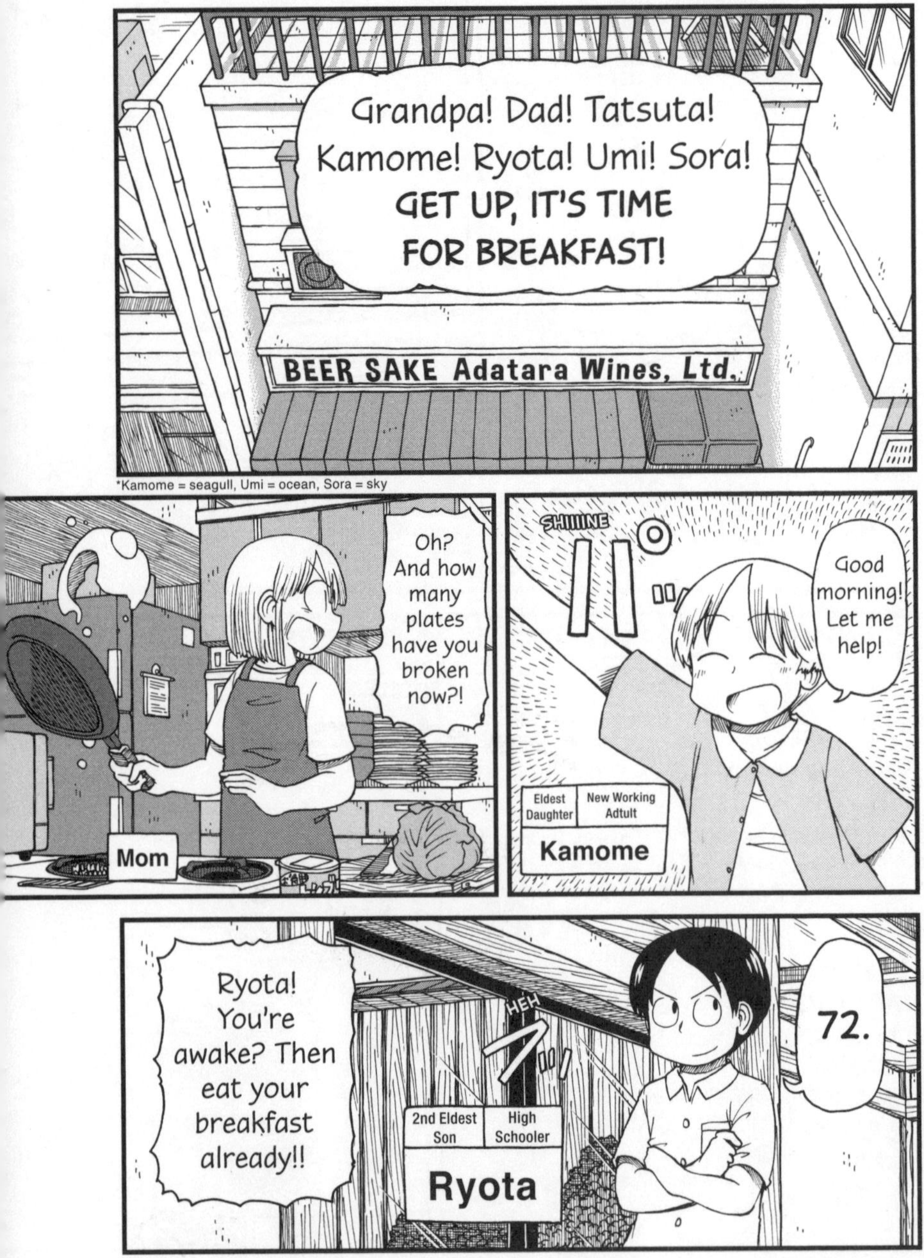
Grandpa! Dad! Tatsuta! Kamome! Ryota! Umi! Sora! GET UP, IT'S TIME FOR BREAKFAST!
BEER SAKE Adatara Wines, Ltd.
SHIIIINE
Good morning! Let me help!
Eldest Daughter
New Working Adtult
Kamome
Oh? And how many plates have you broken now?!
Mom
72.
HEH
Ryota! You're awake? Then eat your breakfast already!!
2nd Eldest Son
High Schooler
Ryota

*Kamome = seagull, Umi = ocean, Sora = sky

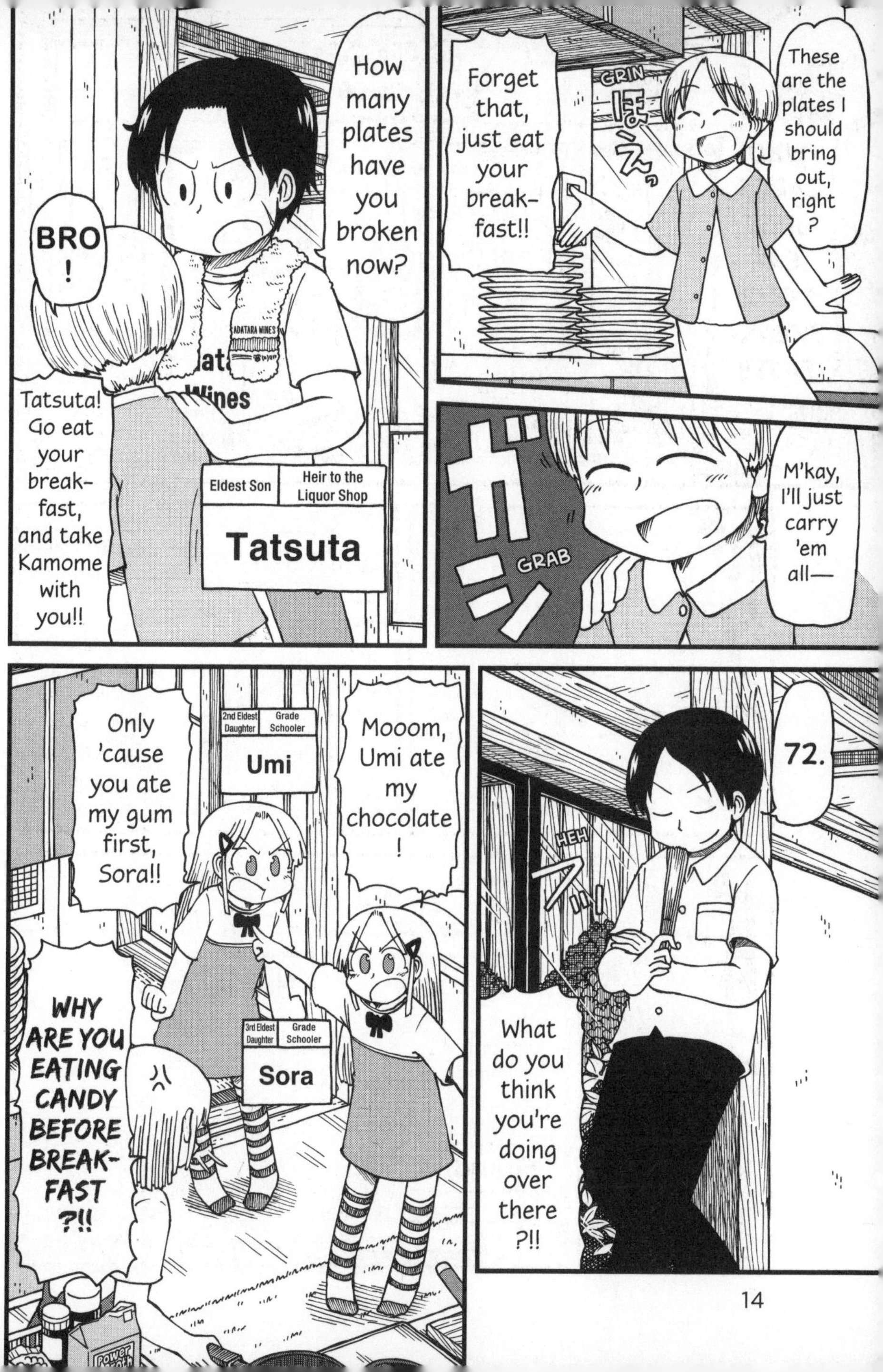

These are the plates I should bring out, right?
GRIN
Forget that, just eat your breakfast!!
M'kay, I'll just carry 'em all—
GRAB
ガシ
How many plates have you broken now?
BRO!
ADATARA WINES
Adatara Wines
Tatsuta! Go eat your breakfast, and take Kamome with you!!
Eldest Son
Heir to the Liquor Shop
Tatsuta
72.
HEH
What do you think you're doing over there?!!
Mooom, Umi ate my chocolate!
2nd Eldest Daughter
Grade Schooler
Umi
Only 'cause you ate my gum first, Sora!!
3rd Eldest Daughter
Grade Schooler
Sora
WHY ARE YOU EATING CANDY BEFORE BREAKFAST?!!

Chapter 27 Good Morning, Adatara

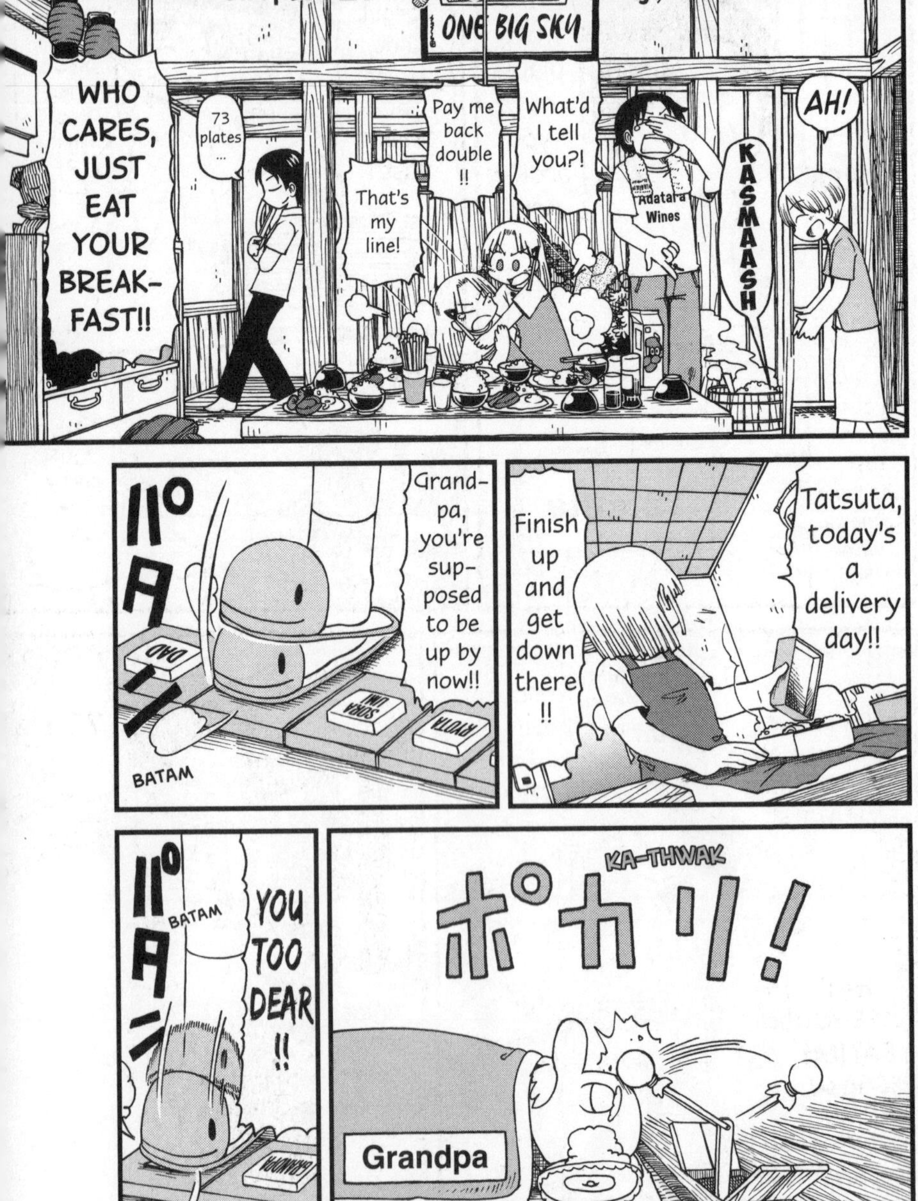

ONE BIG SKY
AH!
KASMAASH
Adatara Wines
What'd I tell you?!
Pay me back double !!
That's my line!
73 plates ...
WHO CARES, JUST EAT YOUR BREAK-FAST!!
Tatsuta, today's a delivery day!!
Finish up and get down there !!
Grand-pa, you're sup-posed to be up by now!!
ハア
BATAM
DAD
SORA UMI
RYOTA
KA-THWAK
ポカリ!
Grandpa
ハア
BATAM
YOU TOO DEAR !!
GRANDPA

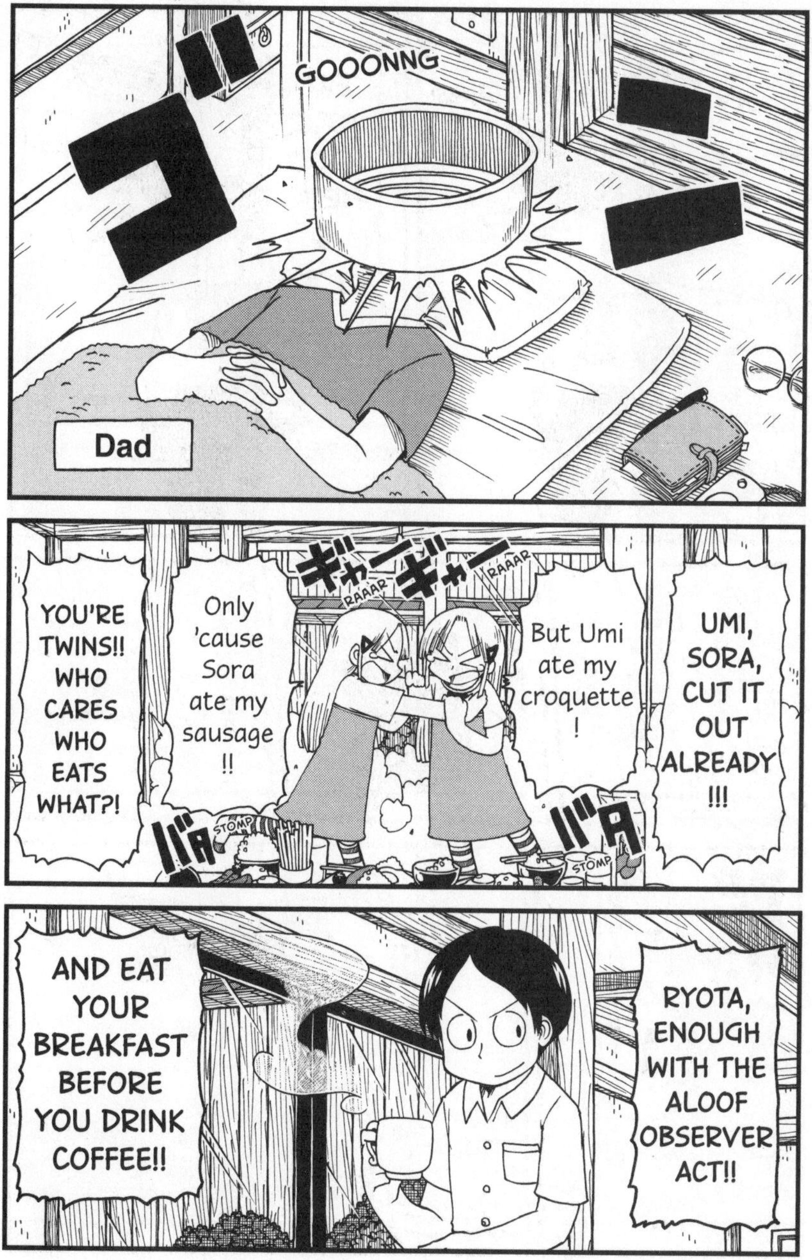
ゴーー
GOOONNG
Dad
ギャーギャー
RAAAR
RAAAR
UMI, SORA, CUT IT OUT ALREADY!!!
But Umi ate my croquette!
Only 'cause Sora ate my sausage!!
YOU'RE TWINS!! WHO CARES WHO EATS WHAT?!
バタ
STOMP
バタ
STOMP
RYOTA, ENOUGH WITH THE ALOOF OBSERVER ACT!!
AND EAT YOUR BREAKFAST BEFORE YOU DRINK COFFEE!!

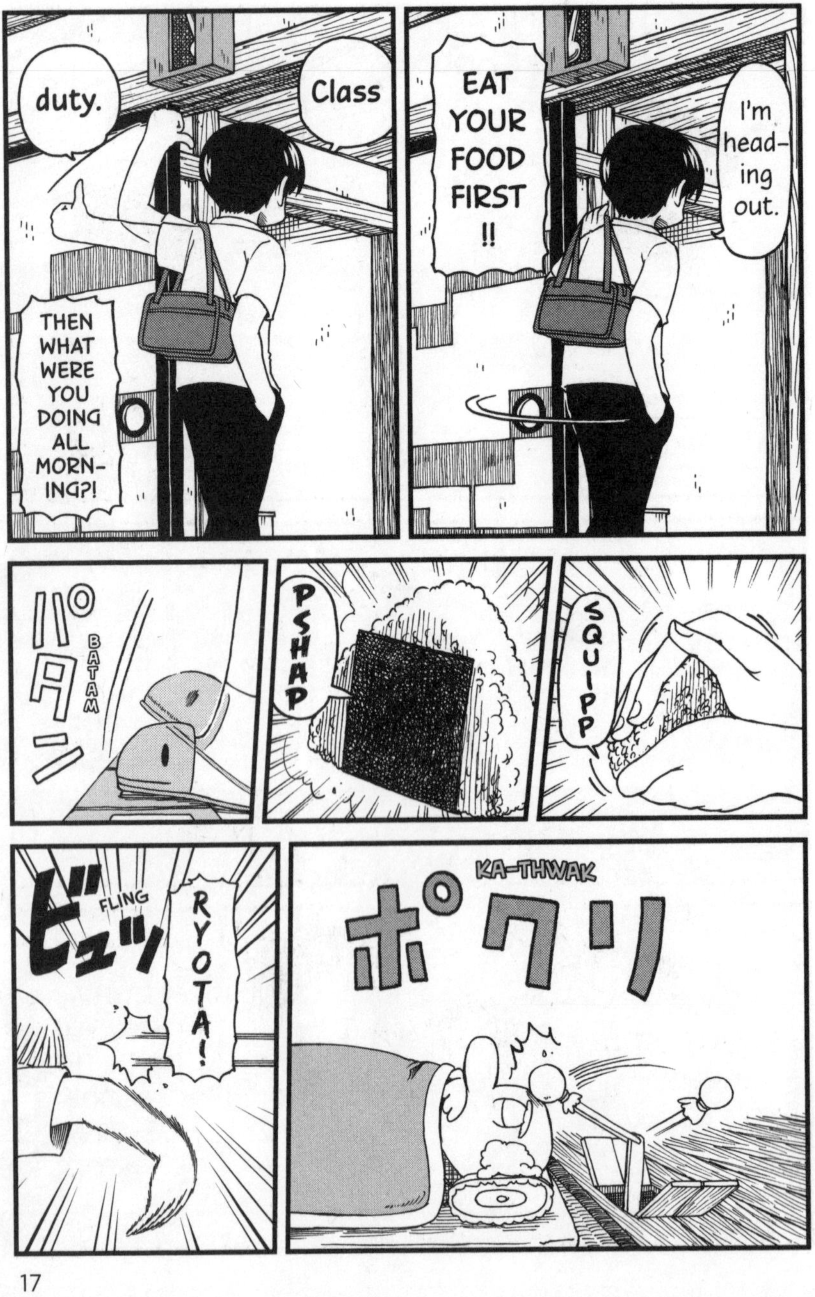
I'm head-ing out.
EAT YOUR FOOD FIRST !!
Class
duty.
THEN WHAT WERE YOU DOING ALL MORN-ING?!
SQUIPP
PSHAP
パタン
BATAM
KA-THWAK
ポクリ
RYOTA!
ビュッ
FLING

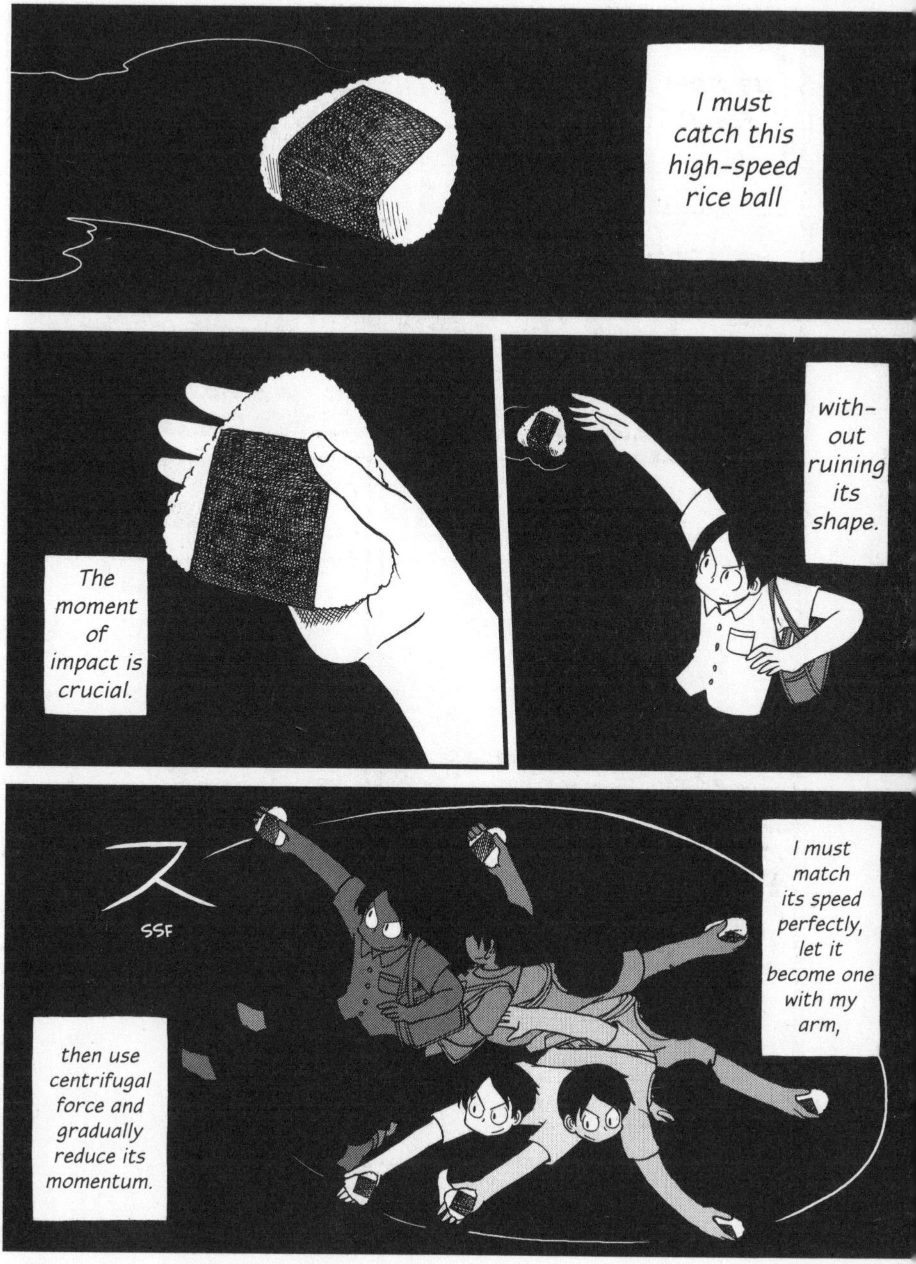
I must catch this high-speed rice ball
with-out ruining its shape.
The moment of impact is crucial.
I must match its speed perfectly, let it become one with my arm,
ス
SSF
then use centrifugal force and gradually reduce its momentum.

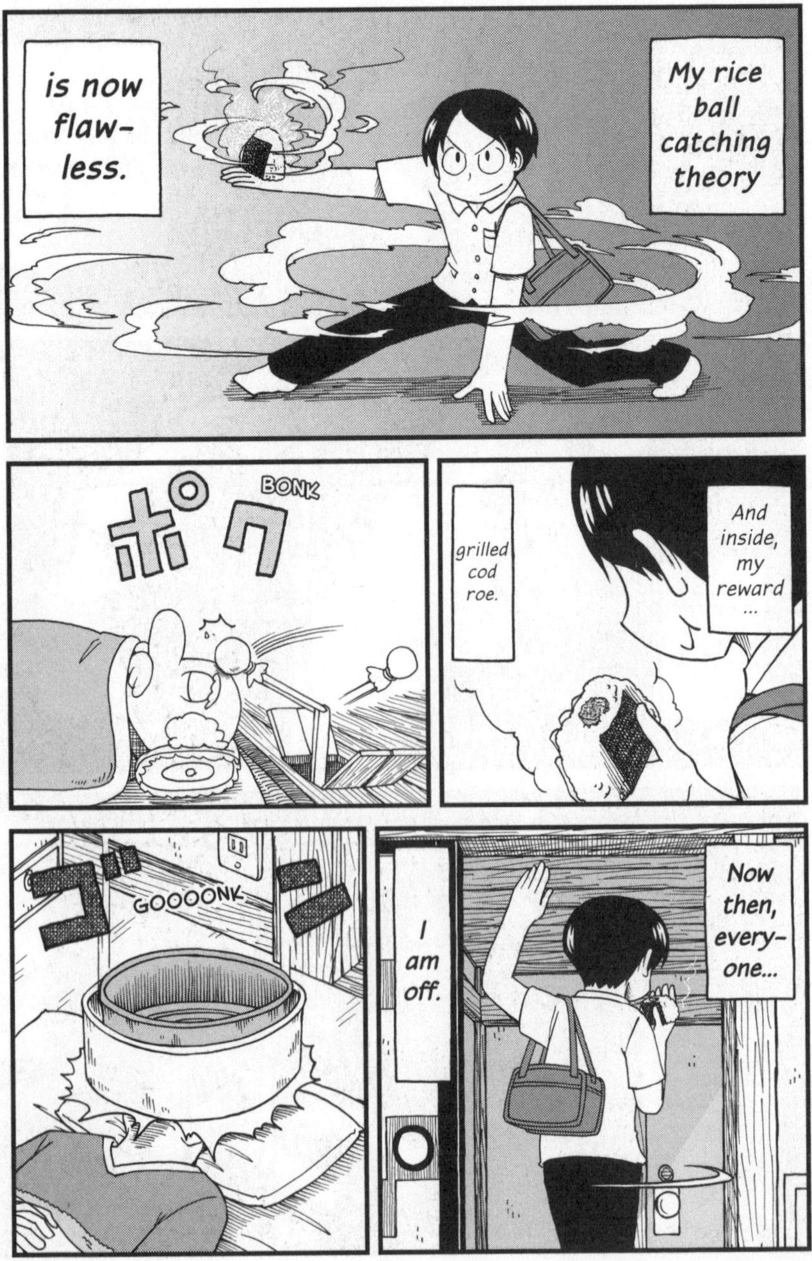
My rice ball catching theory
is now flaw-less.
And inside, my reward ...
grilled cod roe.
ポク
BONK
Now then, every-one...
I am off.
GOOOONK

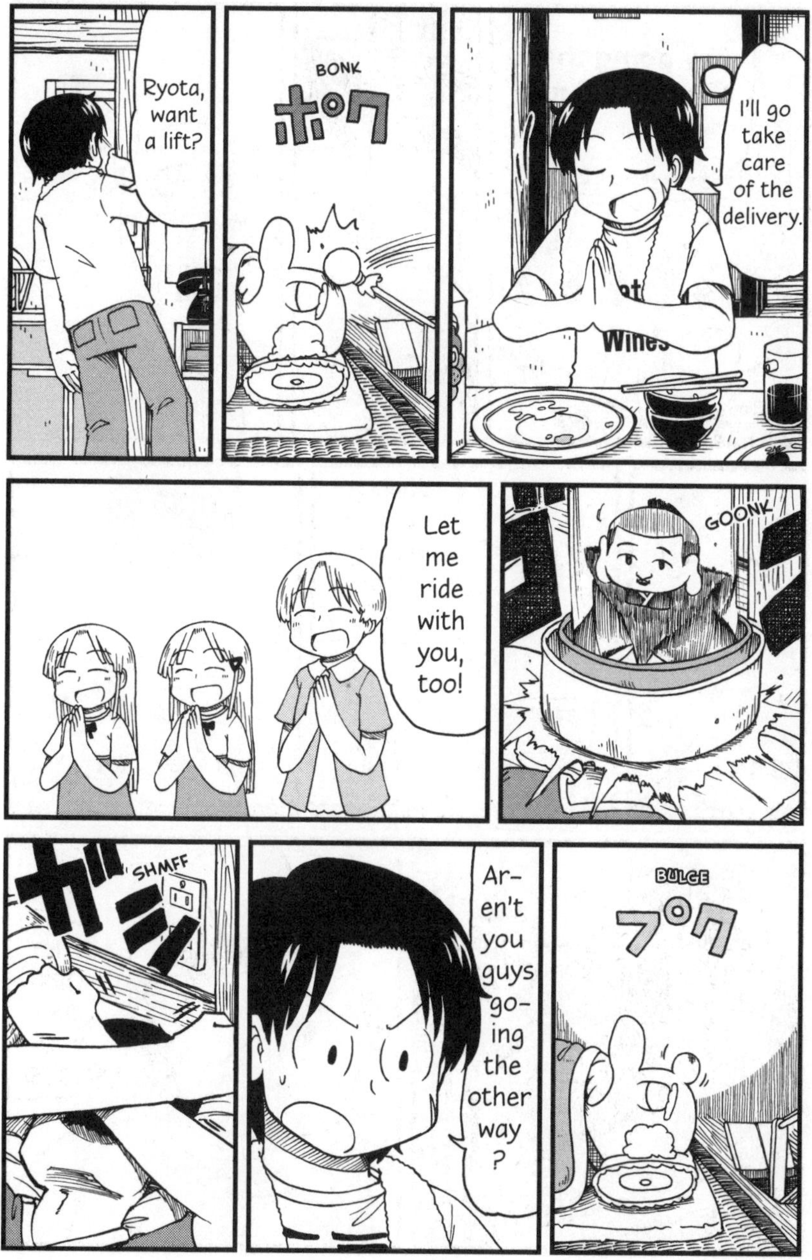
I'll go take care of the delivery.
BONK
ポク
Ryota, want a lift?
GOONK
Let me ride with you, too!
BULGE
プク
Ar-en't you guys go-ing the other way?
SHMFF
ガシ

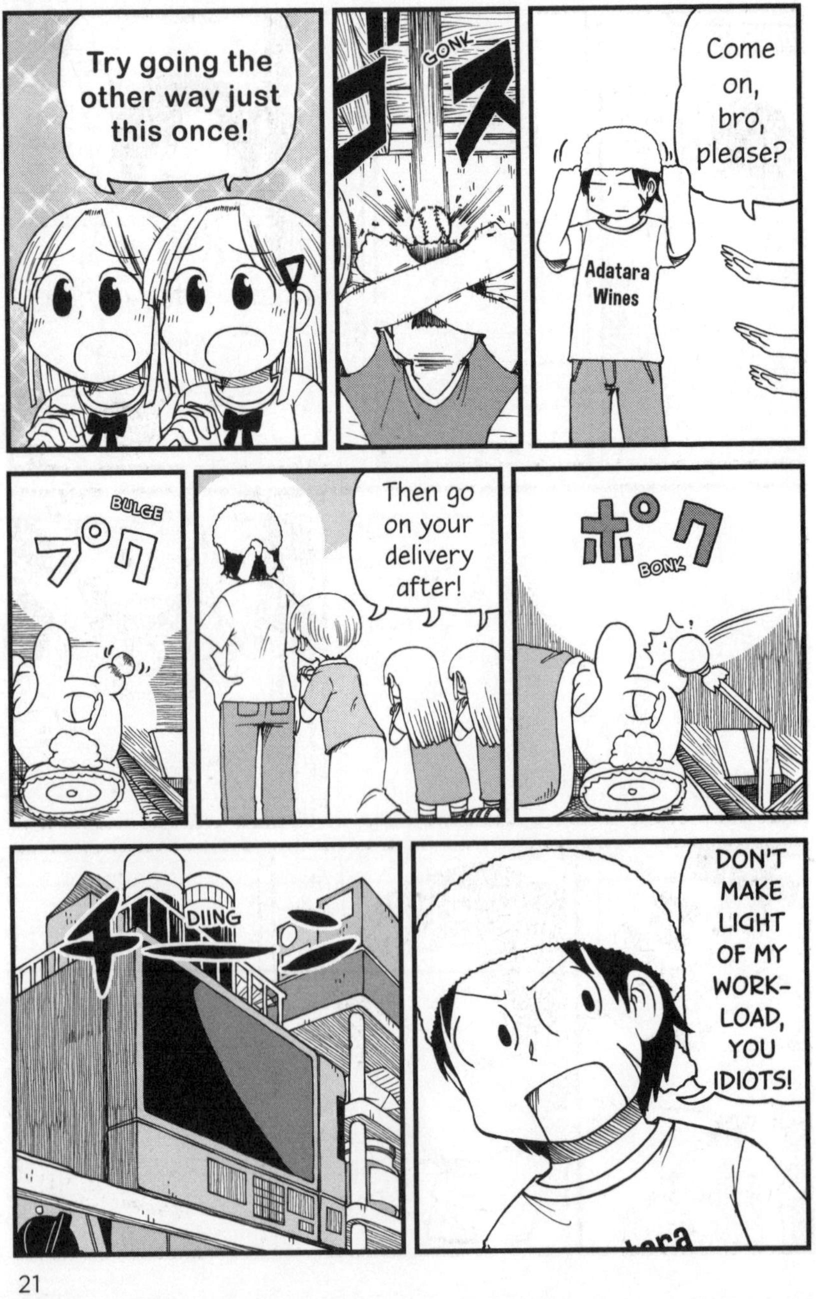
Come on, bro, please?
Adatara Wines
ゴス
GONK
Try going the other way just this once!
ポク
BONK
Then go on your delivery after!
プク
BULGE
DON'T MAKE LIGHT OF MY WORK-LOAD, YOU IDIOTS!
DIING

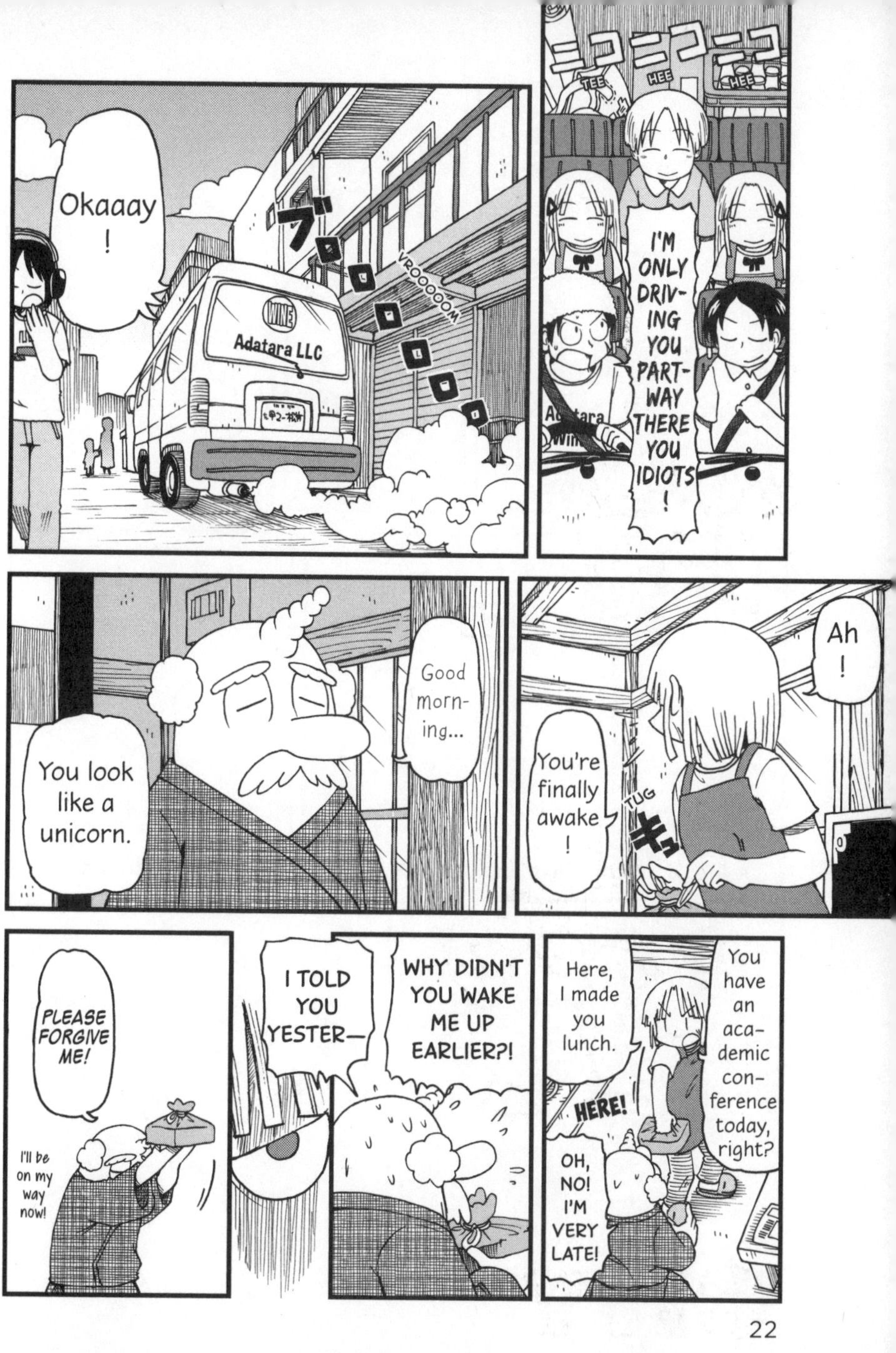
TEE
HEE
HEE
I'M ONLY DRIVING YOU PARTWAY THERE YOU IDIOTS!
Okaaay!
VROOOOOM
WINE
Adatara LLC
Ah!
You're finally awake!
TUG
Good morning...
You look like a unicorn.
You have an academic conference today, right?
Here, I made you lunch.
HERE!
OH, NO! I'M VERY LATE!
WHY DIDN'T YOU WAKE ME UP EARLIER?!
I TOLD YOU YESTER—
PLEASE FORGIVE ME!
I'll be on my way now!

MOM

DAD

CITY

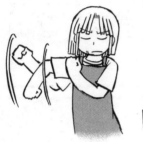

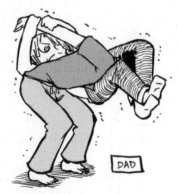

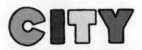

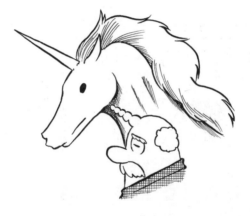

Unicorn

CITY

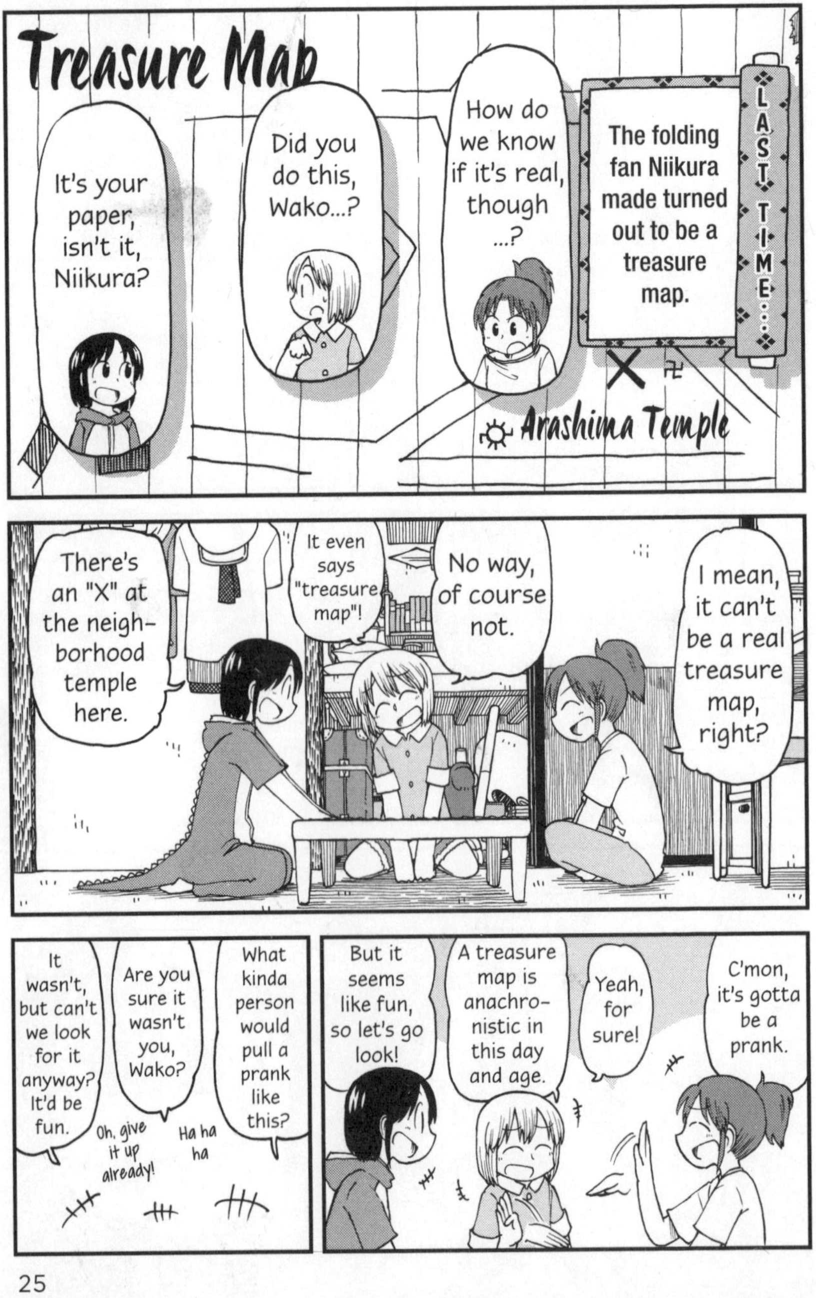
Treasure Map
LAST TIME...
The folding fan Niikura made turned out to be a treasure map.
How do we know if it's real, though ...?
Did you do this, Wako...?
It's your paper, isn't it, Niikura?
Arashima Temple
I mean, it can't be a real treasure map, right?
No way, of course not.
It even says "treasure map"!
There's an "X" at the neighborhood temple here.
C'mon, it's gotta be a prank.
Yeah, for sure!
A treasure map is anachronistic in this day and age.
But it seems like fun, so let's go look!
What kinda person would pull a prank like this?
Ha ha ha
Are you sure it wasn't you, Wako?
Oh, give it up already!
It wasn't, but can't we look for it anyway? It'd be fun.

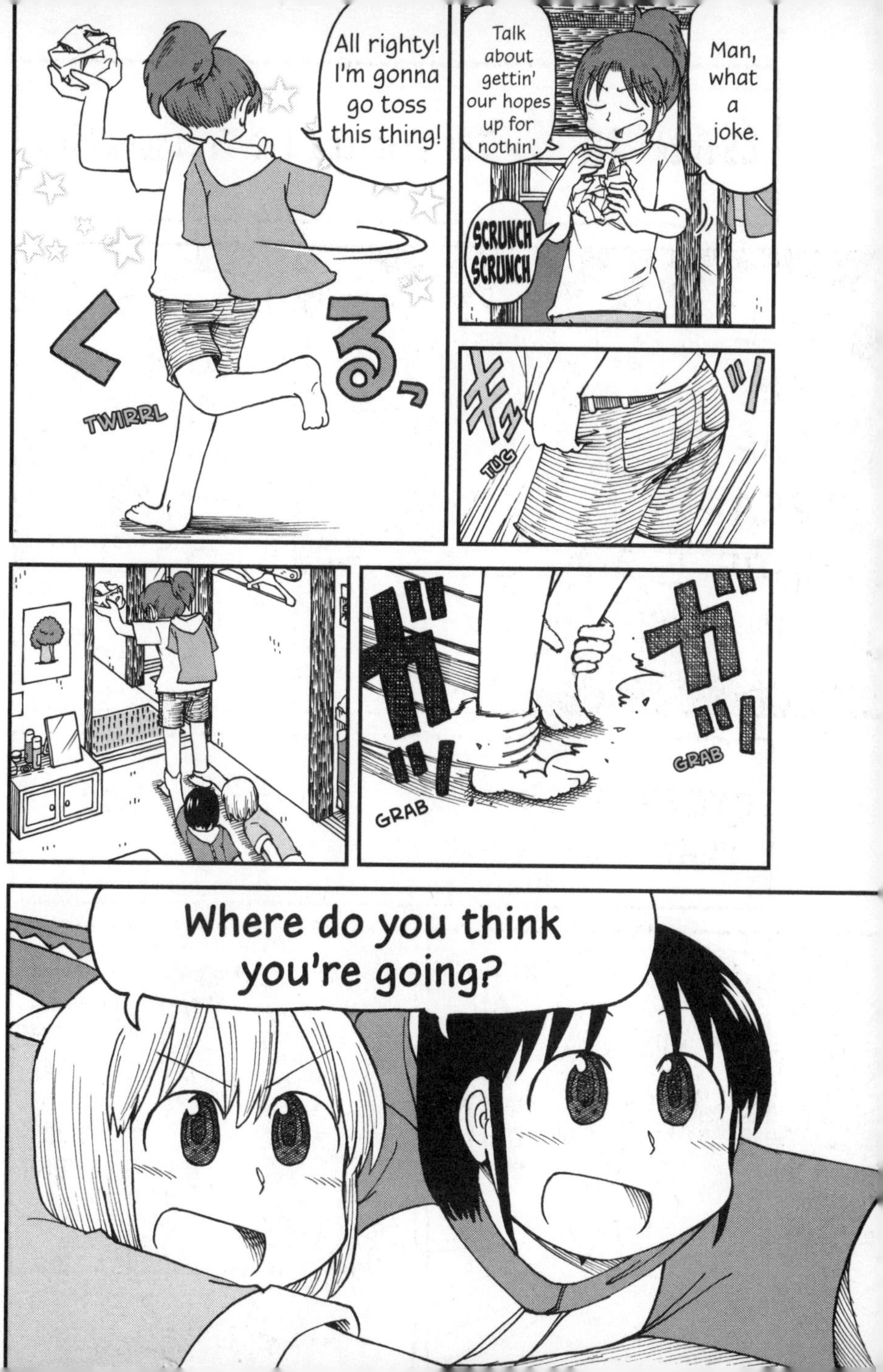
Man, what a joke.
Talk about gettin' our hopes up for nothin'.
SCRUNCH SCRUNCH
キュッ
TUG
All righty! I'm gonna go toss this thing!
くるっ
TWIRRL
ガッ
GRAB
ガッ
GRAB
Where do you think you're going?

Chapter 28 ◇ The Trio and the Treasure Map

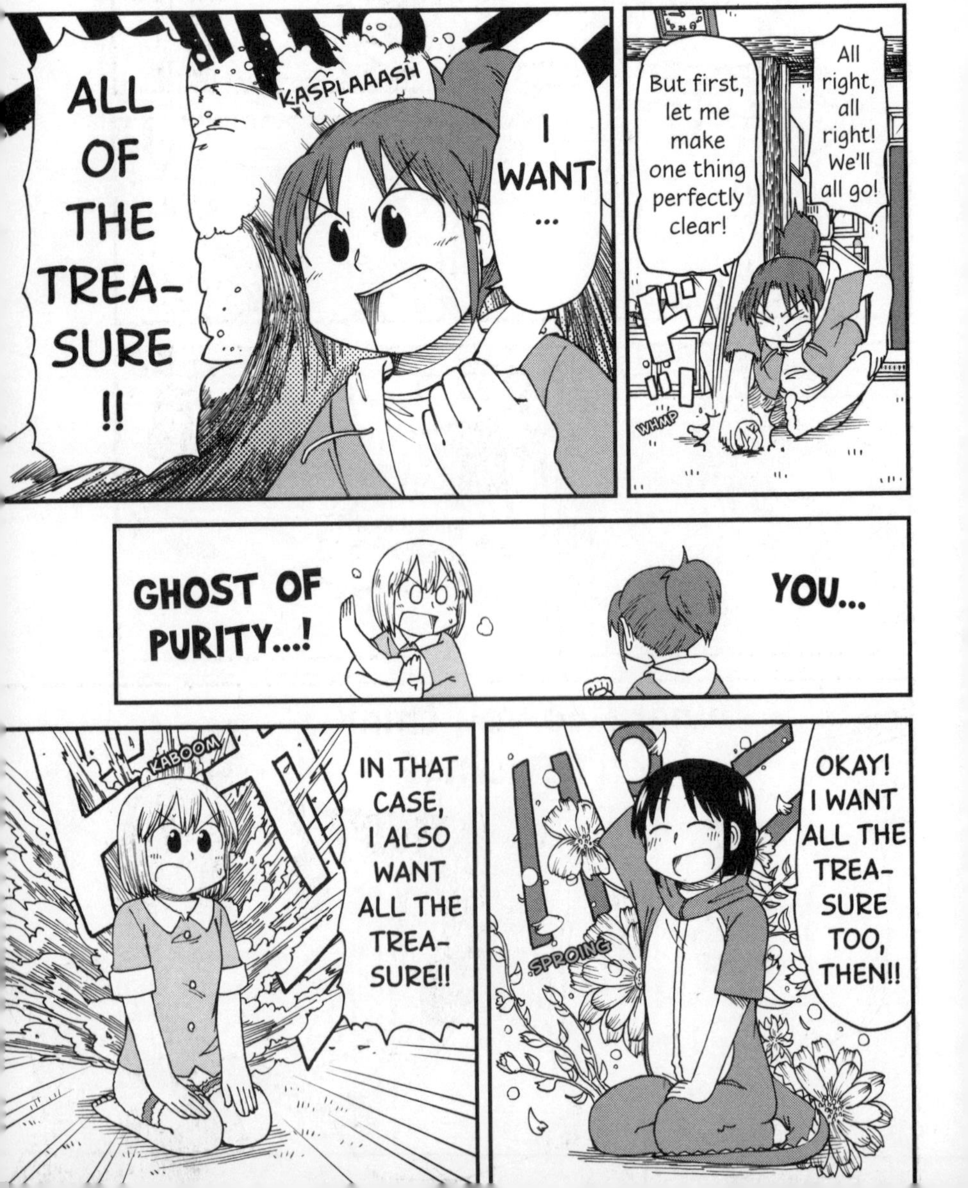
All right, all right! We'll all go!
But first, let me make one thing perfectly clear!
WHMP
I WANT …
KASPLAAASH
ALL OF THE TREA-SURE !!
YOU...
GHOST OF PURITY...!
OKAY! I WANT ALL THE TREA-SURE TOO, THEN!!
SPROING
IN THAT CASE, I ALSO WANT ALL THE TREA-SURE!!
KABOOM

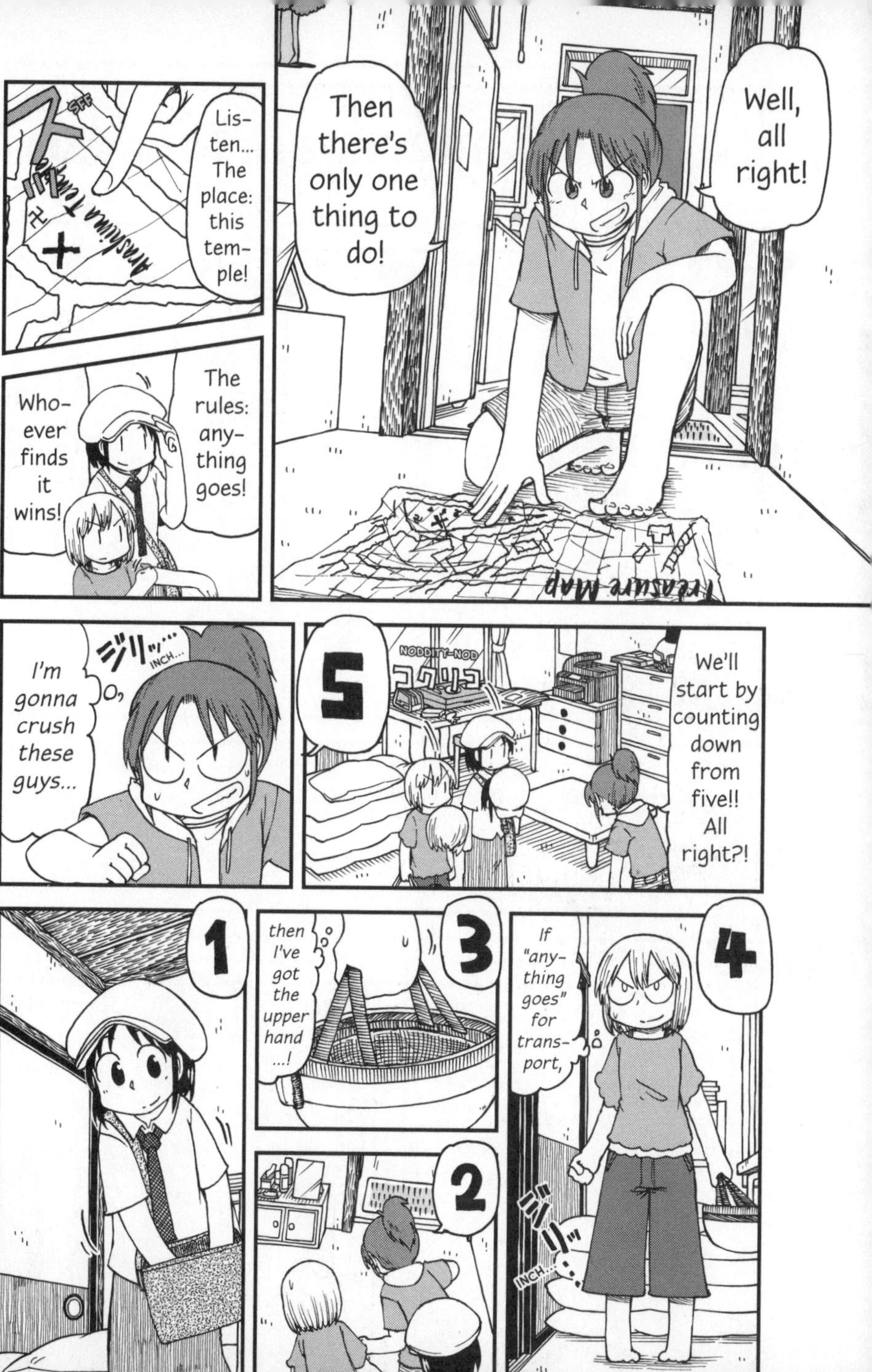
Well, all right!
Then there's only one thing to do!
Treasure Map
Lis-ten... The place: this tem-ple!
SFF
Arashiwa Temple
卍
The rules: any-thing goes!
Who-ever finds it wins!
We'll start by counting down from five!! All right?!
NODDITY-NOD
コクリコ
5
I'm gonna crush these guys...
ジリッ
INCH...
4
If "any-thing goes" for trans-port,
ジリッ
INCH...
3
then I've got the upper hand ...!
2
1

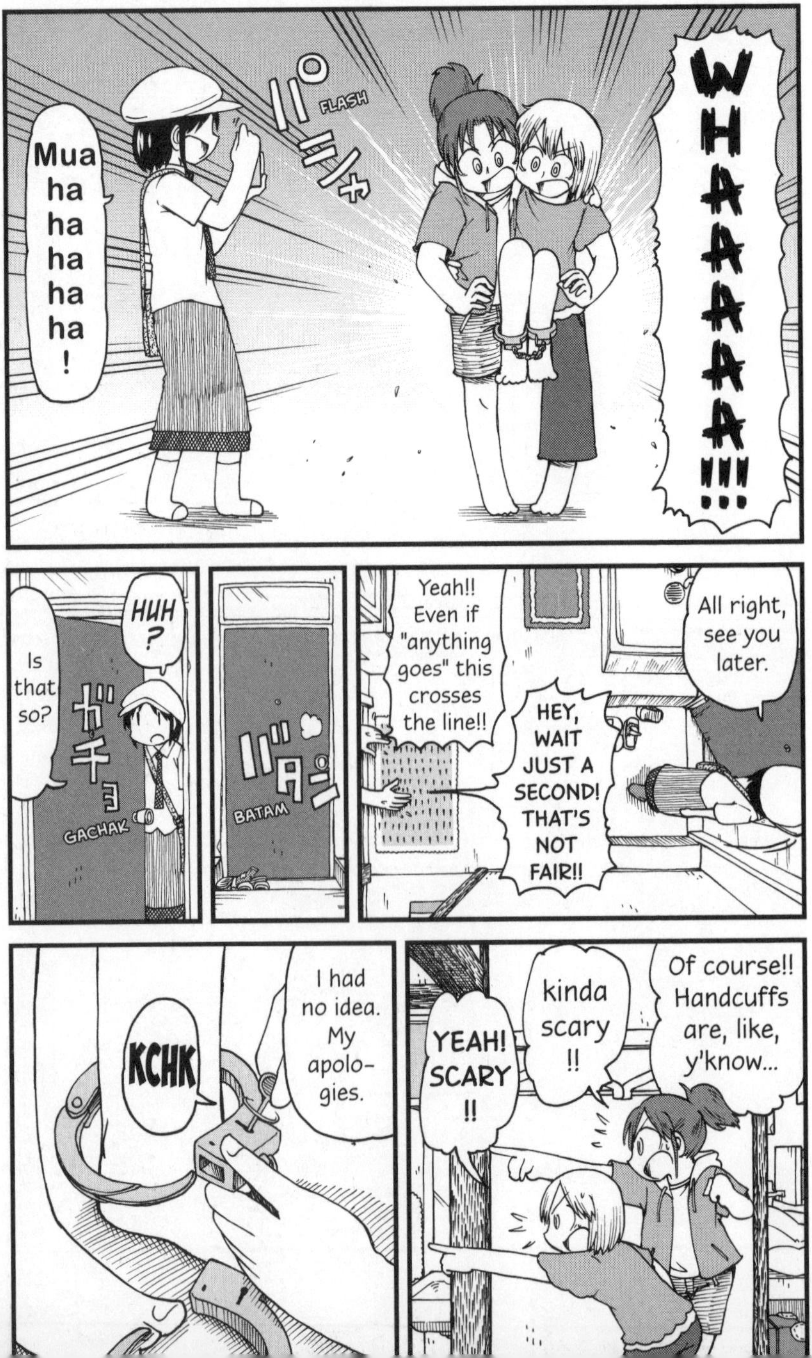

WHAAAAAA!!!
パシャ
FLASH
Mua ha ha ha ha ha ha!
All right, see you later.
Yeah!! Even if "anything goes" this crosses the line!!
HEY, WAIT JUST A SECOND! THAT'S NOT FAIR!!
バタン
BATAM
HUH?
Is that so?
ガチョ
GACHAK
Of course!! Handcuffs are, like, y'know...
kinda scary!!
YEAH! SCARY!!
I had no idea. My apolo-gies.
KCHK

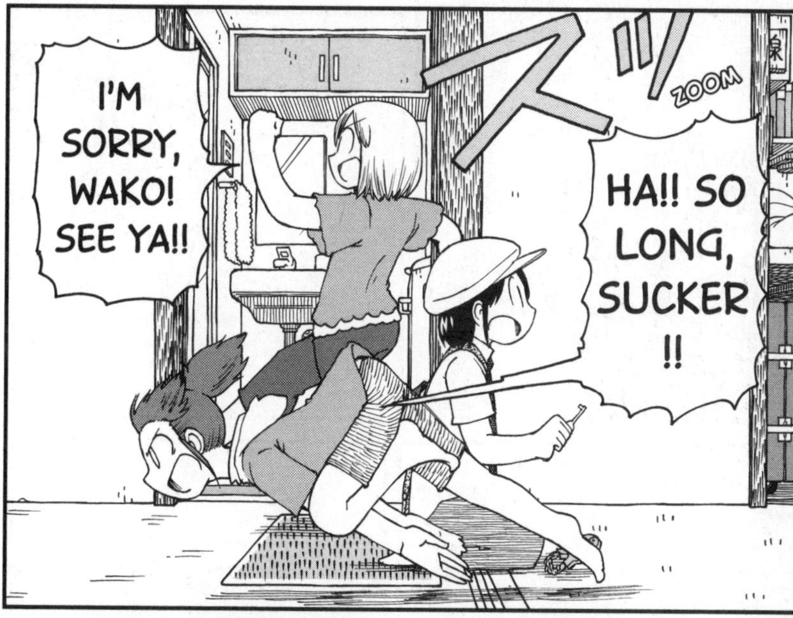
ZOOM
HA!! SO LONG, SUCKER !!
I'M SORRY, WAKO! SEE YA!!

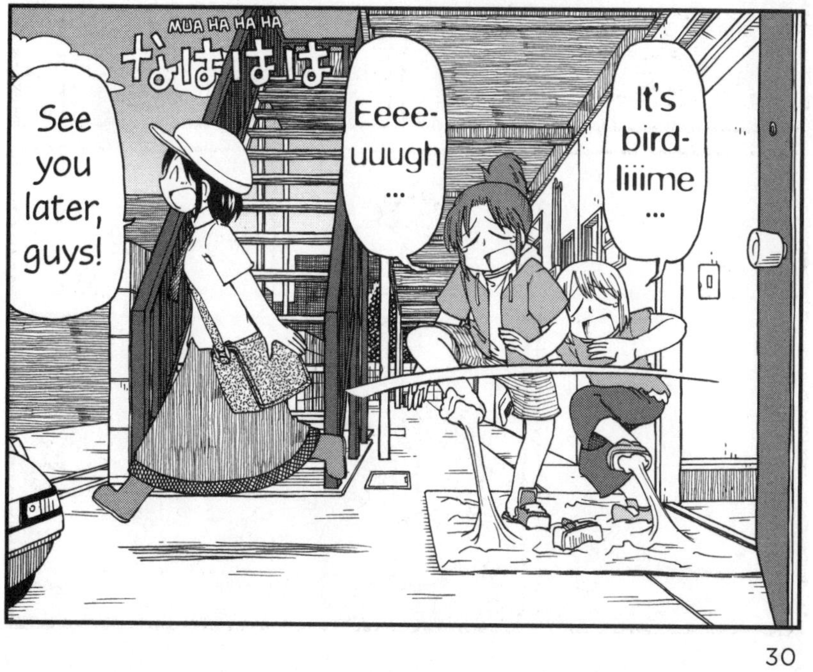
It's bird-liiime ...
Eeee-uuugh ...
MUA HA HA HA
なははは
See you later, guys!

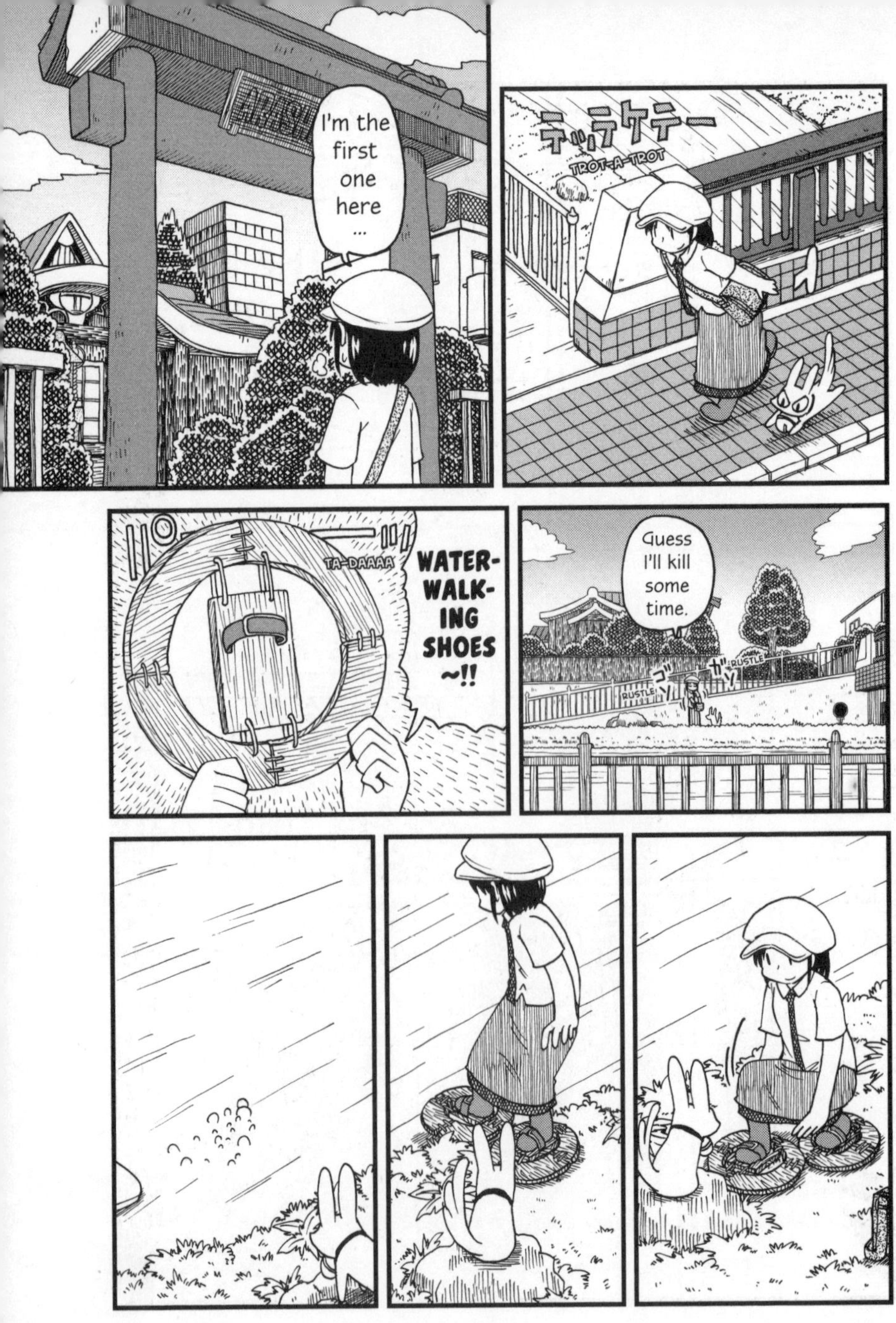
テッテケテー
TROT-A-TROT
I'm the first one here ...
Guess I'll kill some time.
RUSTLE
RUSTLE
TA-DAAAA
WATER-WALKING SHOES ~!!

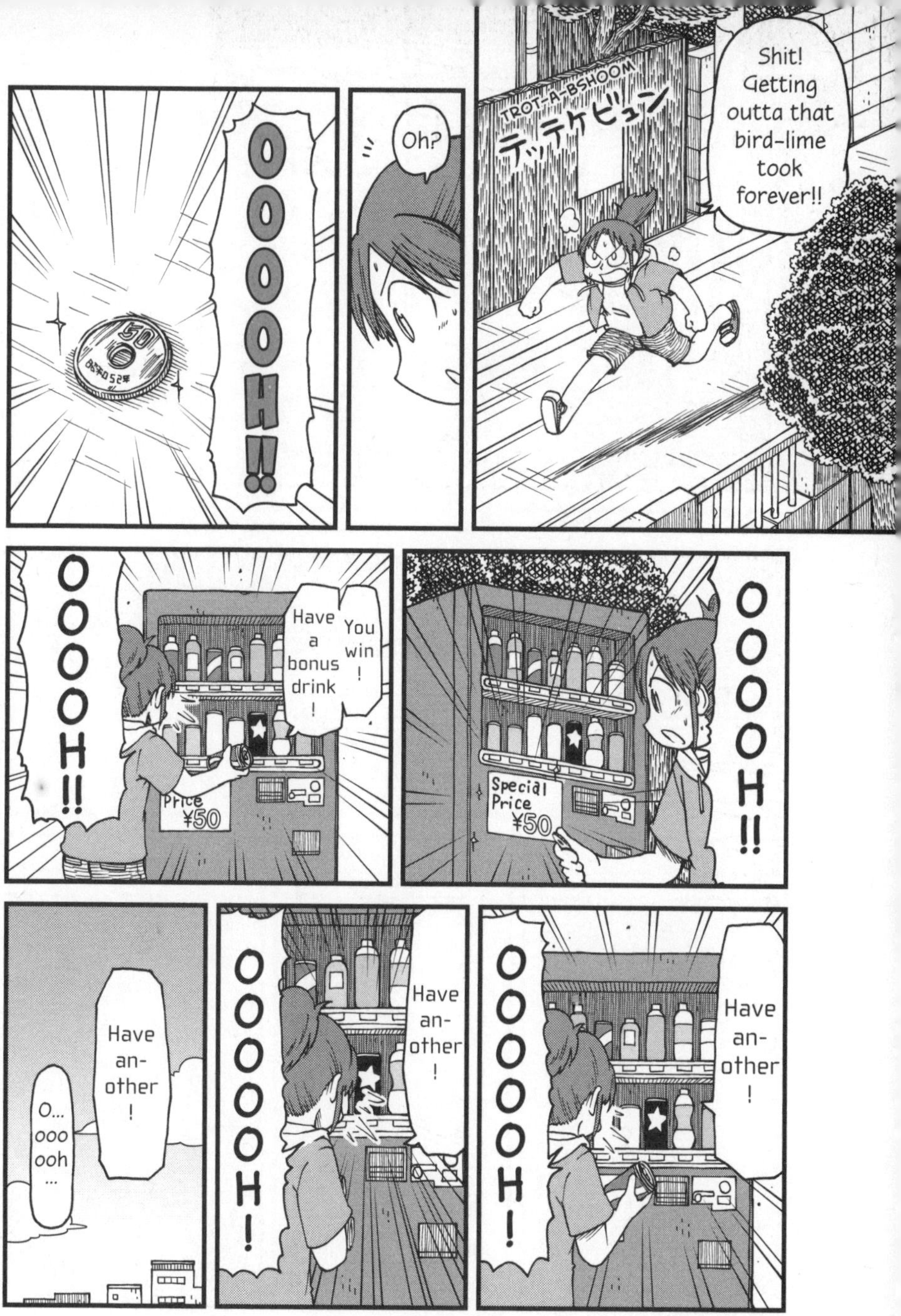
TROT-A-BSHOOM
テッテケビューン
Shit! Getting outta that bird-lime took forever!!
Oh?
OOOOOH!!
OOOOH!!
Special Price ¥50
You win!
Have a bonus drink!
OOOOH!!
Price ¥50
Have an-other!
OOOOOOH!
Have an-other!
OOOOOOH!
Have an-other!
O... ooo ooh ...

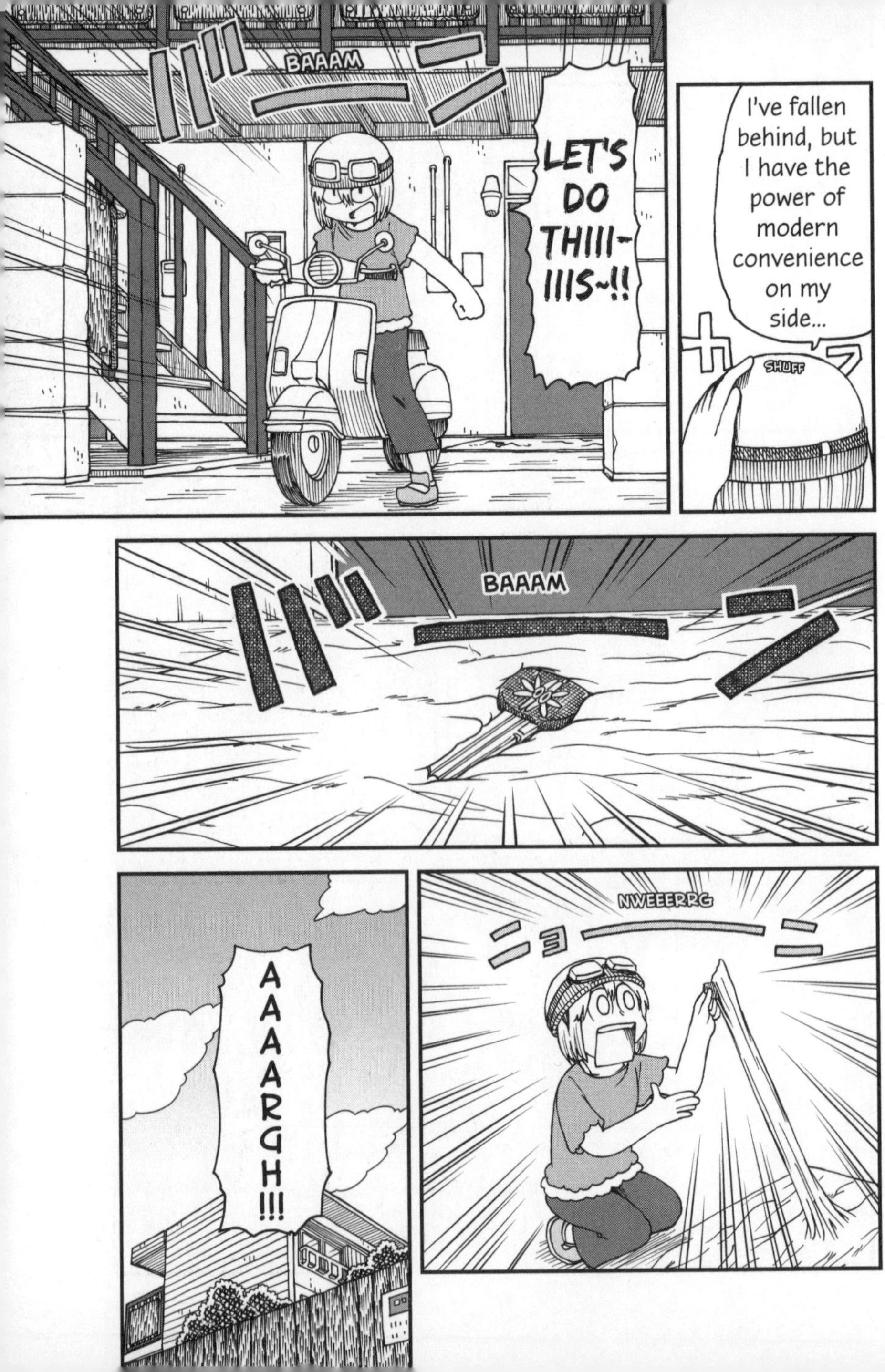
I've fallen behind, but I have the power of modern convenience on my side...
SHUFF
BAAAM
LET'S DO THIIIIIIS~!!
BAAAM
NWEEERRG
AAAAARGH!!!

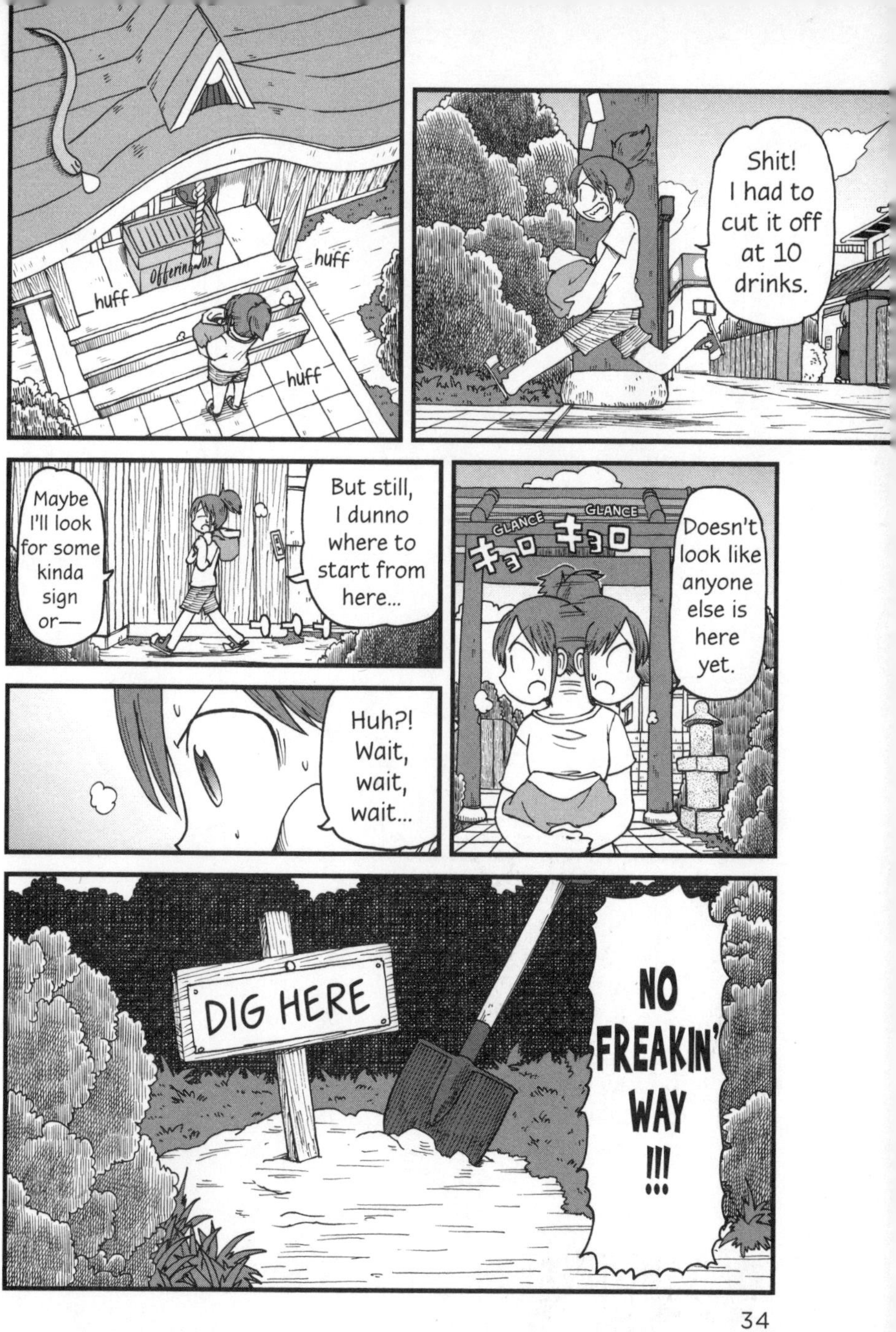
Shit! I had to cut it off at 10 drinks.
Offering box
huff
huff
huff
GLANCE GLANCE
キョロ キョロ
Doesn't look like anyone else is here yet.
But still, I dunno where to start from here...
Maybe I'll look for some kinda sign or—
Huh?! Wait, wait, wait...
NO FREAKIN' WAY !!!
DIG HERE

You win! Have another!
Special price ¥50
You win! Have another!
You win! Have another!

CITY

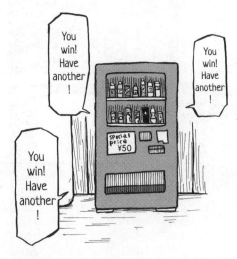

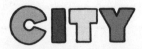

Here are all the ¥50 drinks!

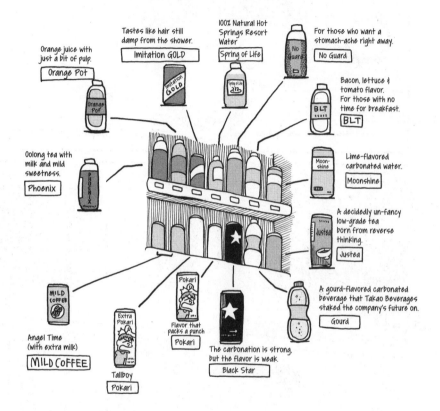

Orange juice with just a bit of pulp.
Orange Pot
Tastes like hair still damp from the shower.
Imitation GOLD
100% Natural Hot Springs Resort Water
Spring of Life
For those who want a stomach-ache right away.
No Guard
Bacon, lettuce & tomato flavor. For those with no time for breakfast.
BLT
Oolong tea with milk and mild sweetness.
Phoenix
Lime-flavored carbonated water.
Moonshine
A decidedly un-fancy low-grade tea born from reverse thinking.
Justea
A gourd-flavored carbonated beverage that Takao Beverages staked the company's future on.
Gourd
Angel Time (with extra milk)
MILD COFFEE
Tallboy
Pokari
Flavor that packs a punch
Pokari
The carbonation is strong, but the flavor is weak.
Black Star

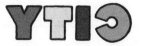

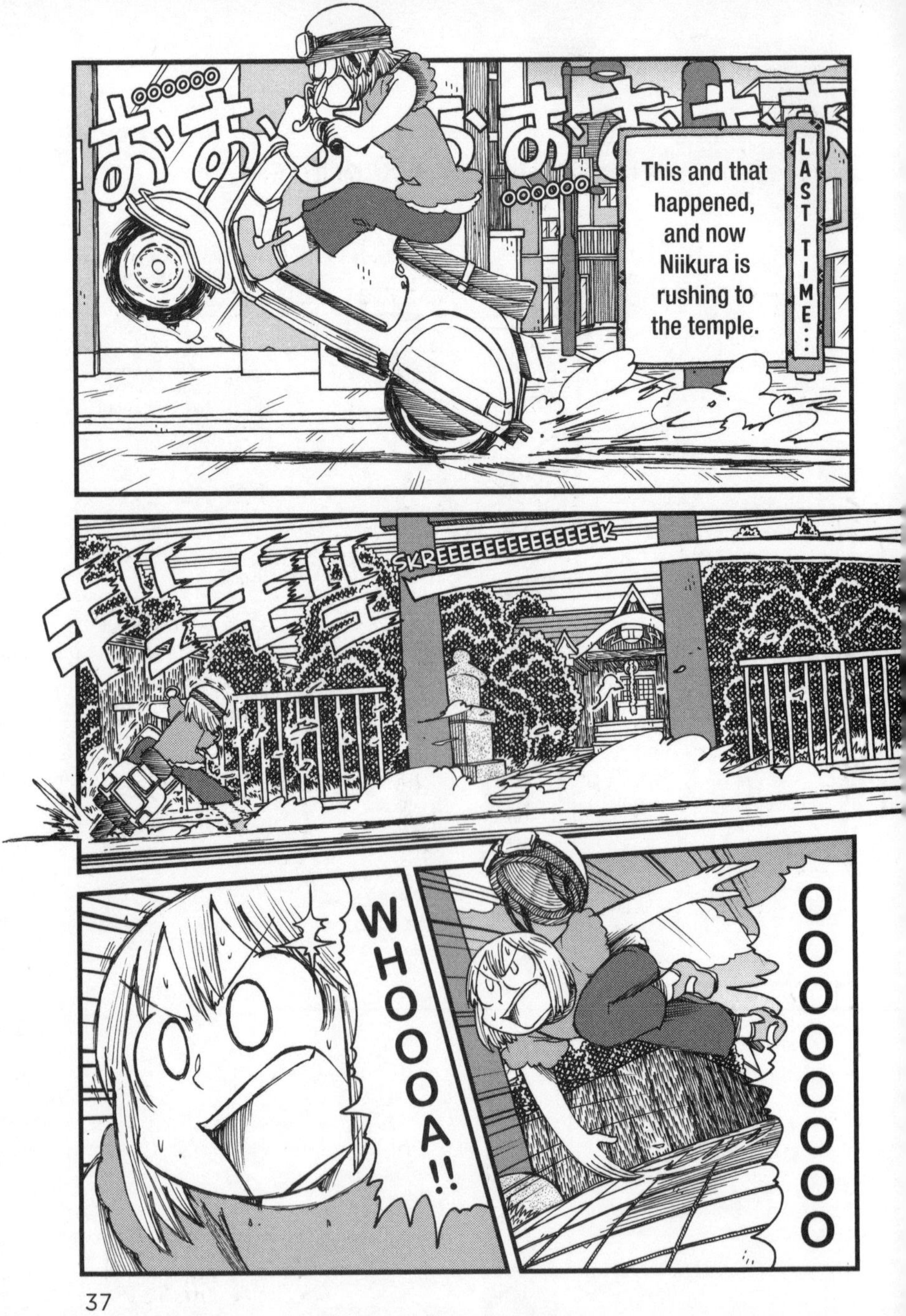
LAST TIME...
This and that happened, and now Niikura is rushing to the temple.
SKREEEEEEEEEEEEEEK
OOOOOOOOOOO
WHOOOOA!!

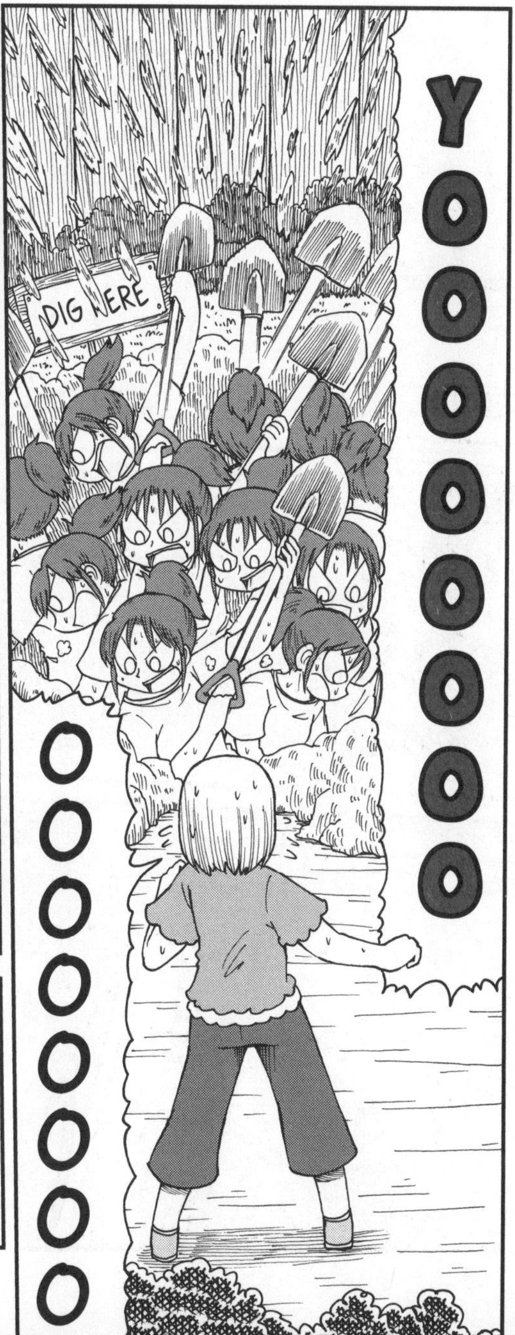
DIG HERE
YOOOOOOOO
OOOOOOOO

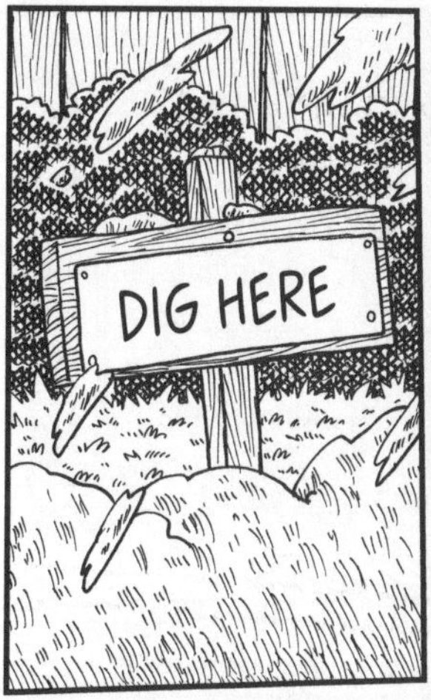
DIG HERE

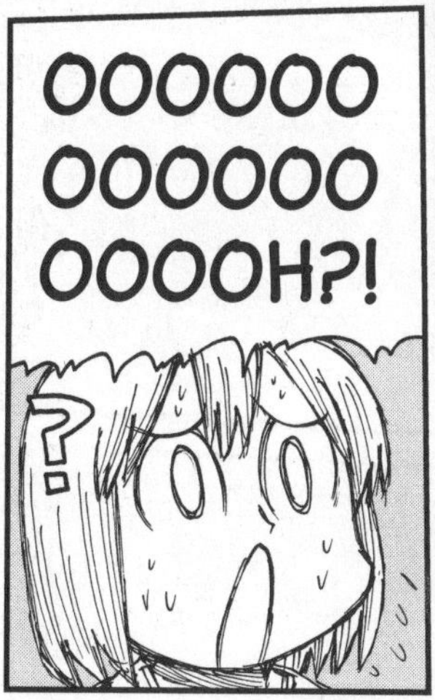
OOOOOO
OOOOOO
OOOOH?!
?!

Chapter 29
Treasure

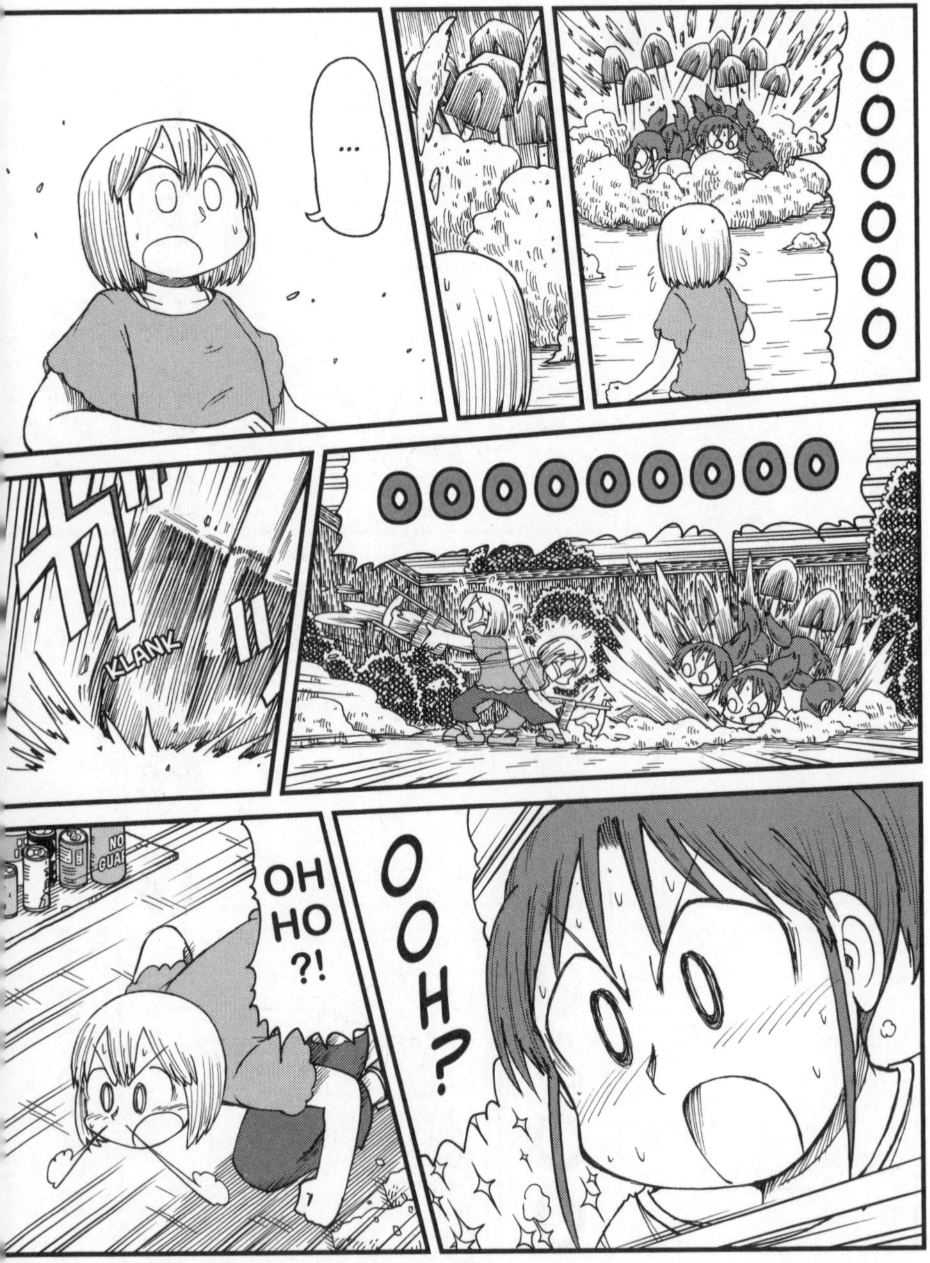
OOOOOO
...
OOOOOOOOOO
KLANK
OOOH?
OH HO ?!

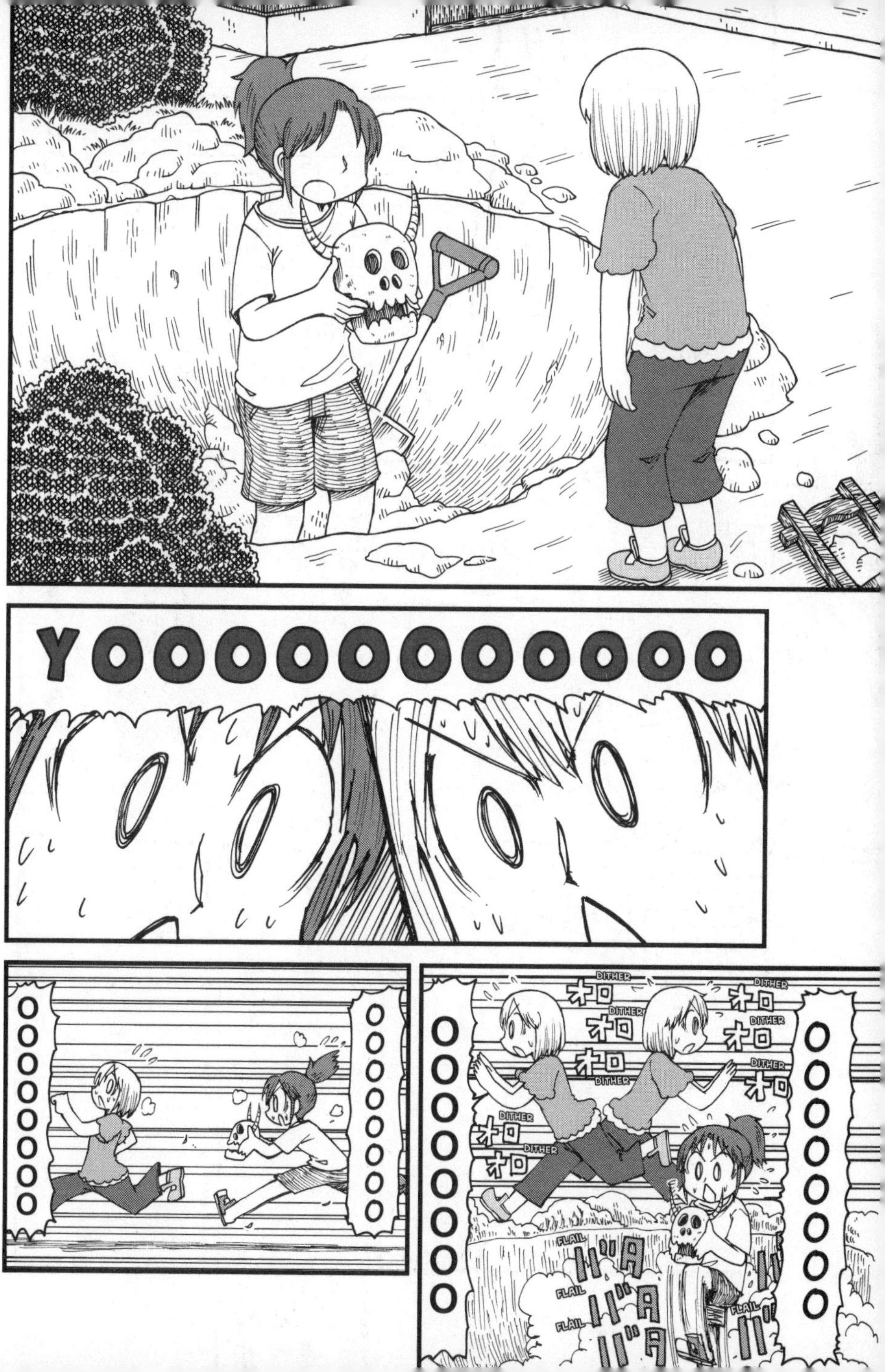
YOOOOOOOOOOO
OOOOOOOOOO
DITHER
オロ
DITHER
オロ
DITHER
オロ
DITHER
オロ
DITHER
オロ
DITHER
オロ
DITHER
オロ
FLAIL
バタ
FLAIL
バタ
FLAIL
バタ
FLAIL
バ
OOOOOOOOOO
OOOOOOOO
OOOOOOOO

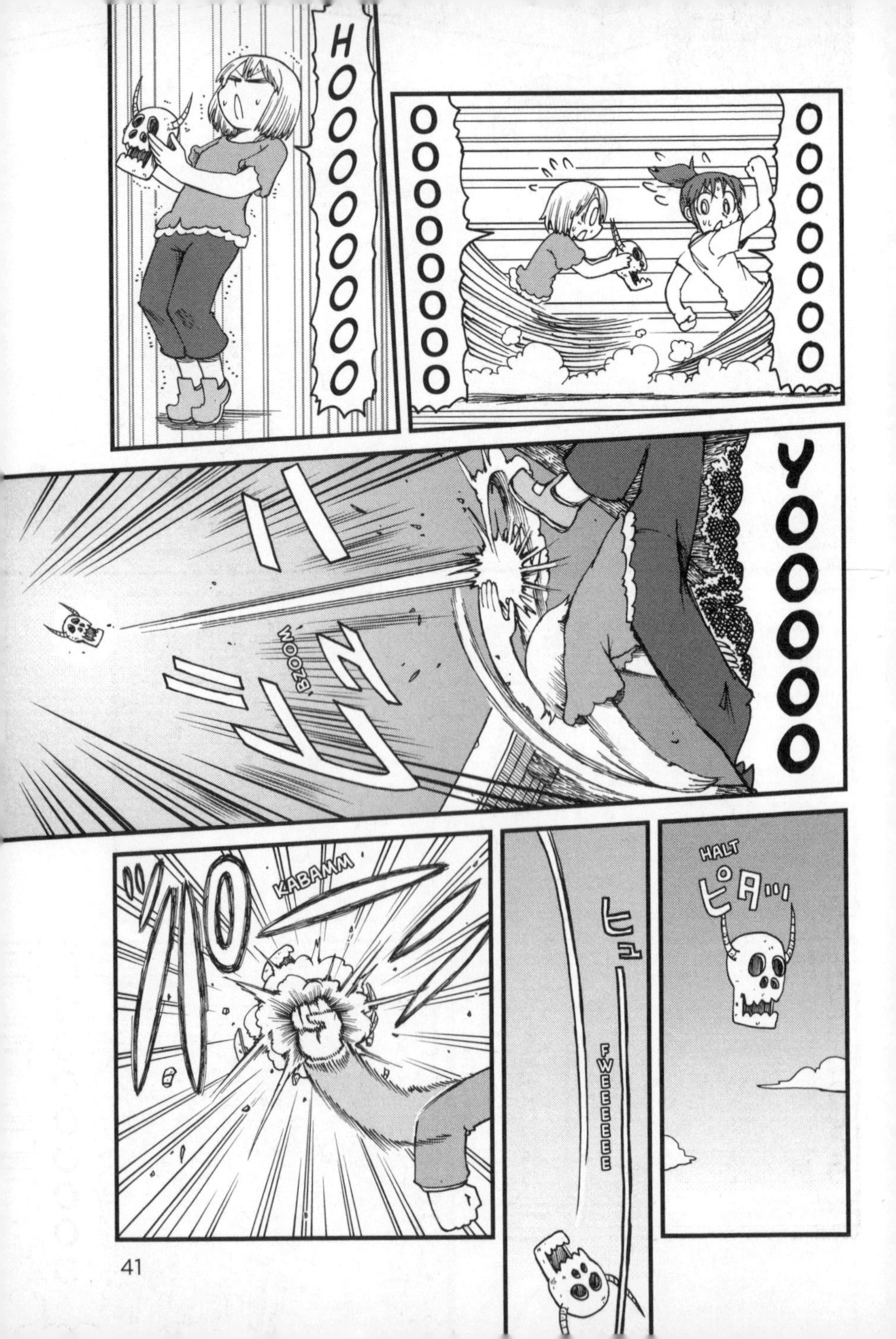

OOOOOOOOO
OOOOOOOOO
HOOOOOOOOOOO
YOOOOOO
BZOOM
HALT
ピタッ
ヒュー
FWEEEEEEE
KABAMM

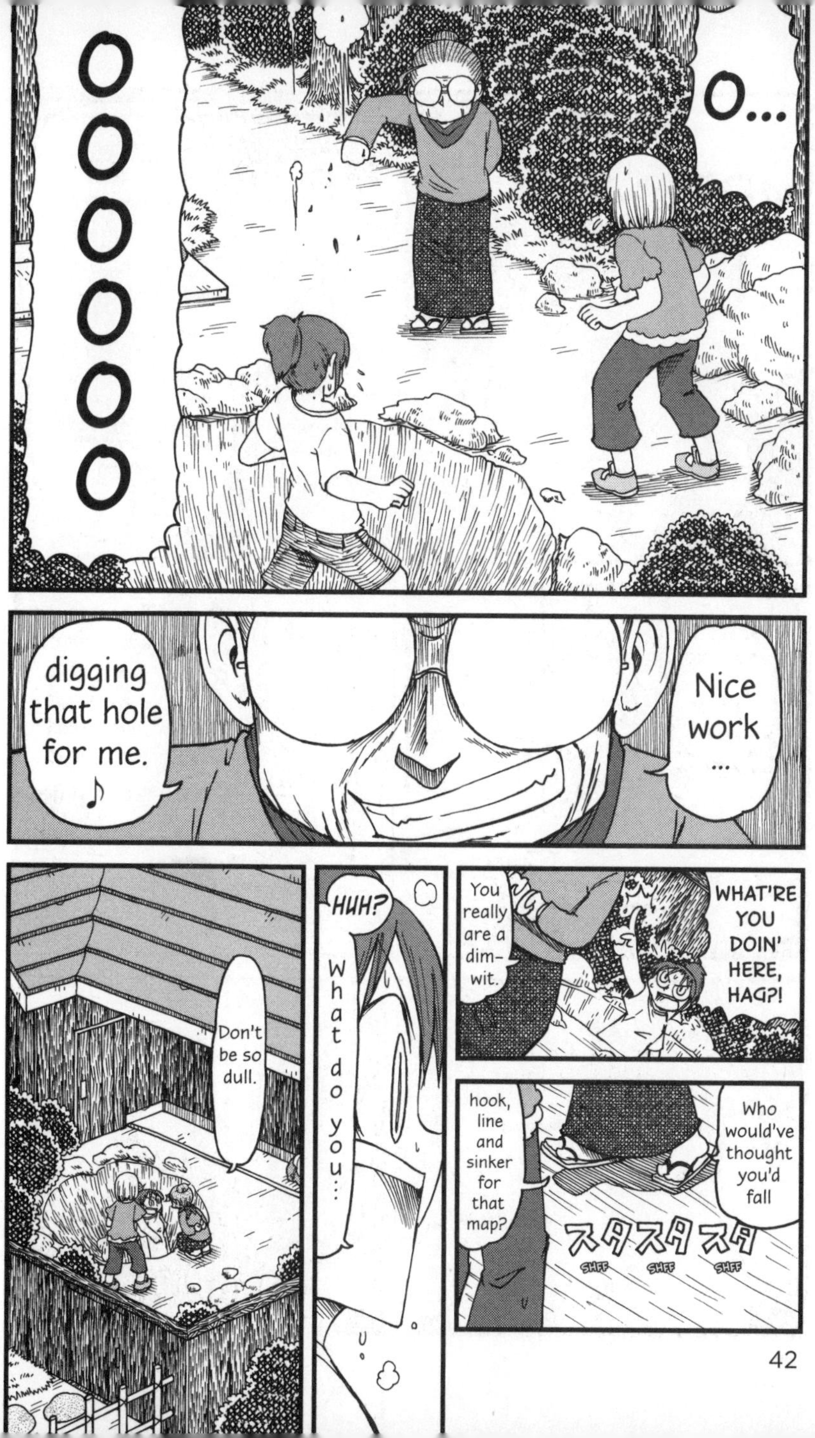
O...
OOOOOO
Nice work ...
digging that hole for me. ♪
WHAT'RE YOU DOIN' HERE, HAG?!
You really are a dim-wit.
Who would've thought you'd fall
hook, line and sinker for that map?
スタスタスタ
SHFF SHFF SHFF
HUH?
What do you...
Don't be so dull.

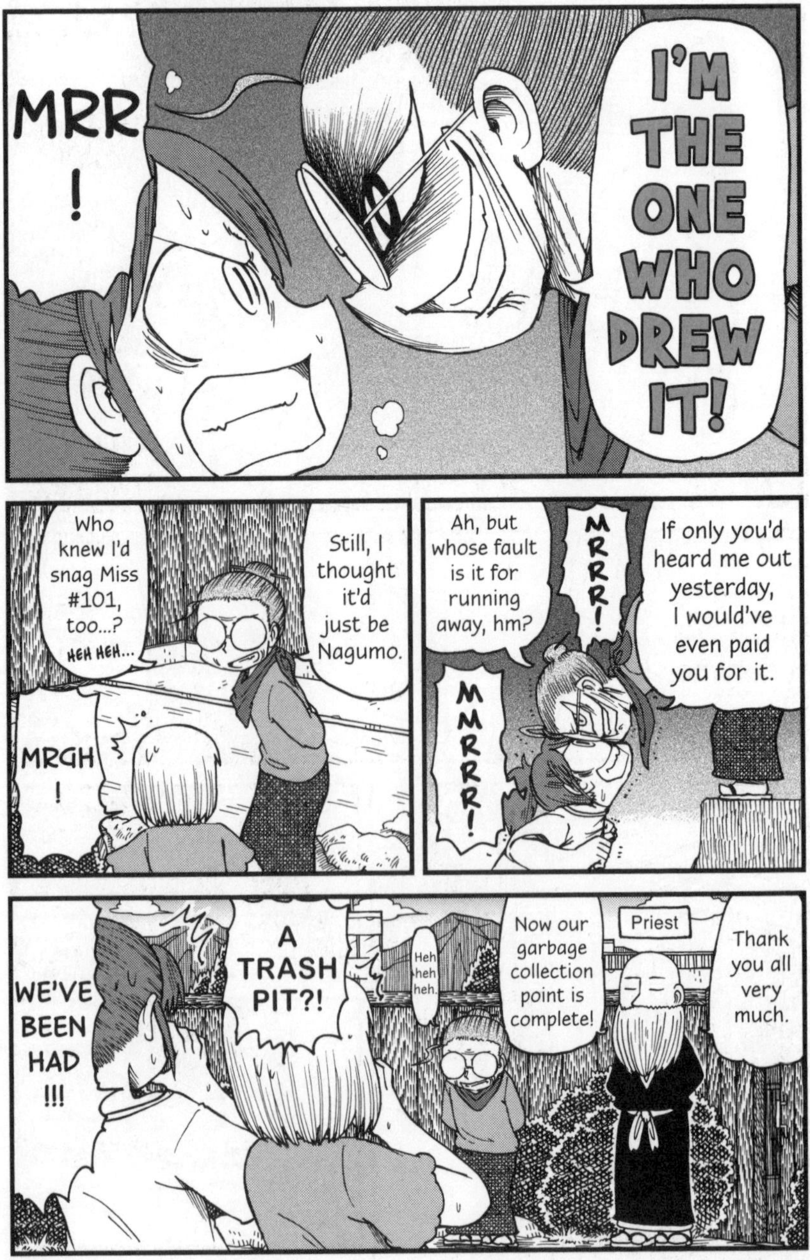
I'M THE ONE WHO DREW IT!
MRR !
If only you'd heard me out yesterday, I would've even paid you for it.
MRRR!
Ah, but whose fault is it for running away, hm?
MMRRR!
Still, I thought it'd just be Nagumo.
Who knew I'd snag Miss #101, too...?
HEH HEH...
MRGH !
Thank you all very much.
Priest
Now our garbage collection point is complete!
Heh heh heh.
A TRASH PIT?!
WE'VE BEEN HAD !!!

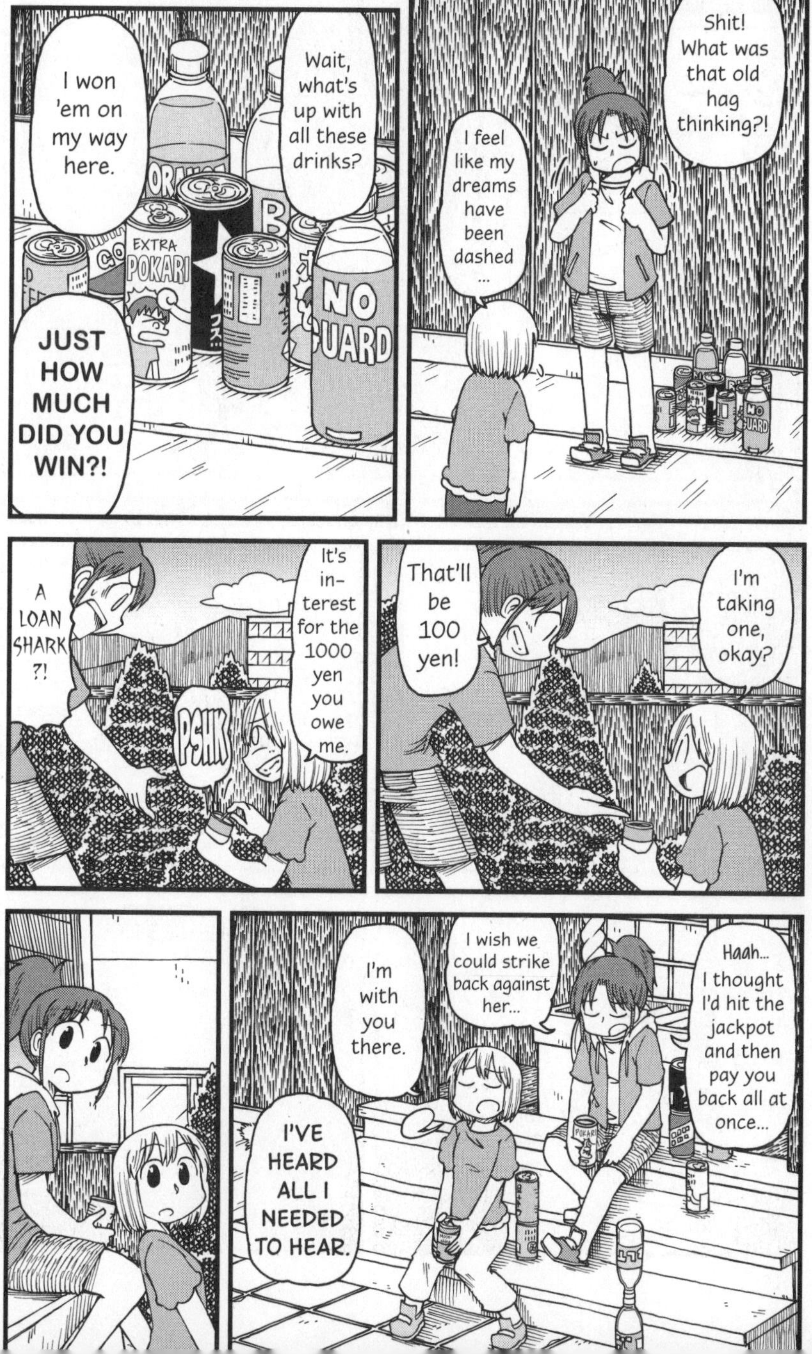
Shit! What was that old hag thinking?!
I feel like my dreams have been dashed...
Wait, what's up with all these drinks?
I won 'em on my way here.
EXTRA POKARI
NO GUARD
JUST HOW MUCH DID YOU WIN?!
I'm taking one, okay?
That'll be 100 yen!
It's in-terest for the 1000 yen you owe me.
PSHK
A LOAN SHARK?!
Haah... I thought I'd hit the jackpot and then pay you back all at once...
I wish we could strike back against her...
I'm with you there.
I'VE HEARD ALL I NEEDED TO HEAR.

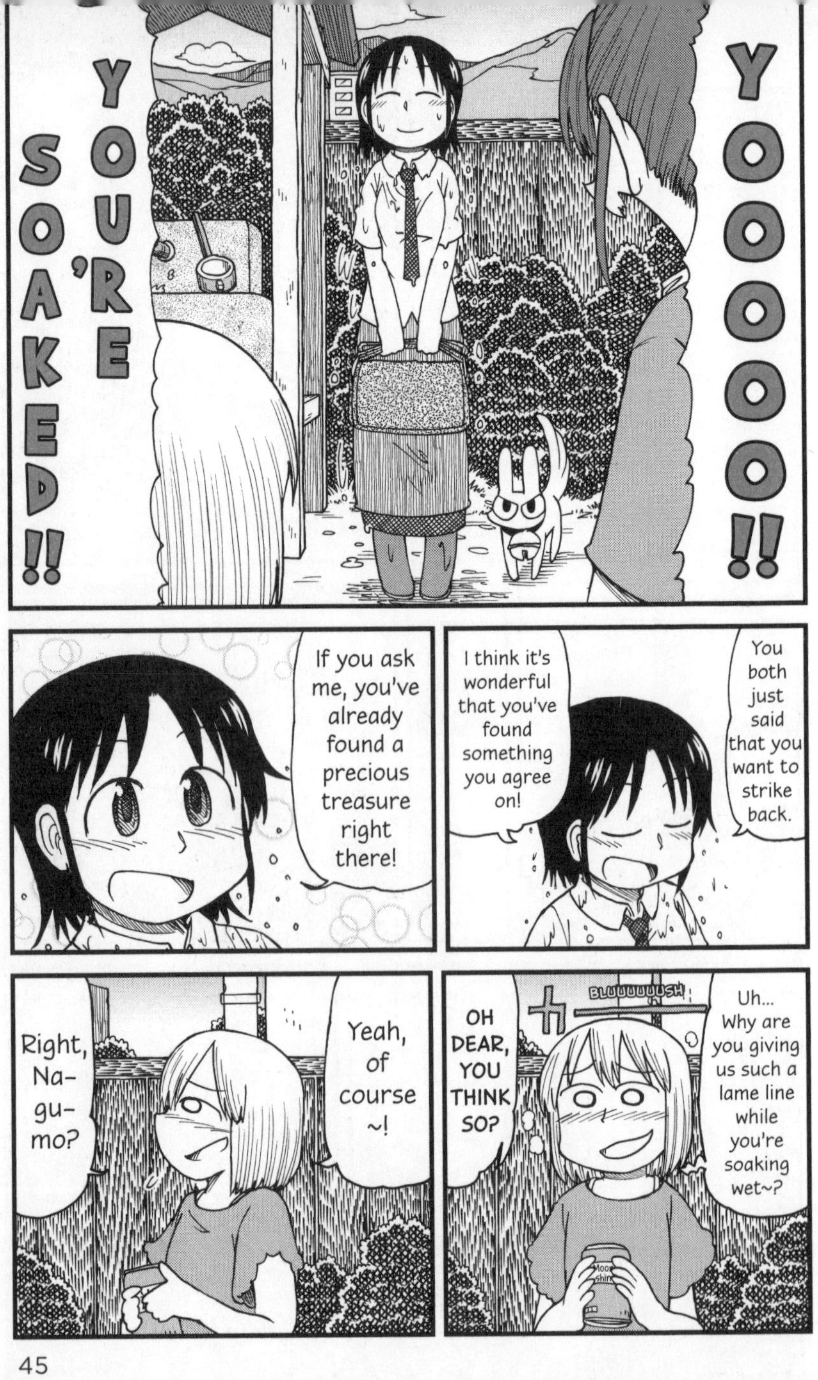
YOOOOOO!!
YOU'RE SOAKED!!
You both just said that you want to strike back.
I think it's wonderful that you've found something you agree on!
If you ask me, you've already found a precious treasure right there!
Uh... Why are you giving us such a lame line while you're soaking wet~?
BLUUUUUUSH
OH DEAR, YOU THINK SO?
Yeah, of course ~!
Right, Na-gumo?

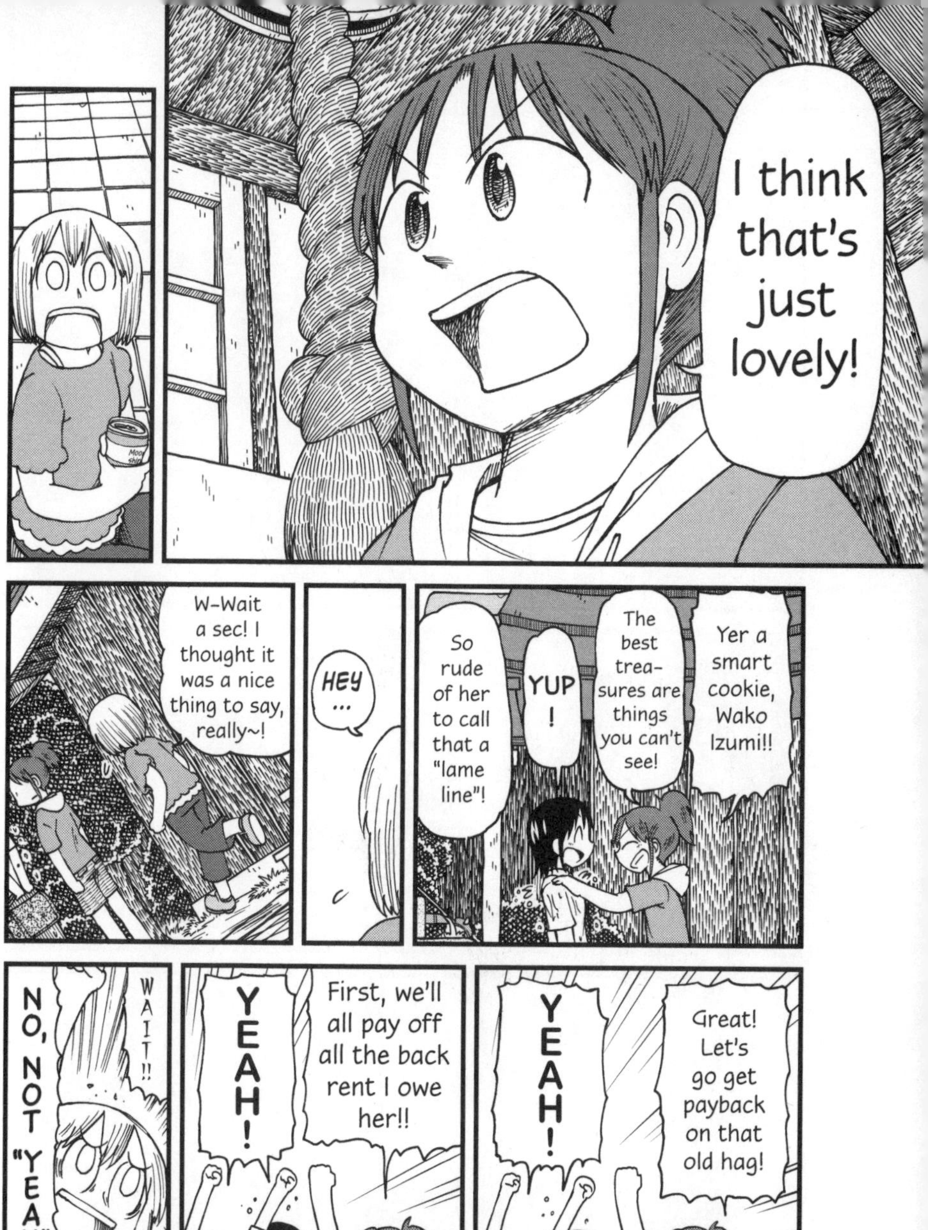
I think that's just lovely!
Yer a smart cookie, Wako Izumi!!
The best trea-sures are things you can't see!
YUP!
So rude of her to call that a "lame line"!
HEY...
W-Wait a sec! I thought it was a nice thing to say, really~!
Great! Let's go get payback on that old hag!
YEAH!
First, we'll all pay off all the back rent I owe her!!
YEAH!
WAIT!!
NO, NOT "YEAH"!!

change of clothes
school
stop by home
work

CITY

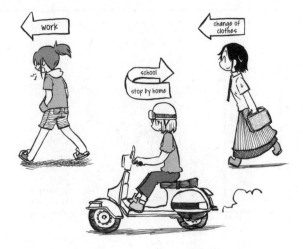

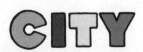

shortcut

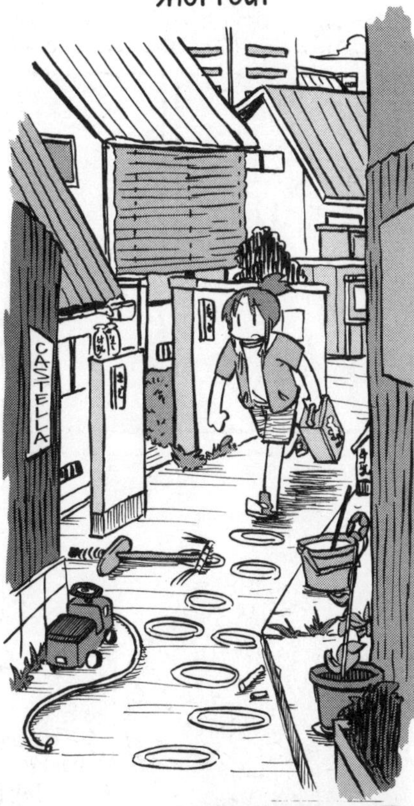
CASTELLA

CITY

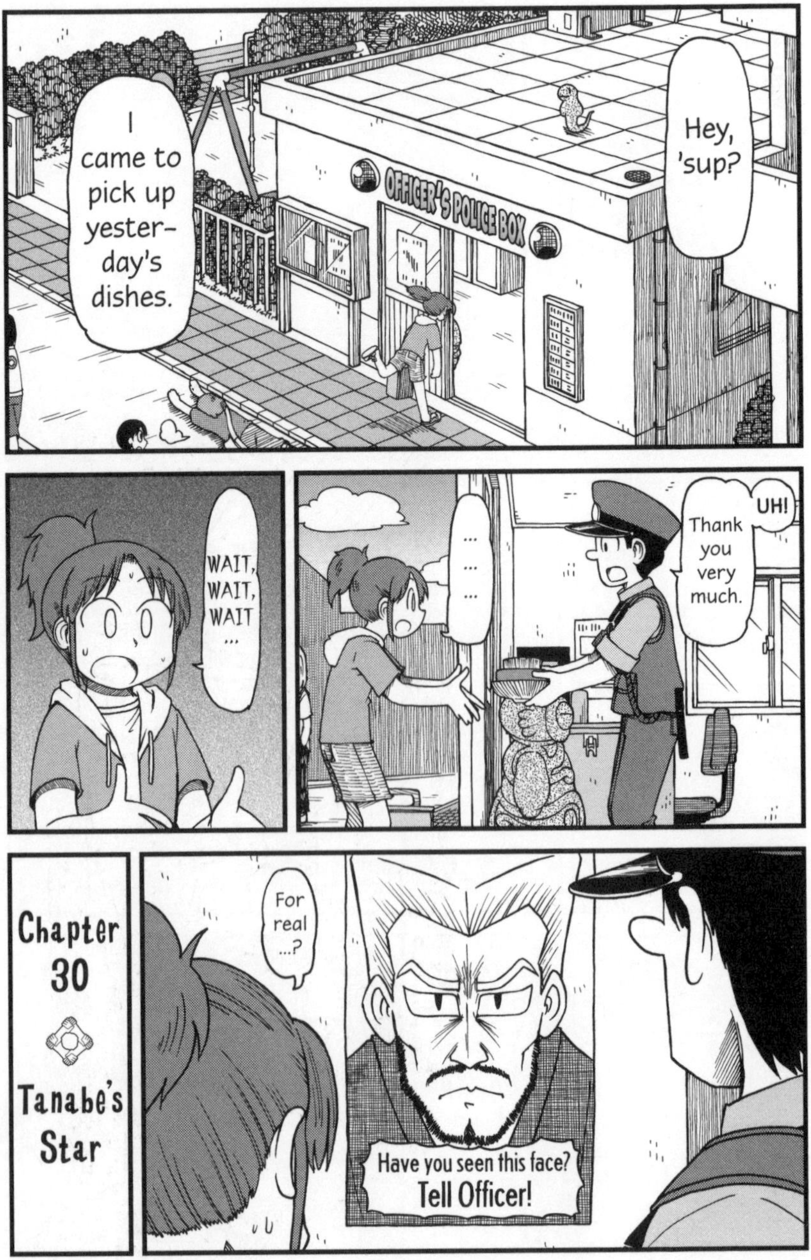
Hey, 'sup?
OFFICER'S POLICE BOX
I came to pick up yester-day's dishes.
UH!
Thank you very much.
... ...
WAIT, WAIT, WAIT ...
For real ...?
Have you seen this face? Tell Officer!
Chapter 30
Tanabe's Star

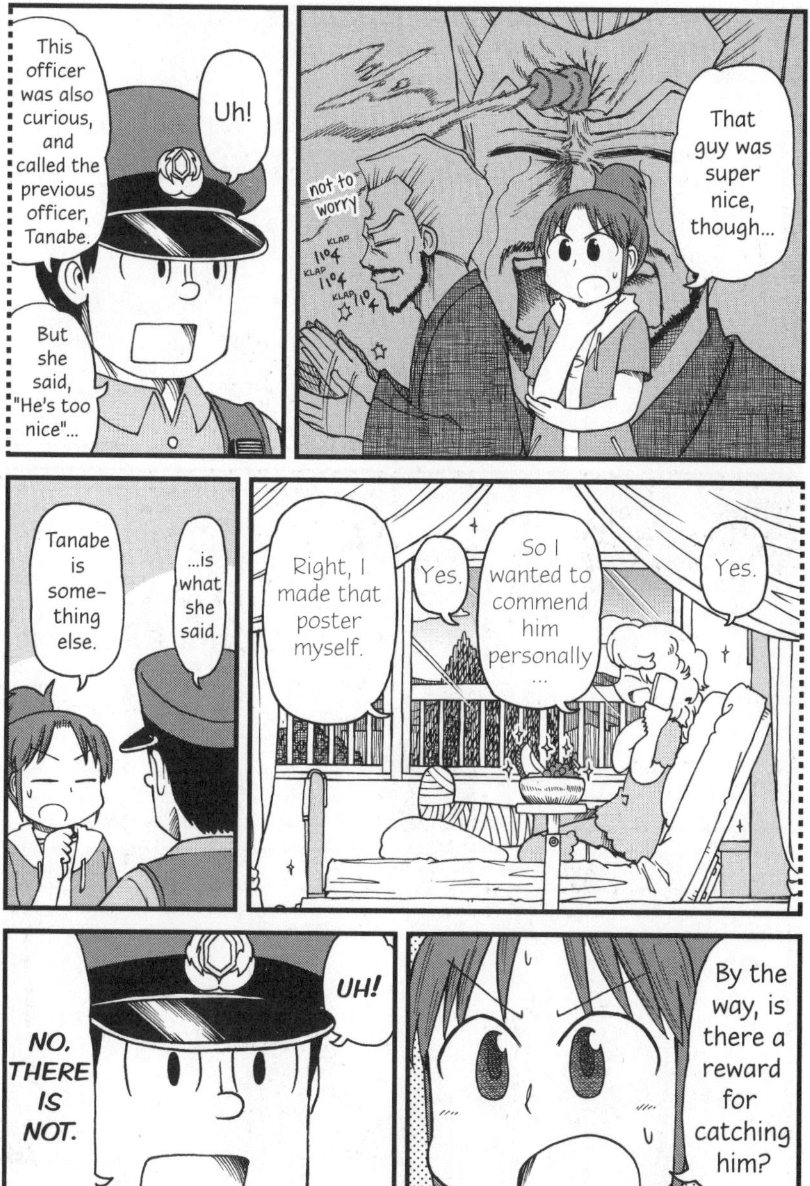
That guy was super nice, though...
not to worry
KLAP
KLAP
KLAP
Uh!
This officer was also curious, and called the previous officer, Tanabe.
But she said, "He's too nice"...
Yes.
So I wanted to commend him personally...
Yes.
Right, I made that poster myself.
Tanabe is some-thing else.
...is what she said.
By the way, is there a reward for catching him?
UH!
NO. THERE IS NOT.

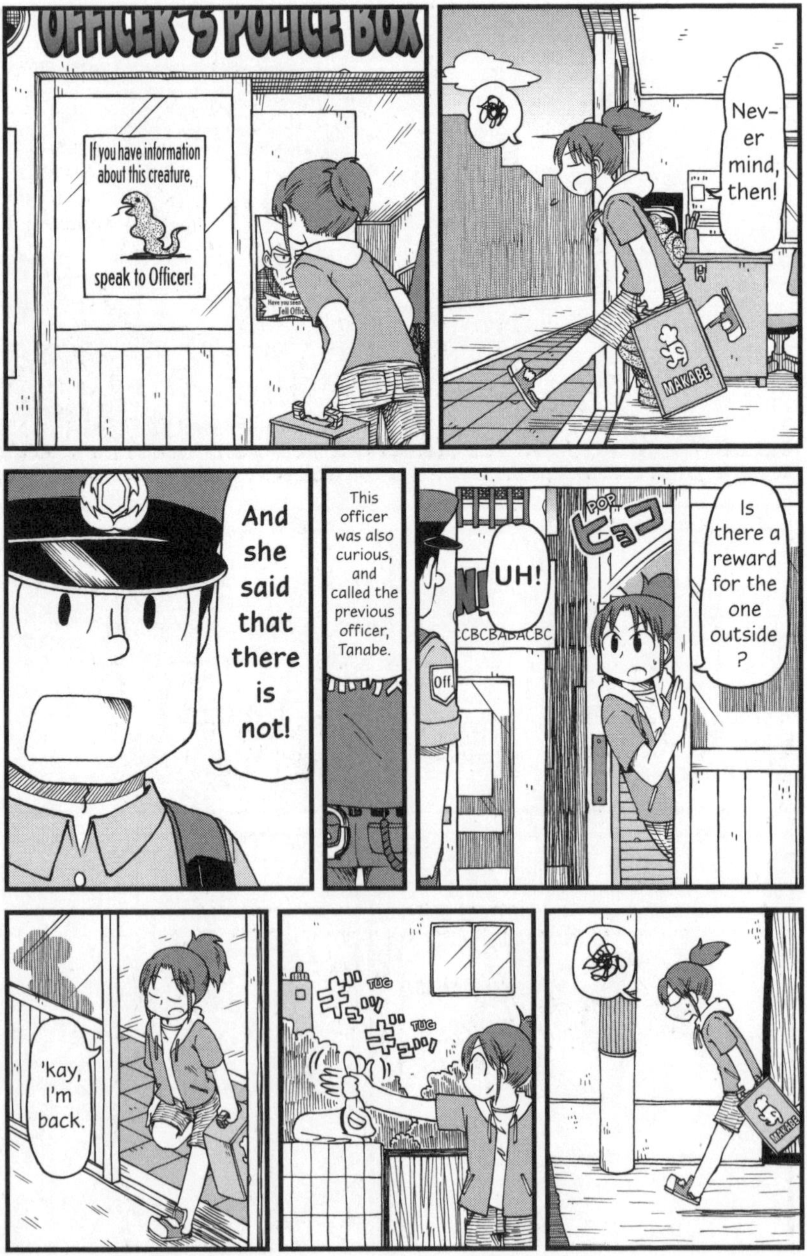
Never mind, then!
MAKABE
OFFICER'S POLICE BOX
If you have information about this creature, speak to Officer!
Is there a reward for the one outside?
POP
UH!
CCBCBABACBC
Off.
This officer was also curious, and called the previous officer, Tanabe.
And she said that there is not!
MAKABE
TUG
TUG
'kay, I'm back.

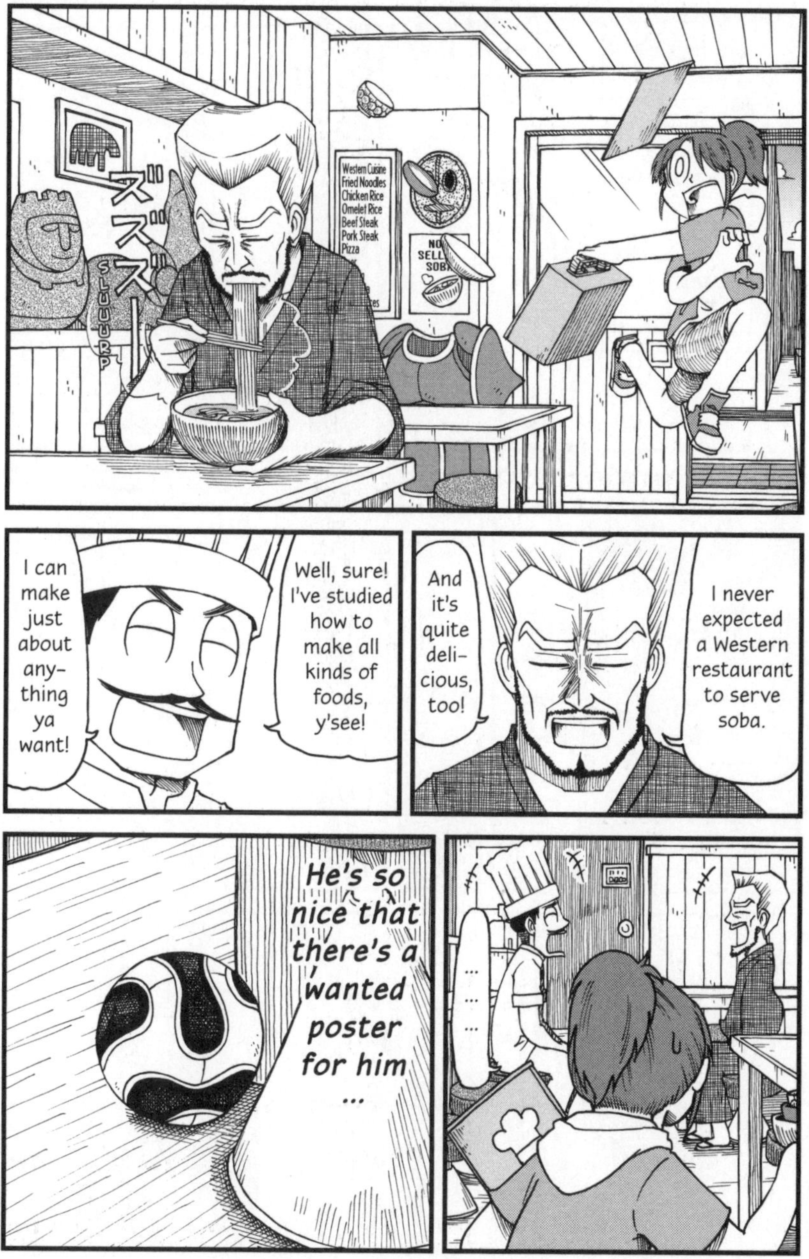
ズズズ
SLUUURP
Western Cuisine
Fried Noodles
Chicken Rice
Omelet Rice
Beef Steak
Pork Steak
Pizza
I never expected a Western restaurant to serve soba.
And it's quite delicious, too!
Well, sure! I've studied how to make all kinds of foods, y'see!
I can make just about anything ya want!
... ...
He's so nice that there's a wanted poster for him ...

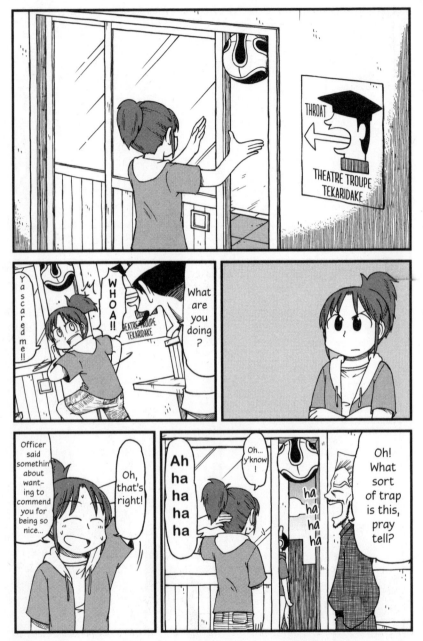

THROAT
THEATRE TROUPE TEKARIDAKE
What are you doing?
WHOA!!
HEATRE TROUPE TEKARIDAKE
Ya scared me!!
Oh! What sort of trap is this, pray tell?
ha ha ha ha
Oh... y'know!
Ah ha ha ha ha
Oh, that's right!
Officer said somethin' about want-ing to commend you for being so nice...

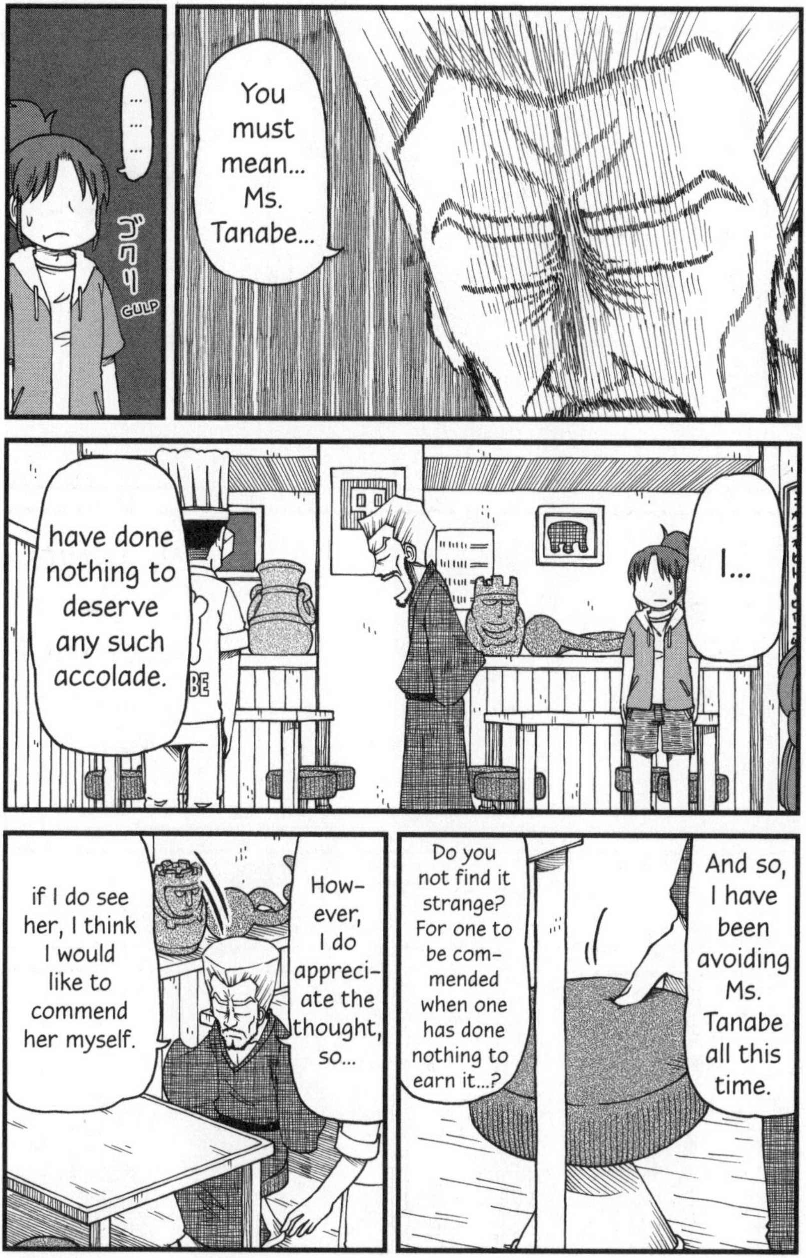
You must mean... Ms. Tanabe...
... ...
ゴクリ
GULP
I...
have done nothing to deserve any such accolade.
And so, I have been avoiding Ms. Tanabe all this time.
Do you not find it strange? For one to be commended when one has done nothing to earn it...?
How-ever, I do appreci-ate the thought, so...
if I do see her, I think I would like to commend her myself.

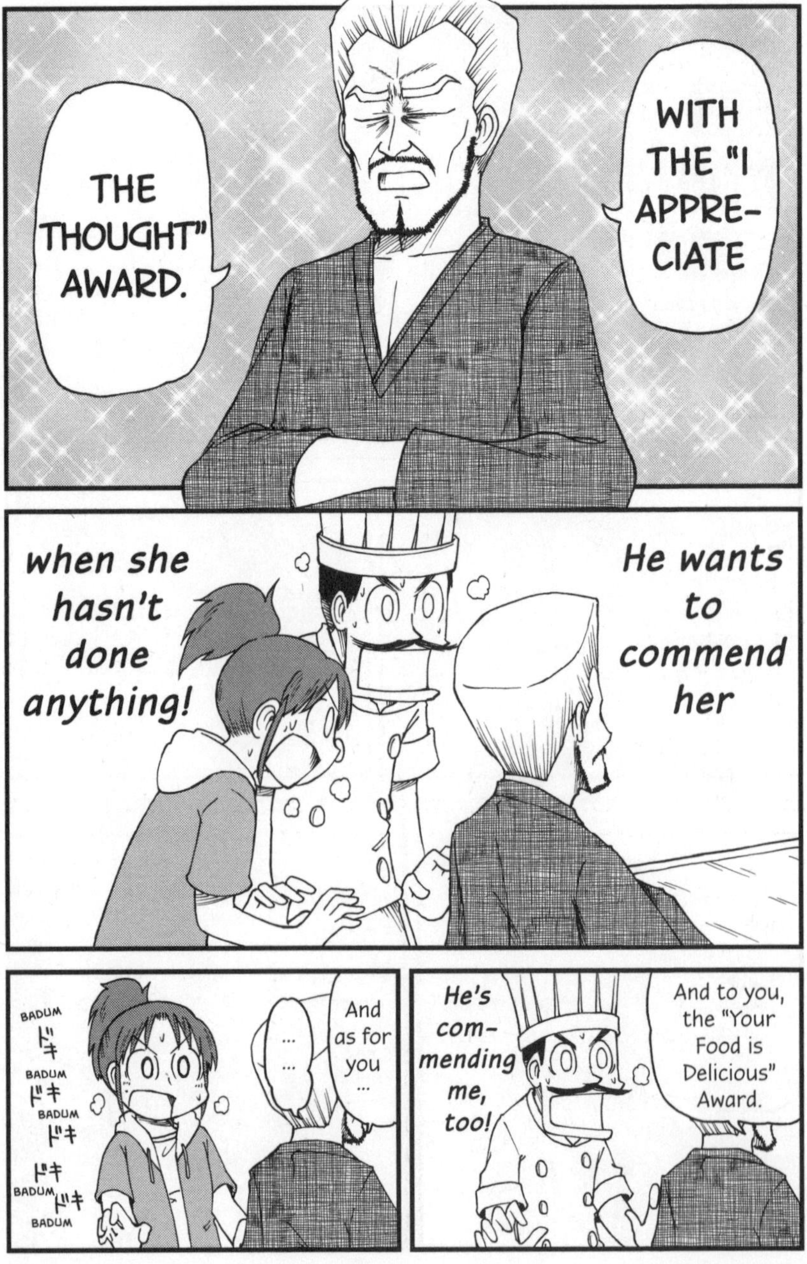
WITH THE "I APPRE-CIATE
THE THOUGHT" AWARD.
He wants to commend her
when she hasn't done anything!
And to you, the "Your Food is Delicious" Award.
He's com-mending me, too!
And as for you ...
... ...
BADUM ドキ BADUM ドキ BADUM ドキ ドキ BADUM ドキ BADUM

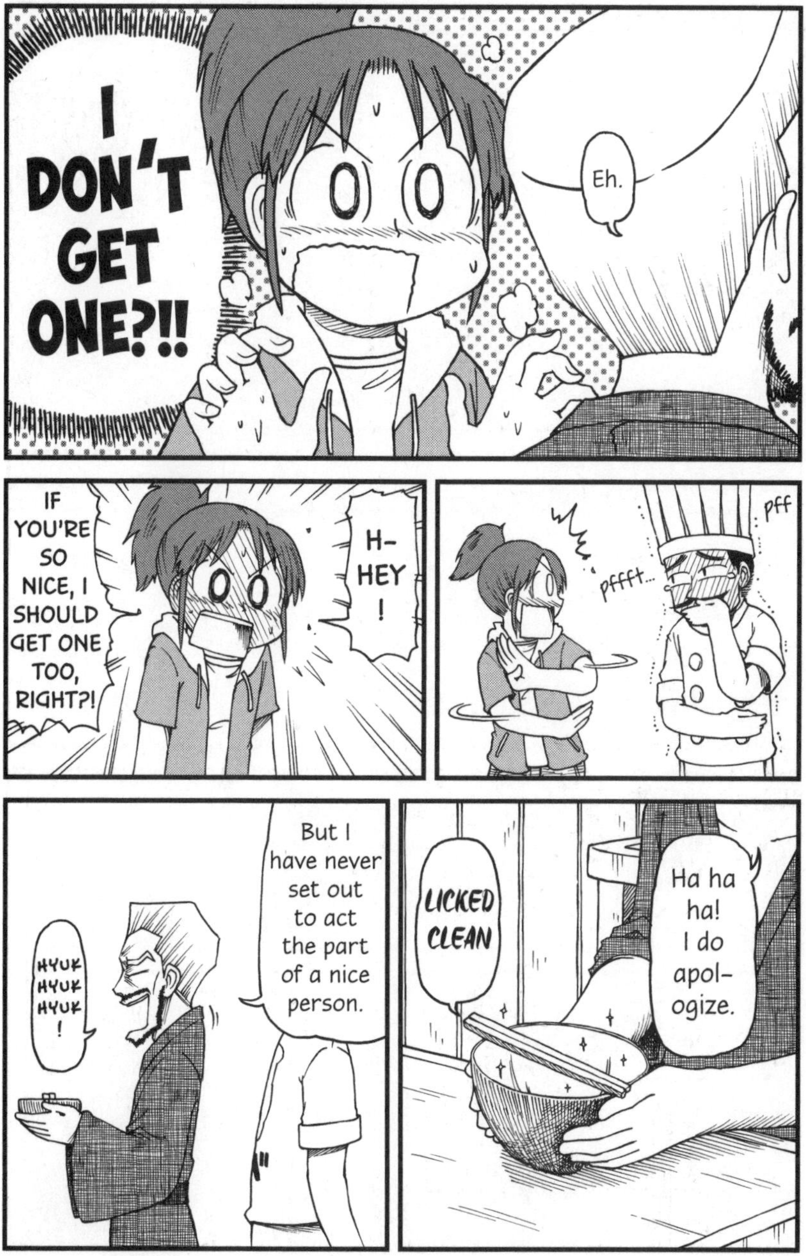
Eh.
I DON'T GET ONE?!!
pff
pffft...
H-HEY!
IF YOU'RE SO NICE, I SHOULD GET ONE TOO, RIGHT?!
Ha ha ha! I do apol-ogize.
LICKED CLEAN
But I have never set out to act the part of a nice person.
HYUK HYUK HYUK!

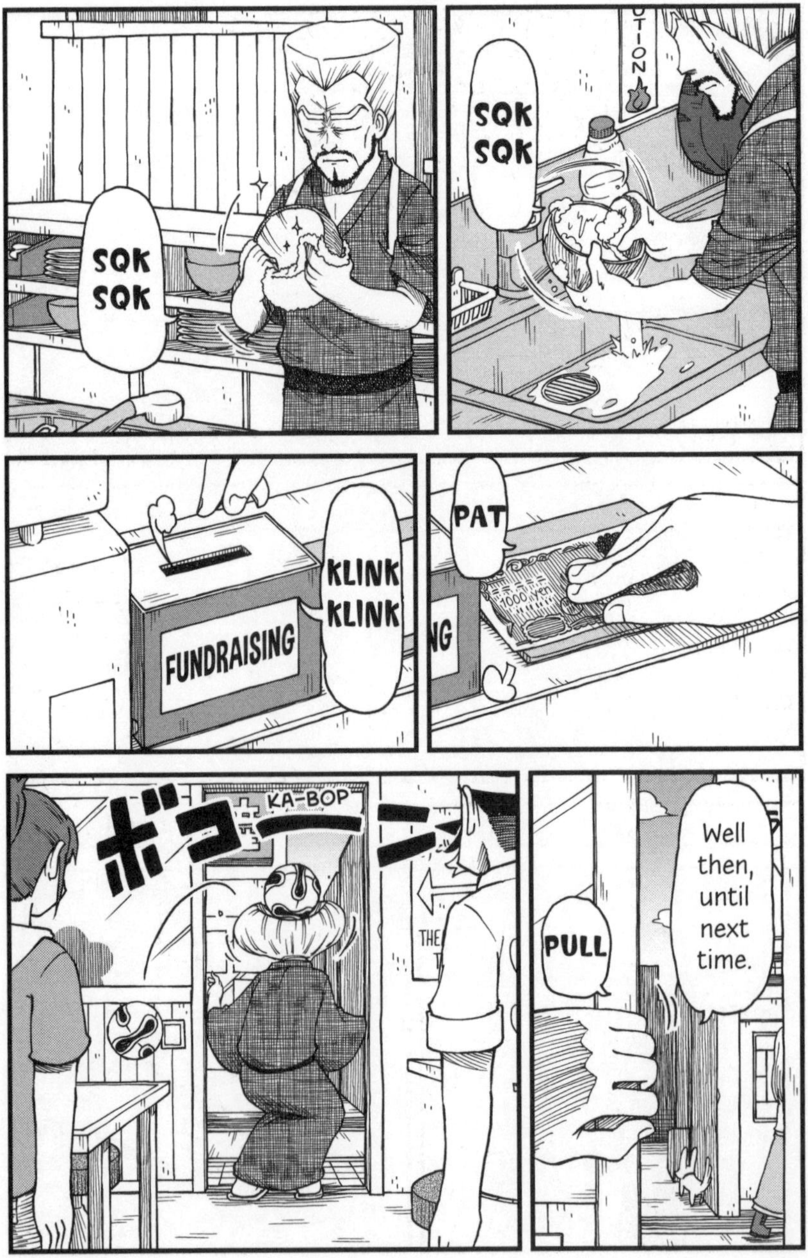
SQK SQK
SQK SQK
PAT
1000 yen
KLINK KLINK
FUNDRAISING
Well then, until next time.
PULL
KA-BOP

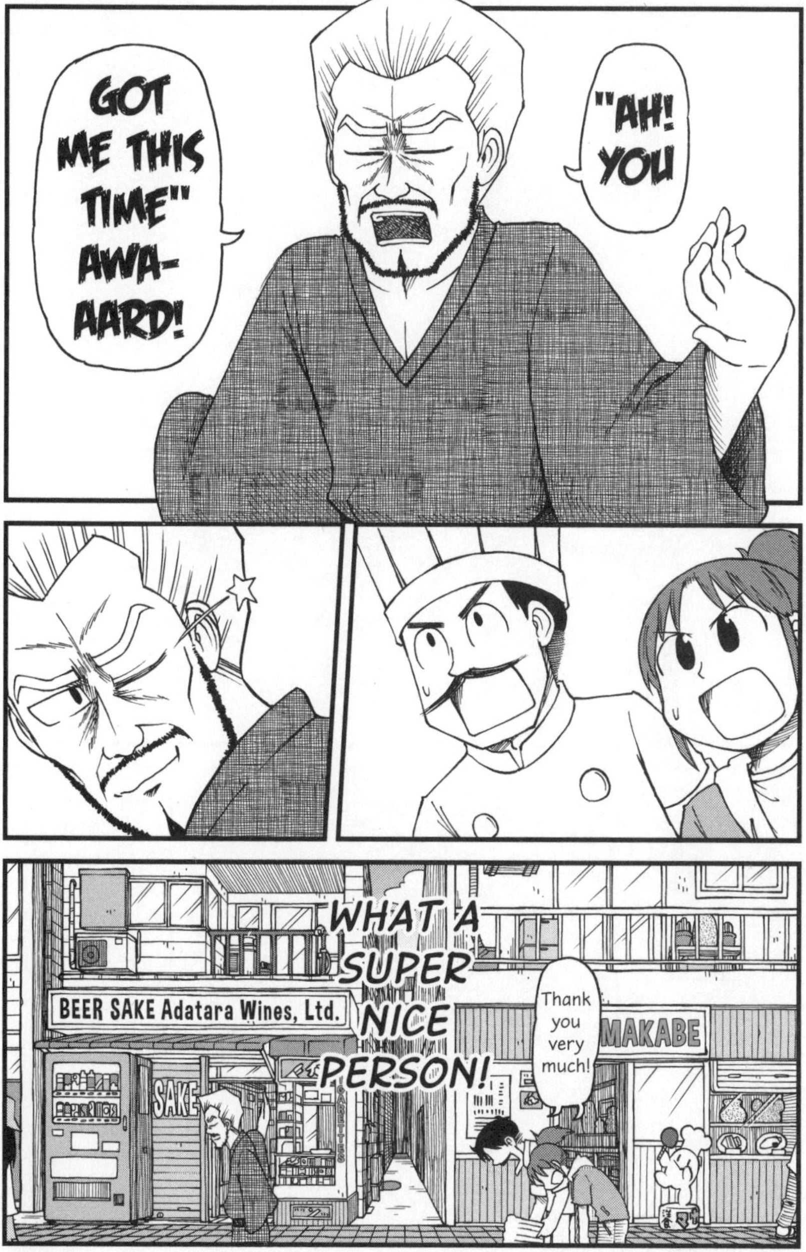
"AH! YOU
GOT ME THIS TIME" AWA-AARD!
WHAT A SUPER NICE PERSON!
Thank you very much!
MAKABE
BEER SAKE Adatara Wines, Ltd.
SAKE

LICKED CLEAN

CITY

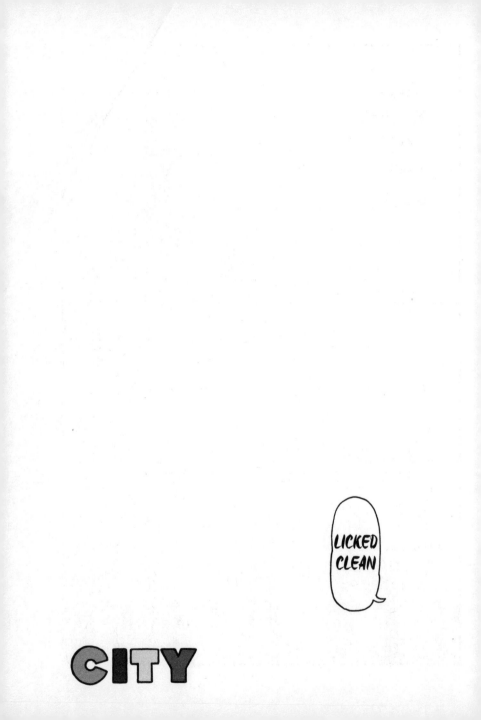

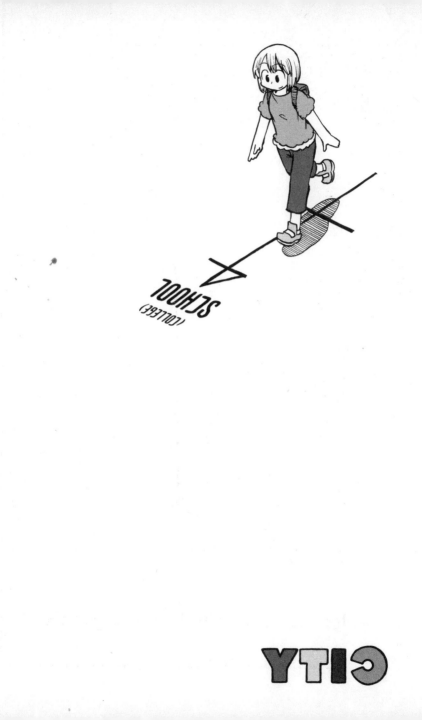

SCHOOL
(COLLEGE)

CITY

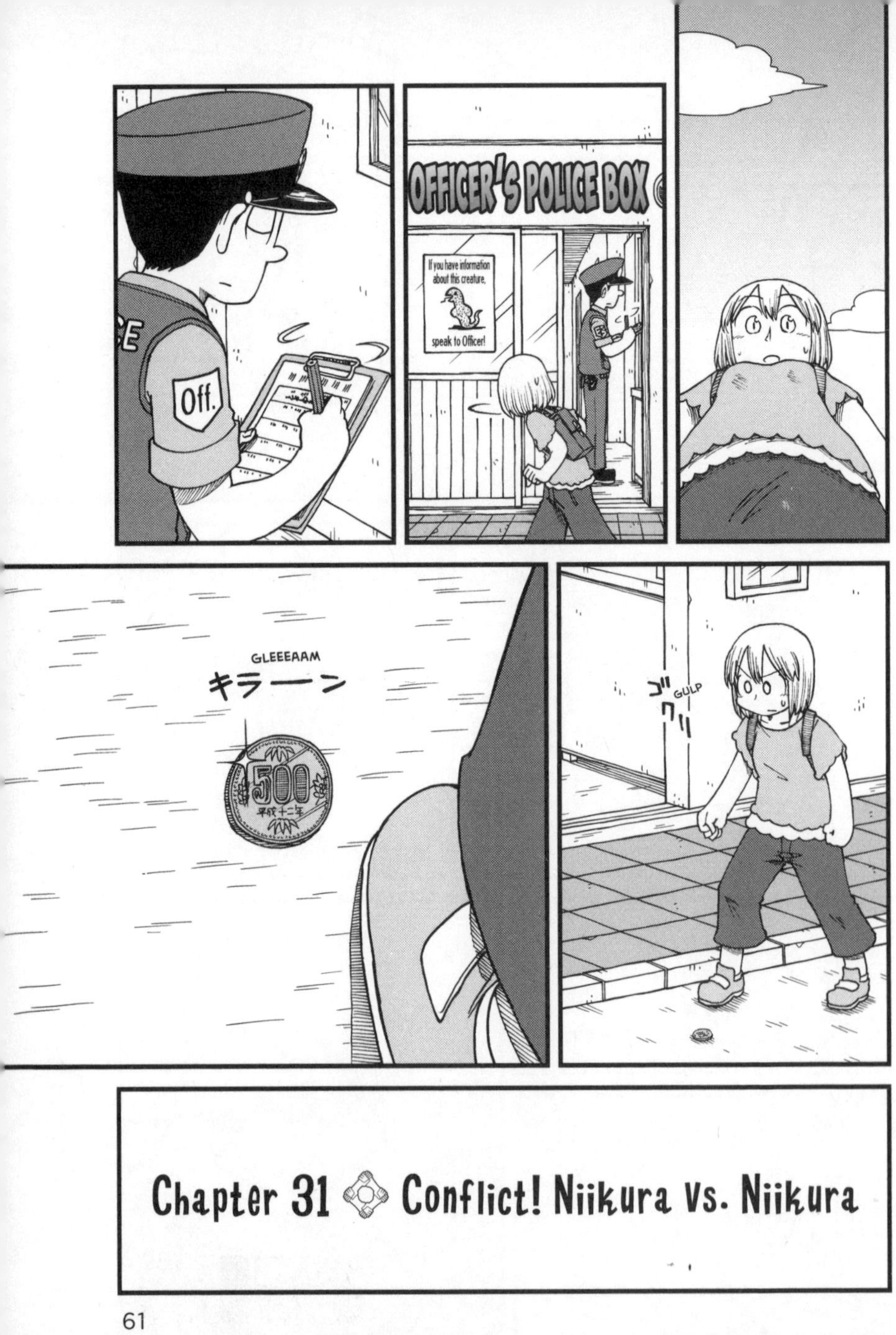
OFFICER'S POLICE BOX
If you have information about this creature, speak to Officer!
Off.
ゴクリ
GULP
キラーーン
GLEEEAAM
500
平成十二年

Chapter 31 Conflict! Niikura Vs. Niikura

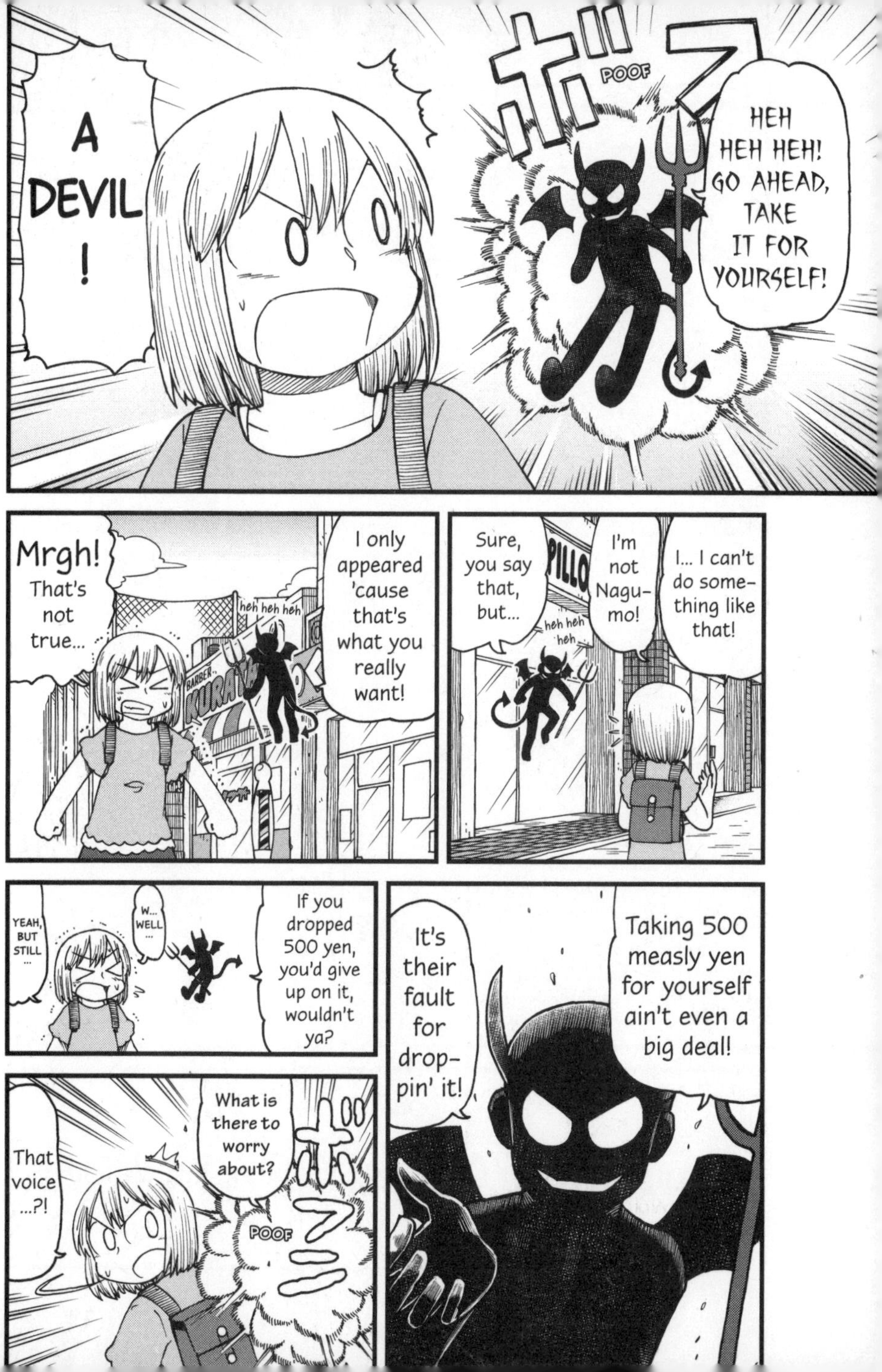
ボフ
POOF
HEH HEH HEH! GO AHEAD, TAKE IT FOR YOURSELF!
A DEVIL !
I... I can't do some-thing like that!
I'm not Nagu-mo!
heh heh heh
Sure, you say that, but...
PILLO
I only appeared 'cause that's what you really want!
heh heh heh
BARBER
Mrgh! That's not true...
Taking 500 measly yen for yourself ain't even a big deal!
It's their fault for drop-pin' it!
If you dropped 500 yen, you'd give up on it, wouldn't ya?
W... WELL ...
YEAH, BUT STILL ...
What is there to worry about?
POOF
That voice ...?!

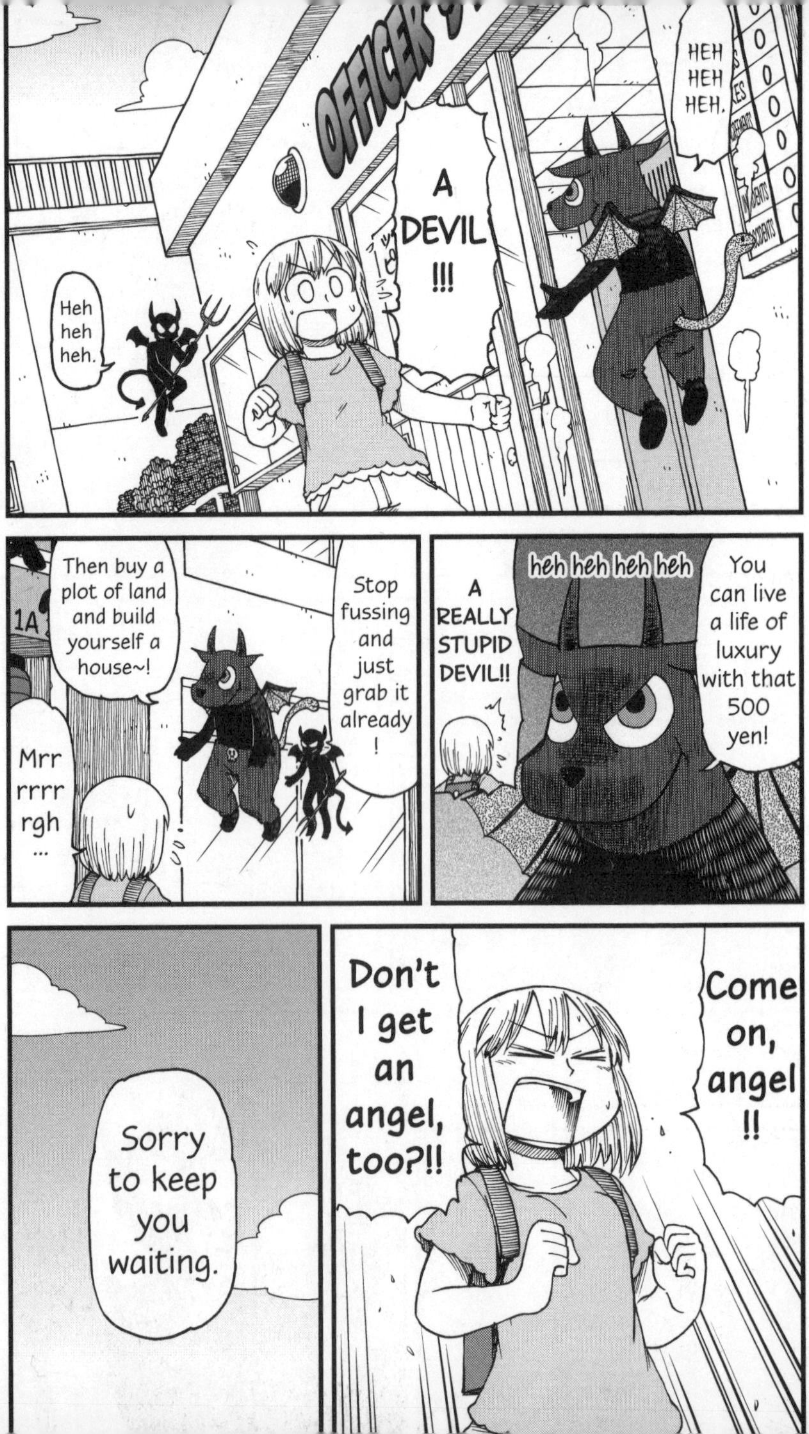
HEH HEH HEH.
A DEVIL !!!
Heh heh heh.
You can live a life of luxury with that 500 yen!
heh heh heh heh
A REALLY STUPID DEVIL!!
Stop fussing and just grab it already!
Then buy a plot of land and build yourself a house~!
Mrr rrrr rgh ...
Come on, angel!!
Don't I get an angel, too?!!
Sorry to keep you waiting.

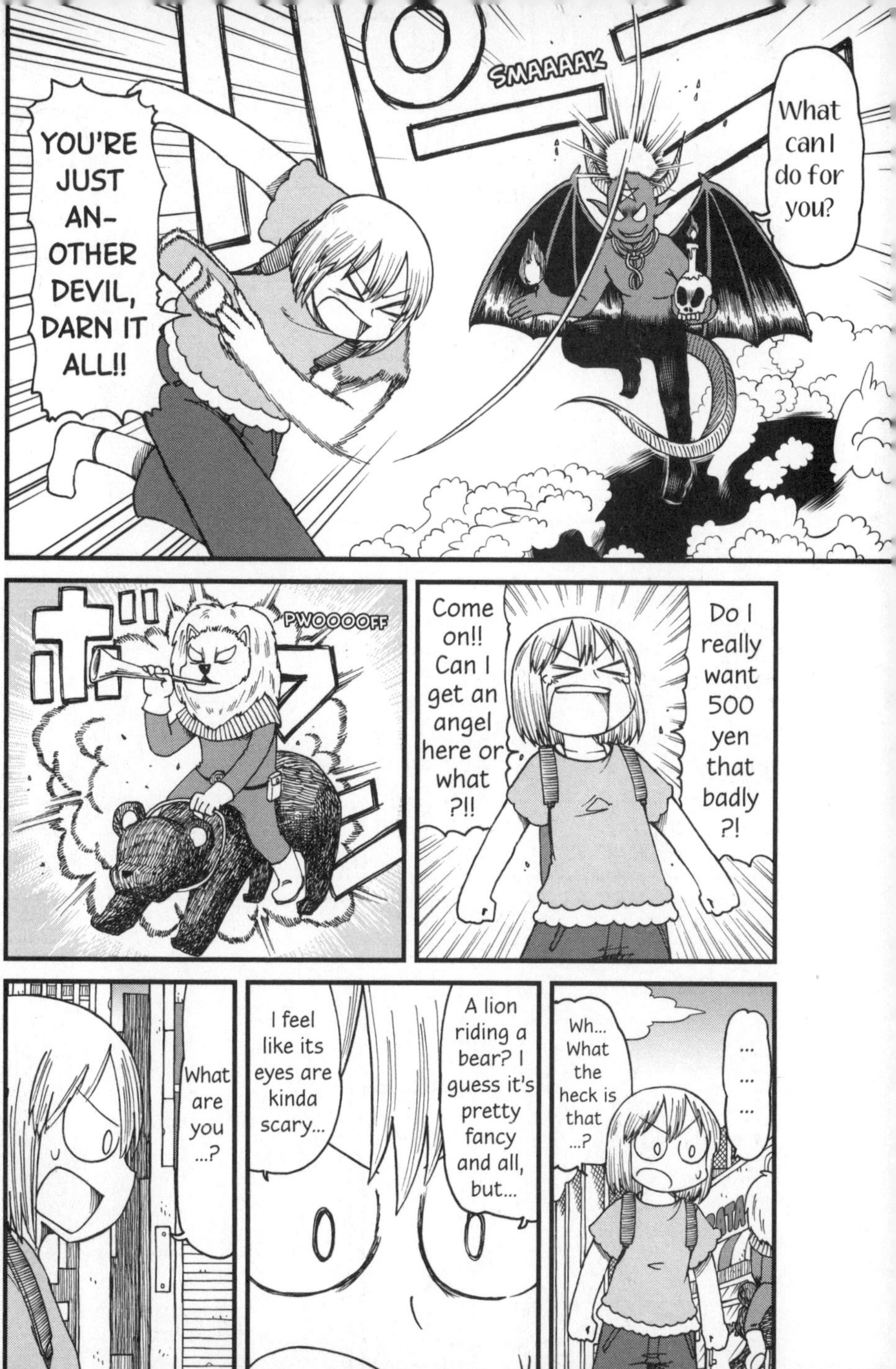
What can I do for you?
SMAAAAK
YOU'RE JUST AN-OTHER DEVIL, DARN IT ALL!!
Do I really want 500 yen that badly?!
Come on!! Can I get an angel here or what?!!
PWOOOOFF
...
...
...
Wh... What the heck is that...?
A lion riding a bear? I guess it's pretty fancy and all, but...
I feel like its eyes are kinda scary...
What are you...?

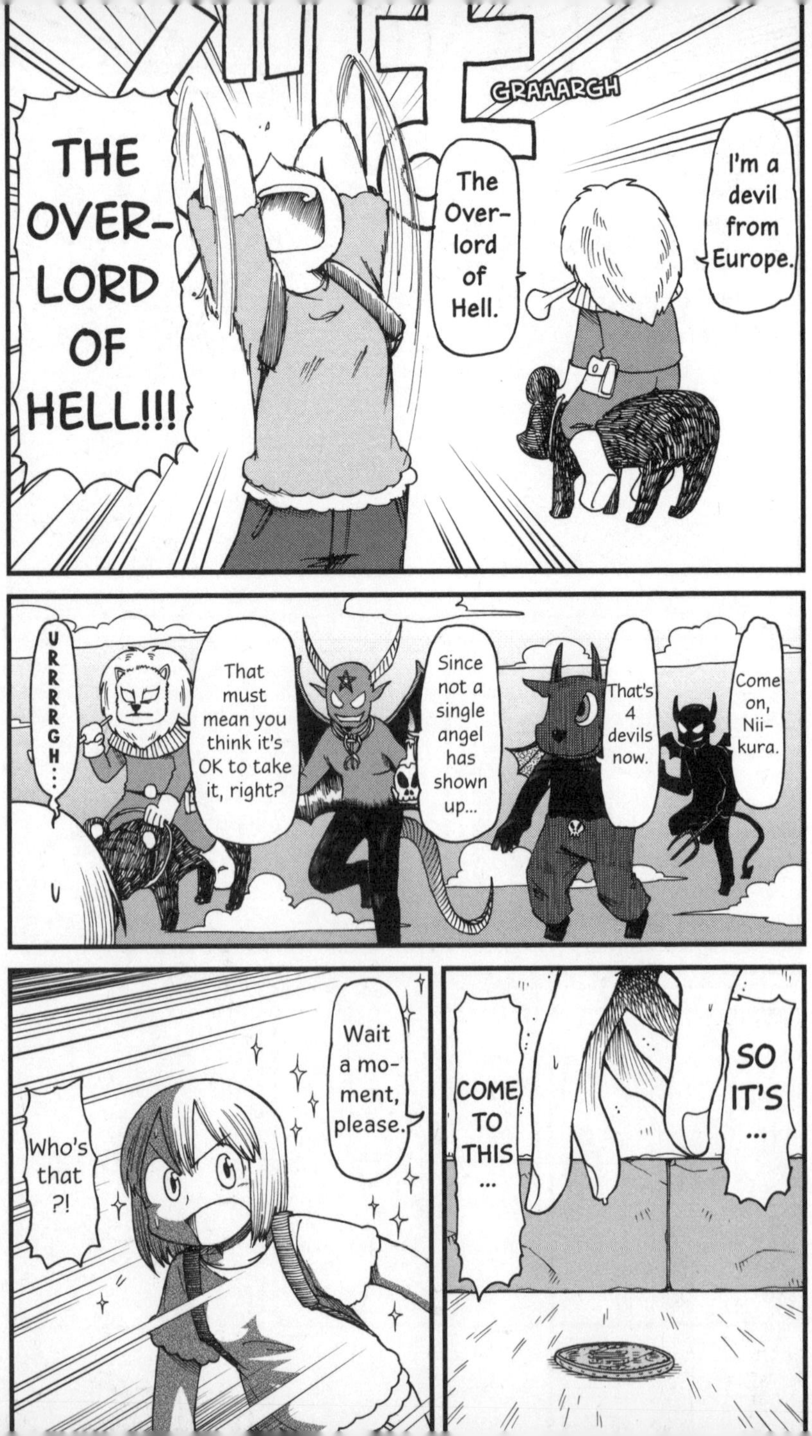
I'm a devil from Europe.
The Over-lord of Hell.
GRAAARGH
THE OVER-LORD OF HELL!!!
Come on, Nii-kura.
That's 4 devils now.
Since not a single angel has shown up...
That must mean you think it's OK to take it, right?
URRRRGH...
SO IT'S ...
COME TO THIS ...
Wait a mo-ment, please.
Who's that ?!

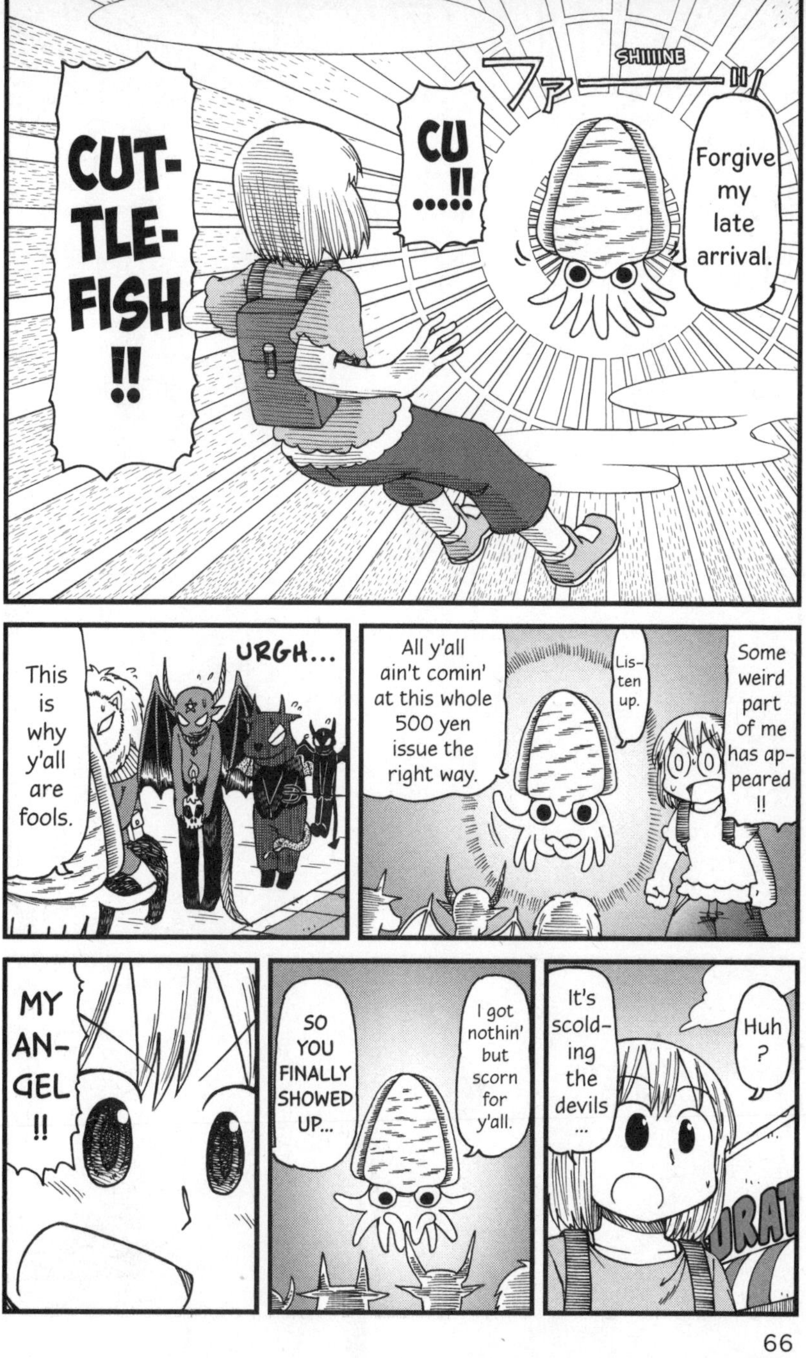
SHIIIINE
ファー
Forgive my late arrival.
CU ...!!
CUT-TLE-FISH !!
Some weird part of me has ap-peared !!
Lis-ten up.
All y'all ain't comin' at this whole 500 yen issue the right way.
URGH...
This is why y'all are fools.
Huh ?
It's scold-ing the devils ...
URAT
I got nothin' but scorn for y'all.
SO YOU FINALLY SHOWED UP...
MY AN-GEL !!

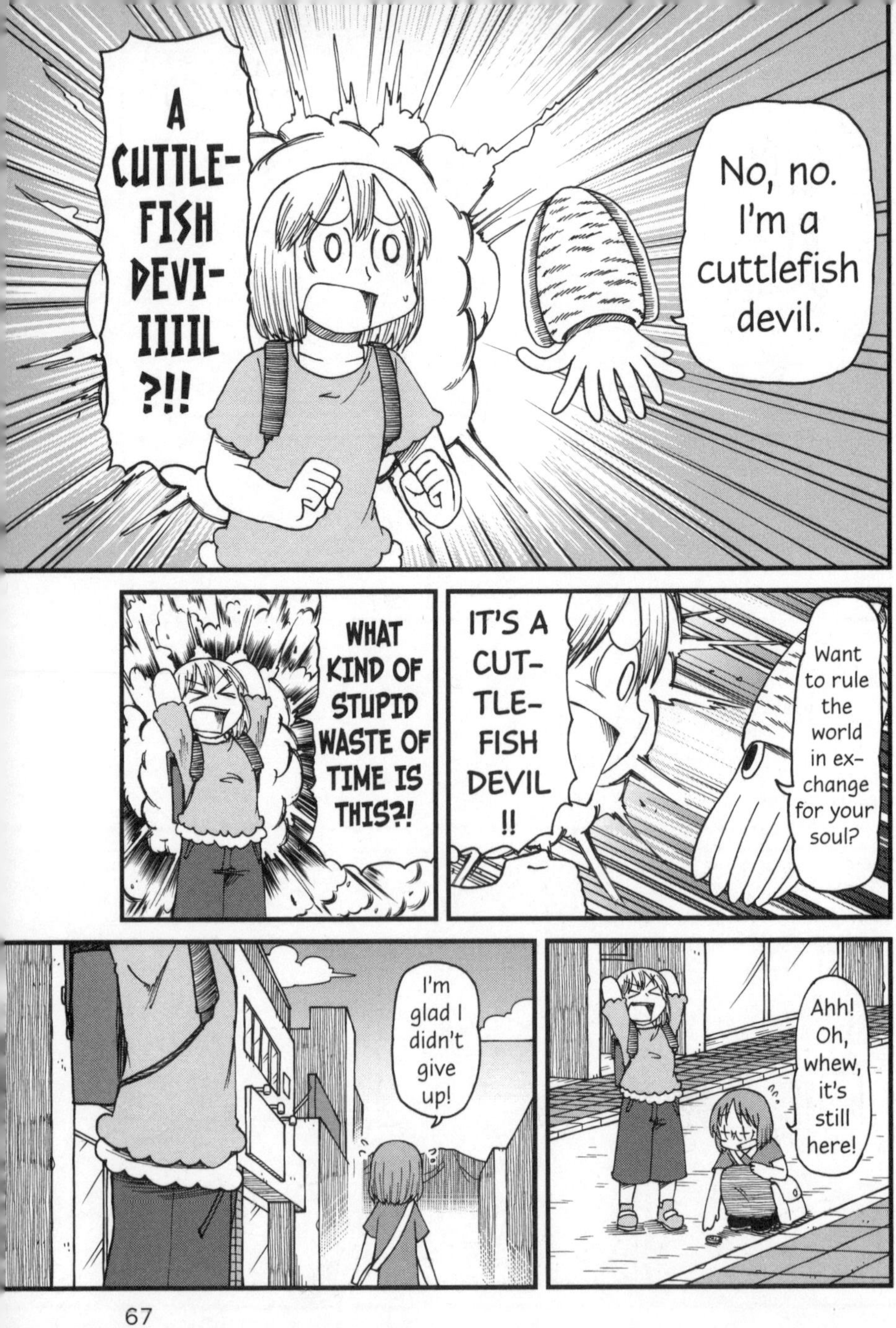
No, no. I'm a cuttlefish devil.
A CUTTLE-FISH DEVI-IIIIL?!!
Want to rule the world in ex-change for your soul?
IT'S A CUT-TLE-FISH DEVIL!!
WHAT KIND OF STUPID WASTE OF TIME IS THIS?!
Ahh! Oh, whew, it's still here!
I'm glad I didn't give up!

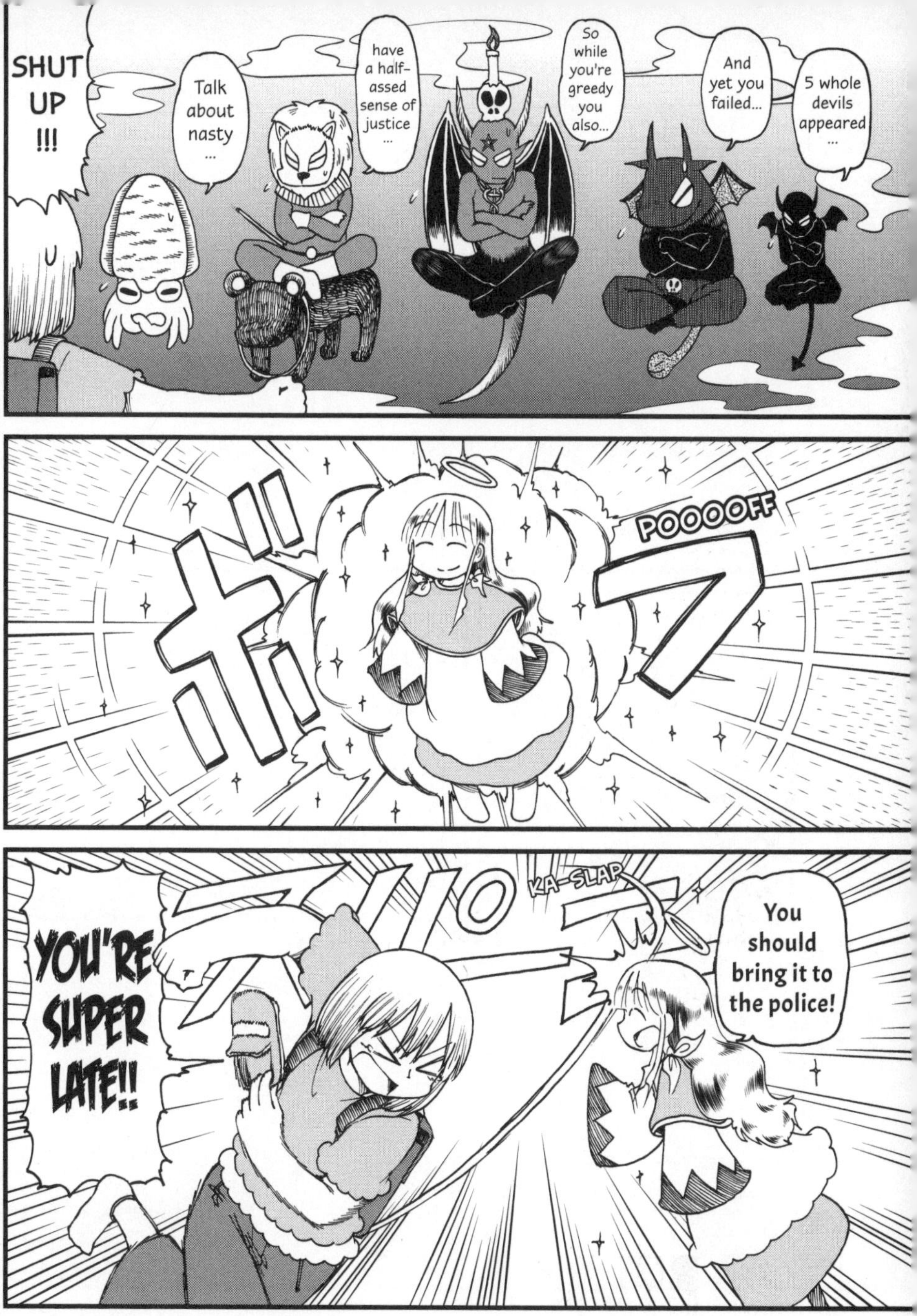
5 whole devils appeared ...
And yet you failed...
So while you're greedy you also...
have a half-assed sense of justice ...
Talk about nasty ...
SHUT UP !!!
POOOOFF
You should bring it to the police!
KA-SLAP
YOU'RE SUPER LATE!!

500

CITY

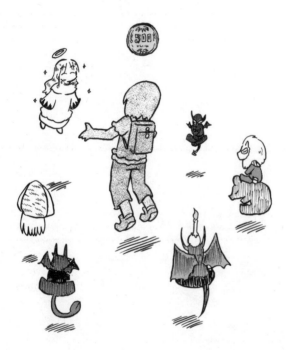

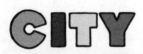

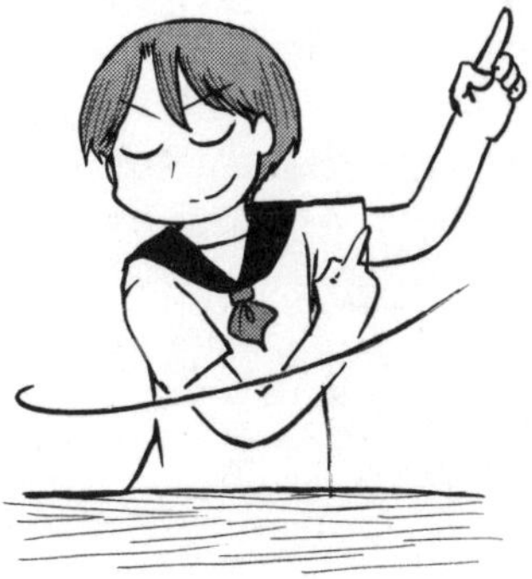

CITY

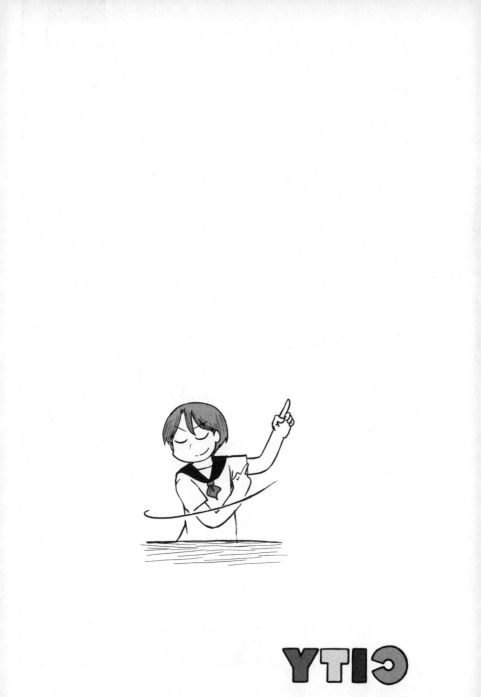

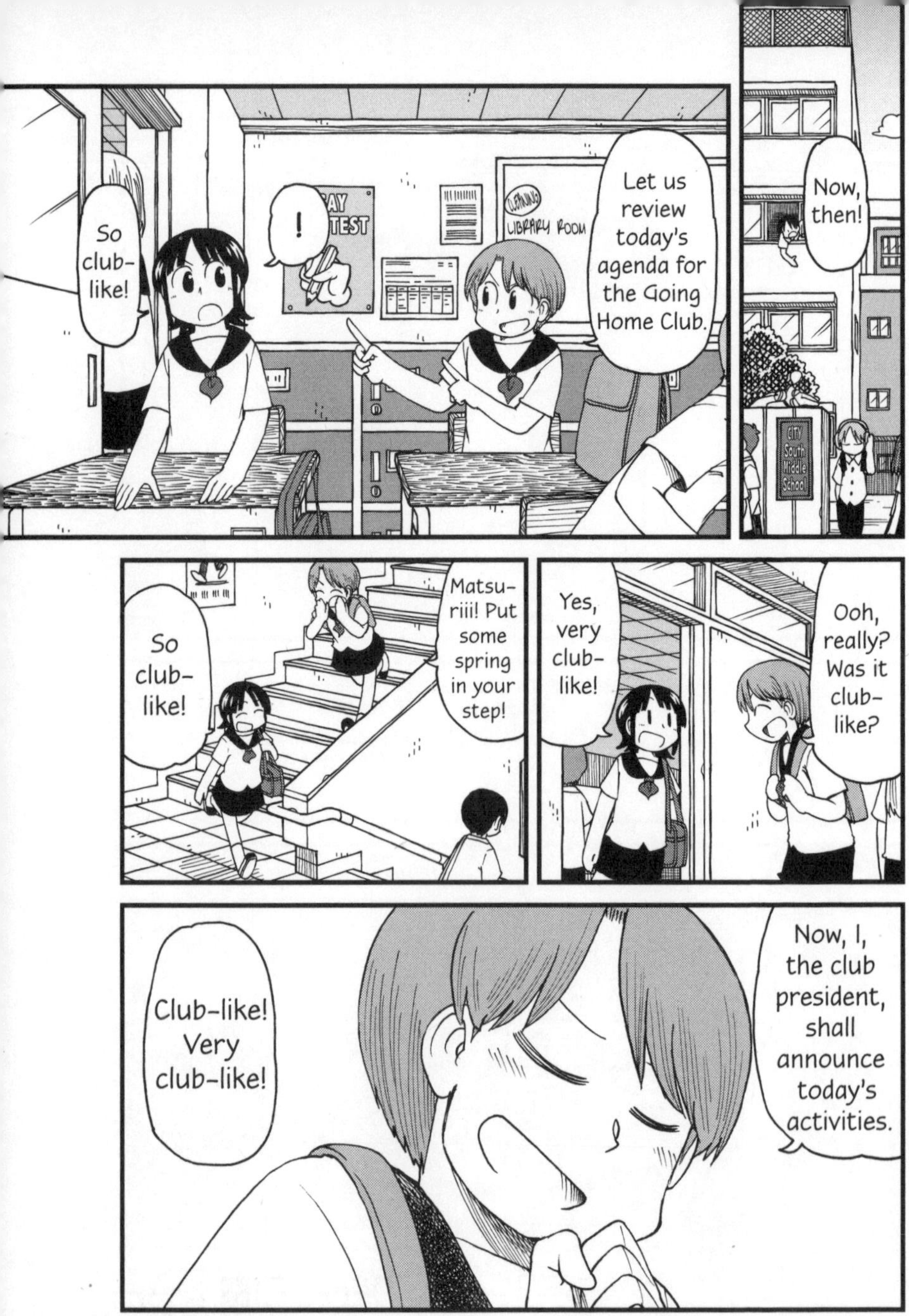
Now, then!
CITY South Middle School
Let us review today's agenda for the Going Home Club.
LIBRARY ROOM
!
So club-like!
Ooh, really? Was it club-like?
Yes, very club-like!
Matsu-riii! Put some spring in your step!
So club-like!
Now, I, the club president, shall announce today's activities.
Club-like! Very club-like!

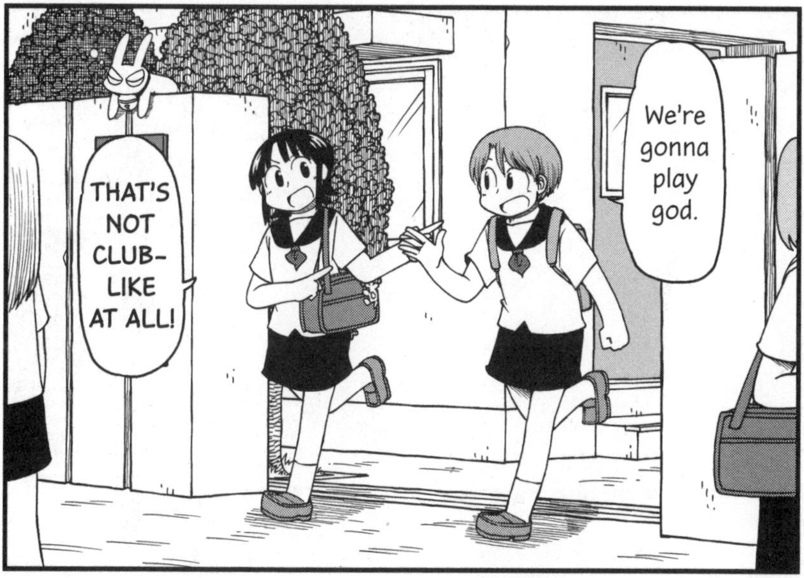
We're gonna play god.
THAT'S NOT CLUB-LIKE AT ALL!

Chapter 30 Playing God

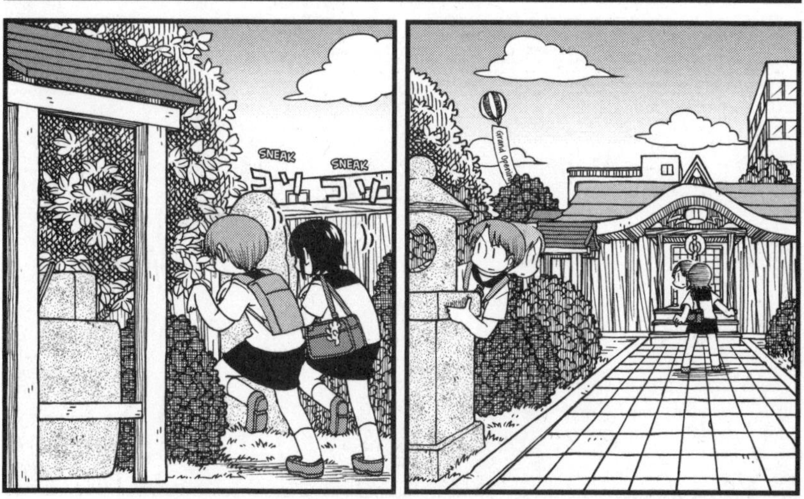
SNEAK
SNEAK

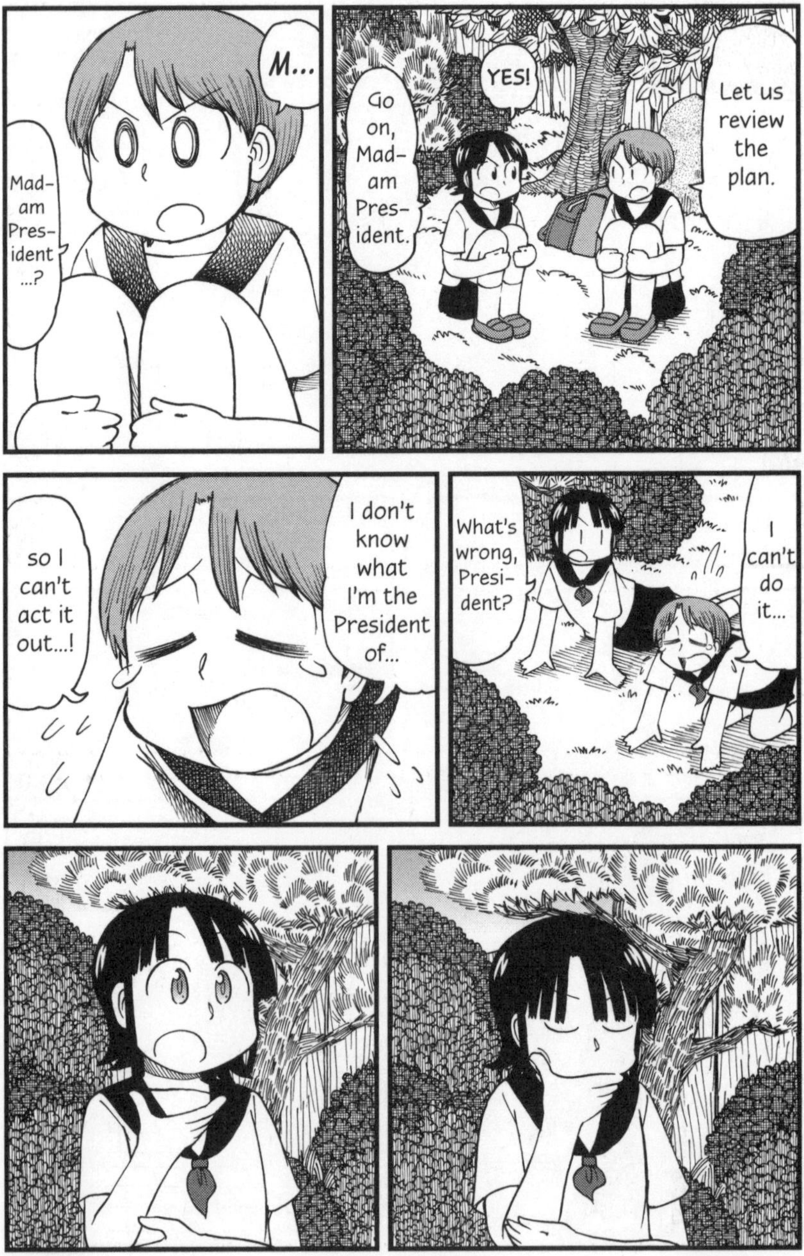
Let us review the plan.
YES!
Go on, Madam President.
M...
Madam President...?
I can't do it...
What's wrong, President?
I don't know what I'm the President of...
so I can't act it out...!

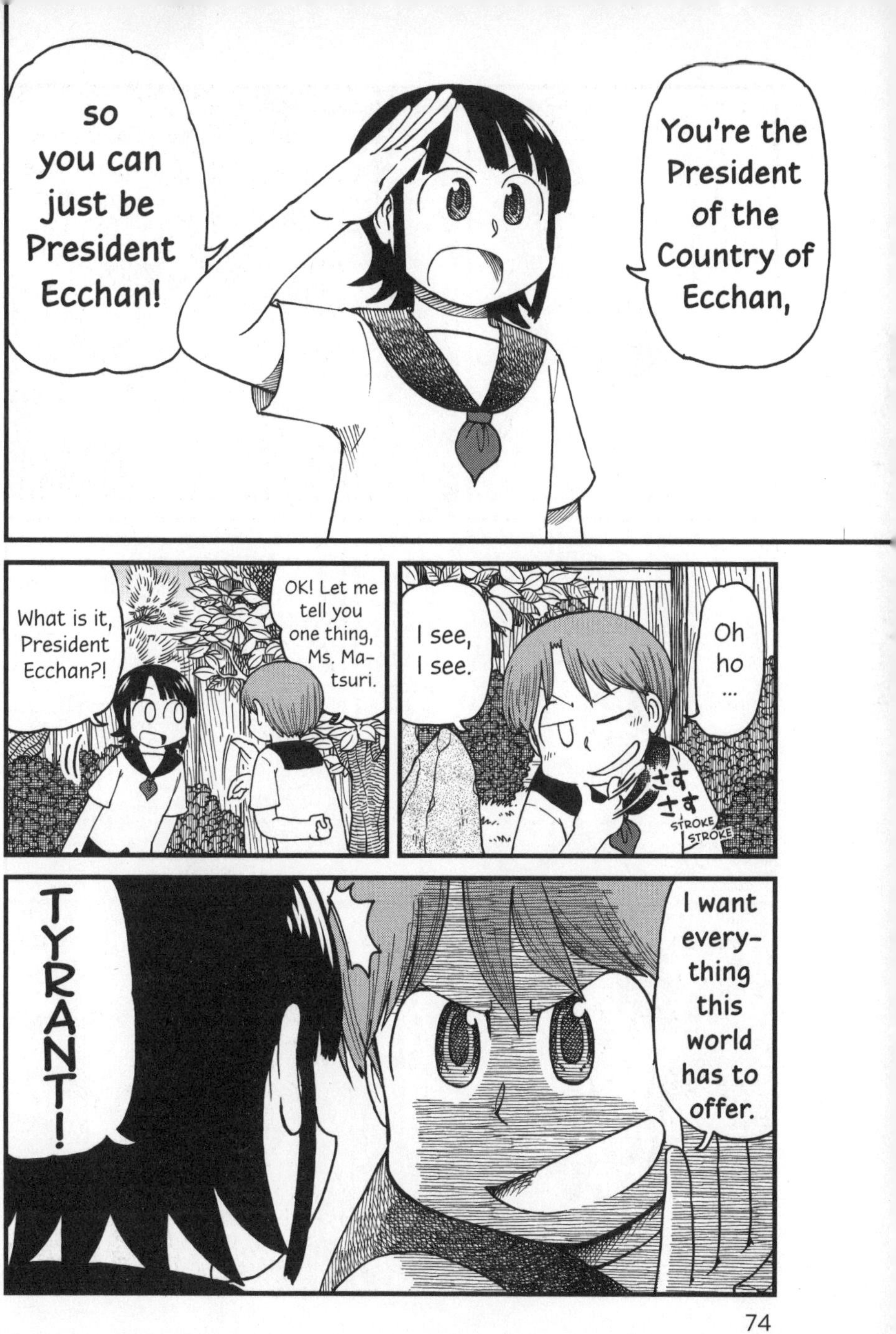
You're the President of the Country of Ecchan,
so you can just be President Ecchan!
Oh ho ...
I see, I see.
さすさす
STROKE STROKE
OK! Let me tell you one thing, Ms. Matsuri.
What is it, President Ecchan?!
I want everything this world has to offer.
TYRANT!

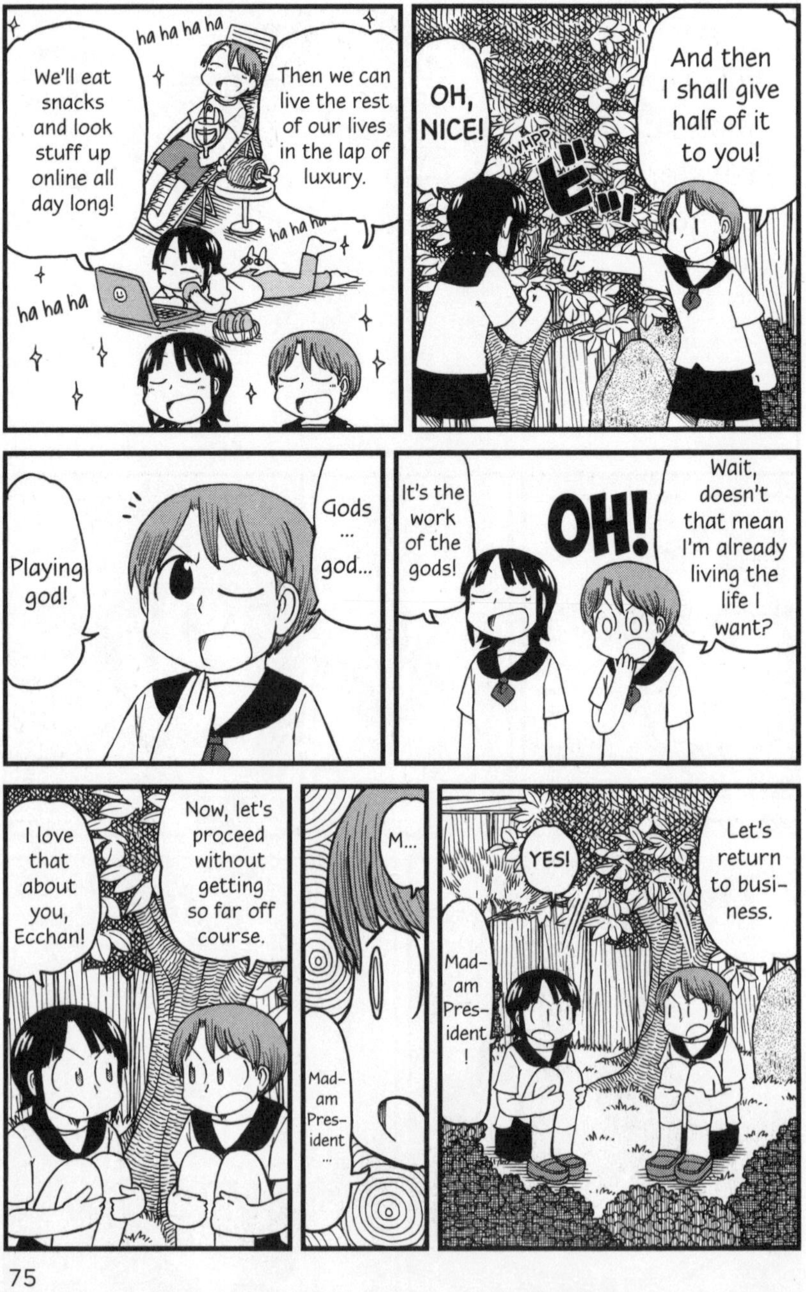
And then I shall give half of it to you!
WHPP
OH, NICE!
Then we can live the rest of our lives in the lap of luxury.
ha ha ha ha
We'll eat snacks and look stuff up online all day long!
ha ha ha
ha ha ha
Wait, doesn't that mean I'm already living the life I want?
OH!
It's the work of the gods!
Gods ... god...
Playing god!
Let's return to busi-ness.
YES!
Mad-am Pres-ident!
M...
Mad-am Pres-ident ...
Now, let's proceed without getting so far off course.
I love that about you, Ecchan!

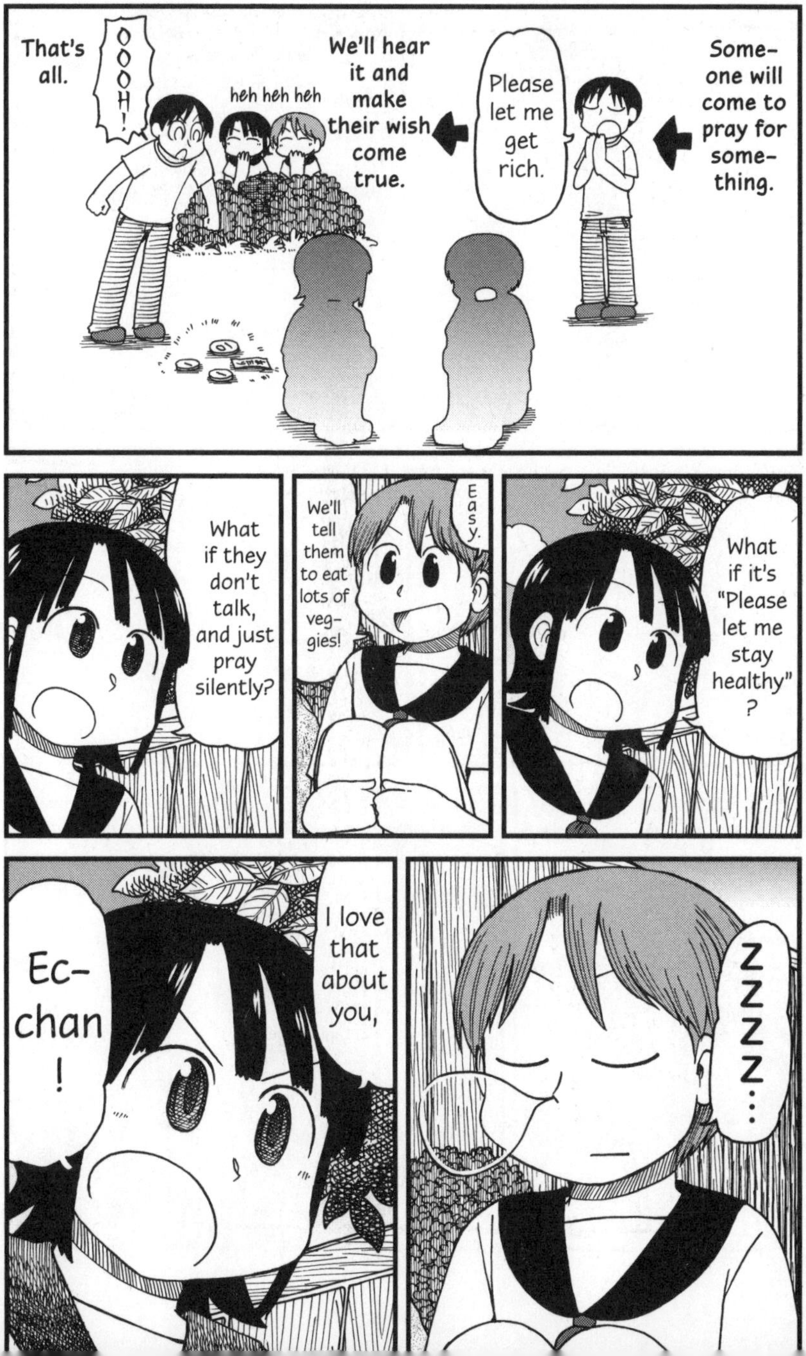
Some-one will come to pray for some-thing.
Please let me get rich.
We'll hear it and make their wish come true.
heh heh heh
OOOH!
That's all.
What if it's "Please let me stay healthy"?
Easy.
We'll tell them to eat lots of veg-gies!
What if they don't talk, and just pray silently?
ZZZZ...
I love that about you,
Ec-chan!

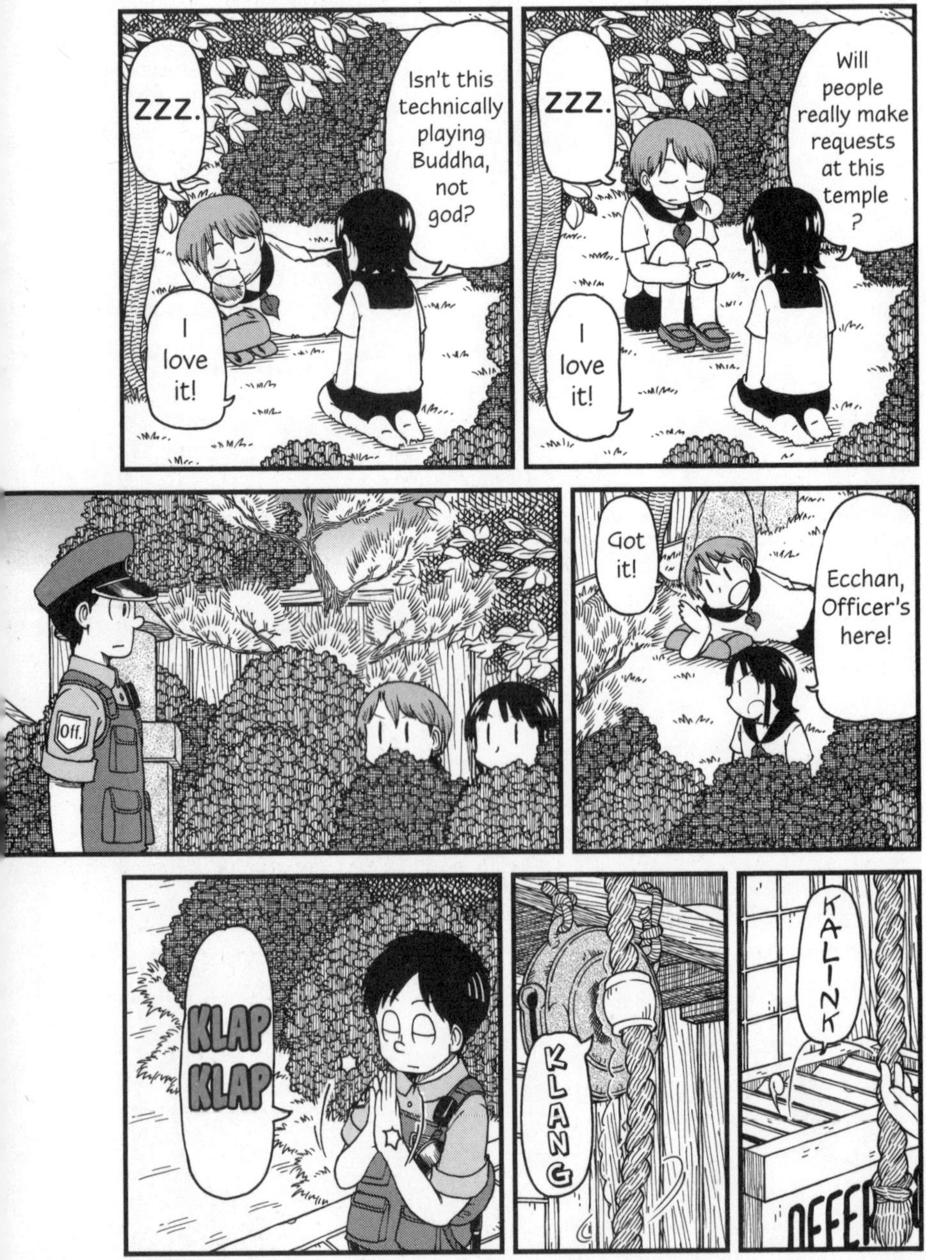
Will people really make requests at this temple?
ZZZ.
I love it!
Isn't this technically playing Buddha, not god?
ZZZ.
I love it!
Ecchan, Officer's here!
Got it!
Off.
KALINK
KLANG
KLAP KLAP

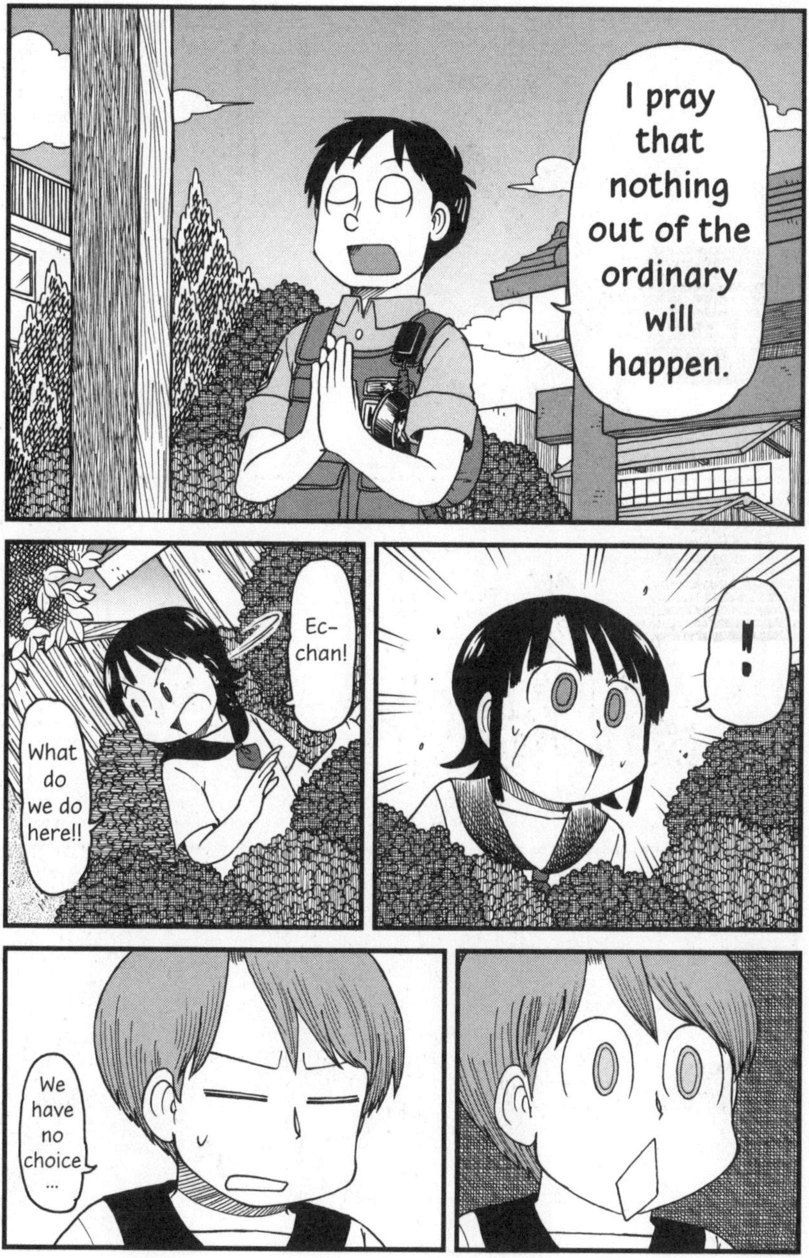
I pray that nothing out of the ordinary will happen.
!
Ec-chan!
What do we do here!!
We have no choice ...

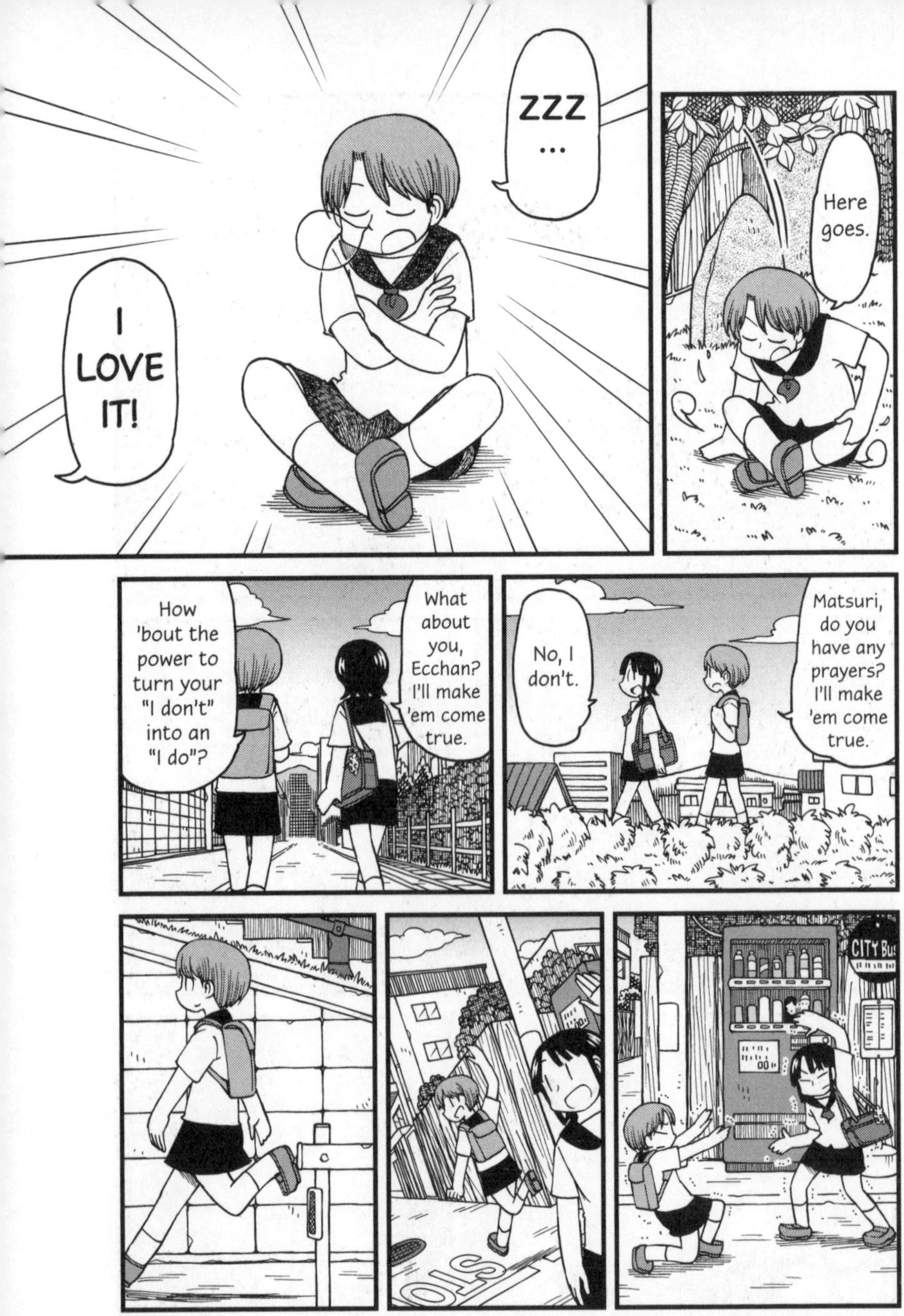
Here goes.
ZZZ ...
I LOVE IT!
Matsuri, do you have any prayers? I'll make 'em come true.
No, I don't.
What about you, Ecchan? I'll make 'em come true.
How 'bout the power to turn your "I don't" into an "I do"?
CITY Bus

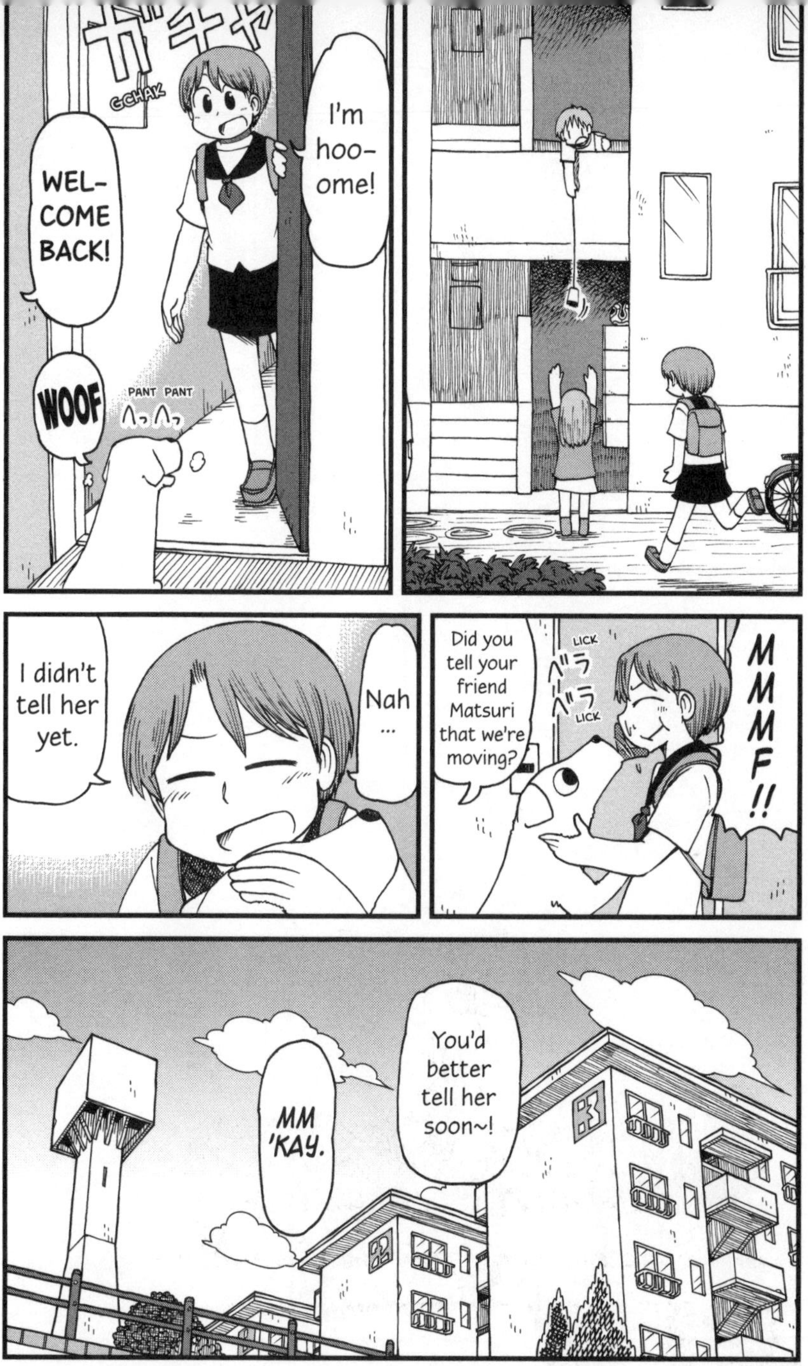
GCHAK
I'm hoo-ome!
WEL-COME BACK!
WOOF
PANT PANT
ヘっヘっ
MMMMF!!
LICK
ベラ
ベラ
LICK
Did you tell your friend Matsuri that we're moving?
Nah ...
I didn't tell her yet.
You'd better tell her soon~!
MM 'KAY.

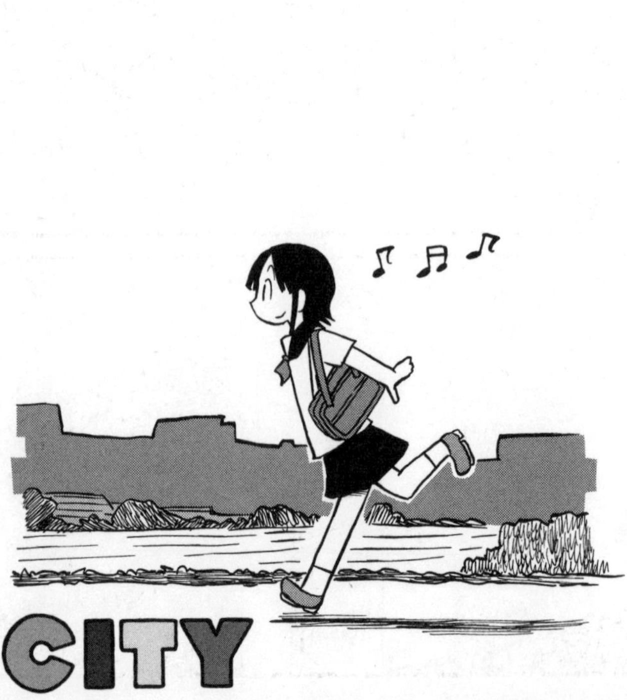
CITY

CITY

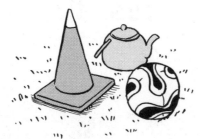

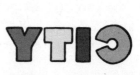

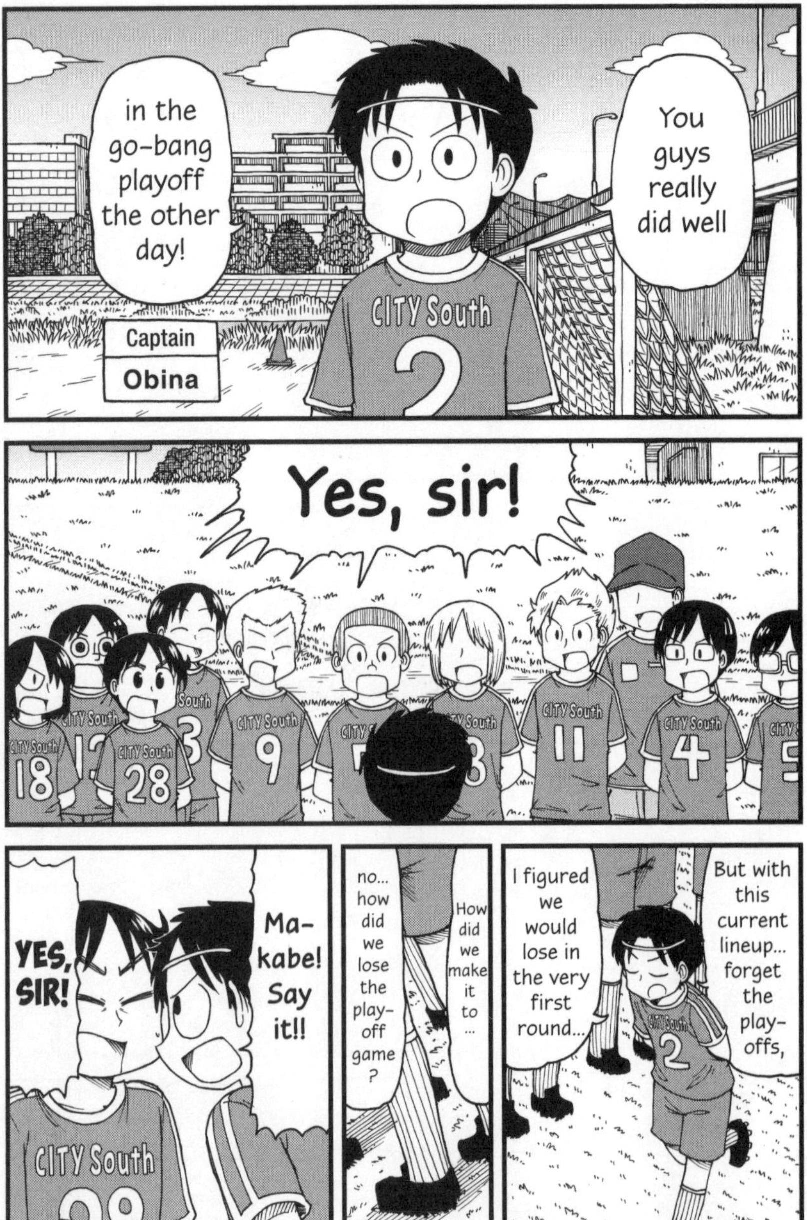
You guys really did well
in the go-bang playoff the other day!
Captain
Obina
Yes, sir!
But with this current lineup... forget the play-offs,
I figured we would lose in the very first round...
How did we make it to ...
no... how did we lose the play-off game ?
Ma-kabe! Say it!!
YES, SIR!

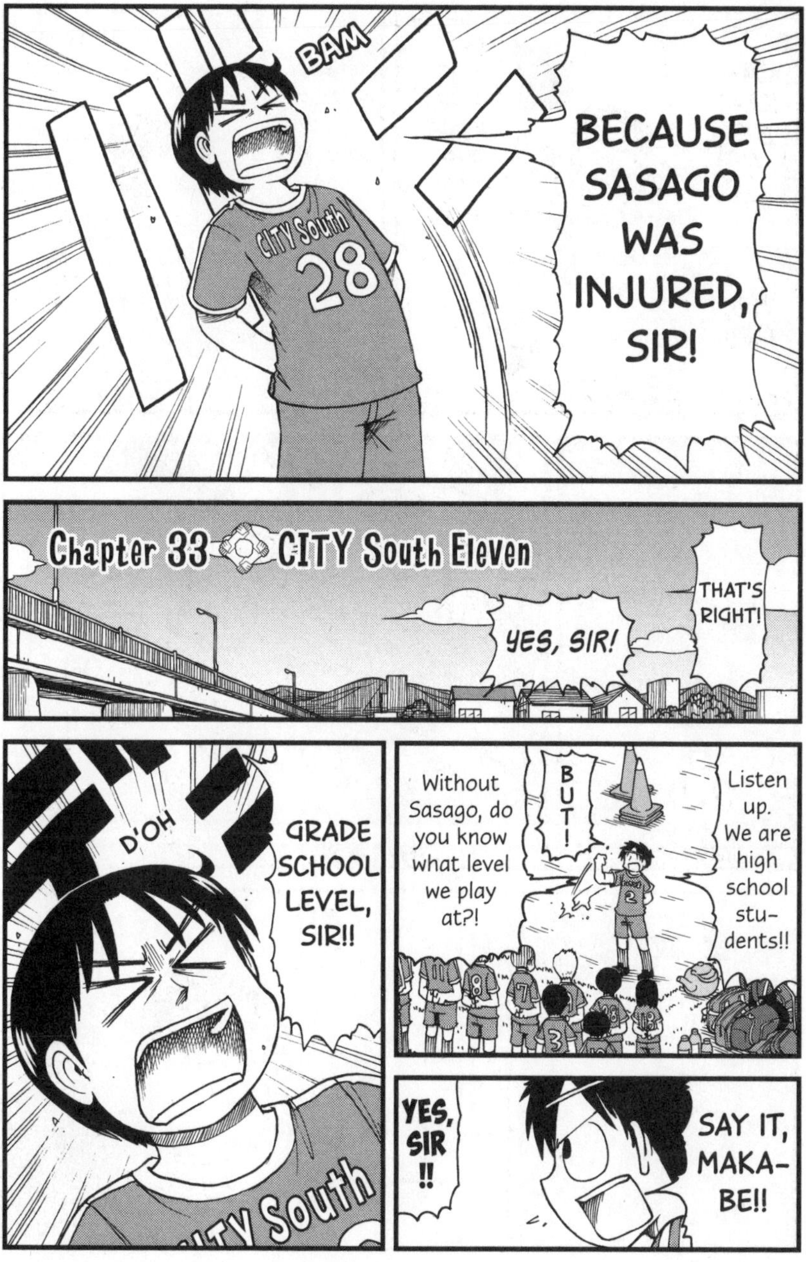
BECAUSE SASAGO WAS INJURED, SIR!
BAM
CITY South 28
Chapter 33 CITY South Eleven
THAT'S RIGHT!
YES, SIR!
Listen up. We are high school stu-dents!!
BUT!
Without Sasago, do you know what level we play at?!
SAY IT, MAKA-BE!!
YES, SIR!!
GRADE SCHOOL LEVEL, SIR!!
D'OH
CITY South

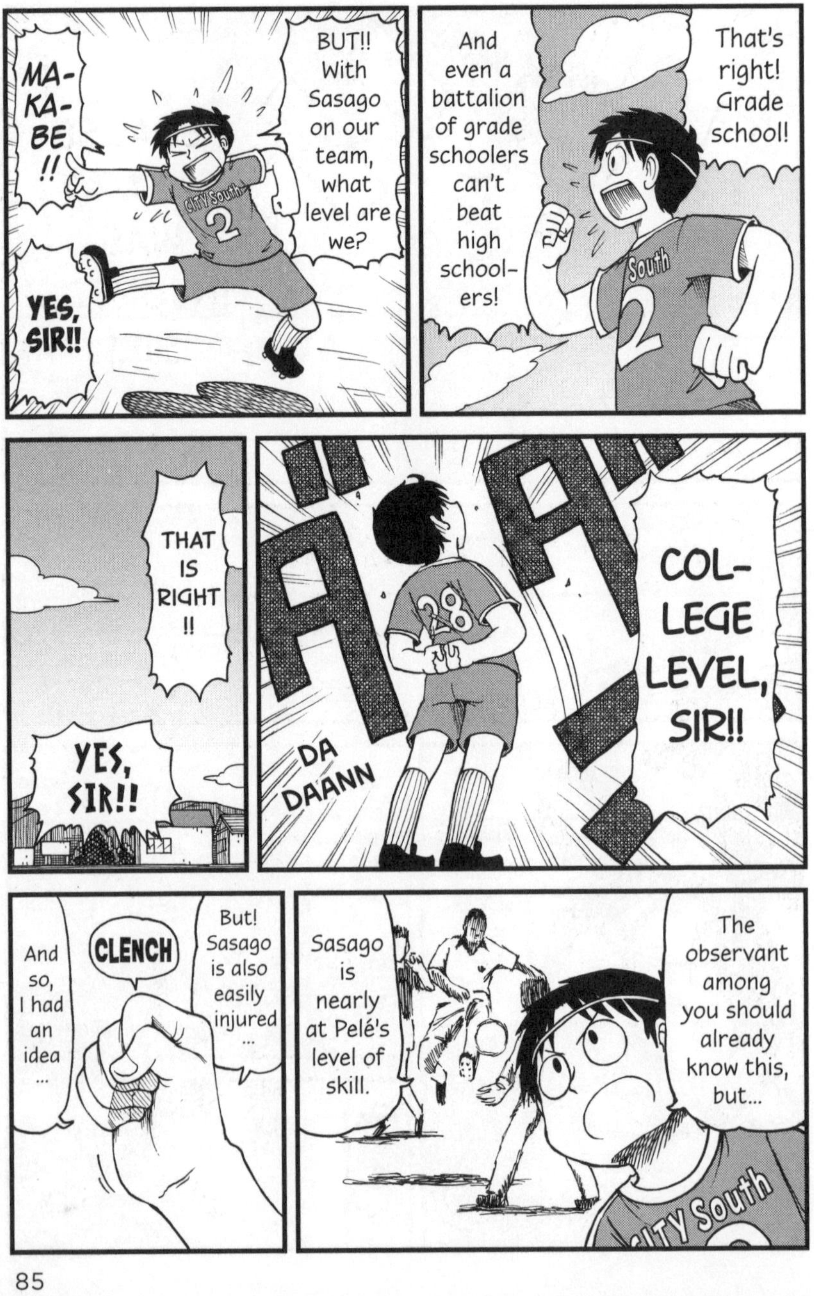
That's right! Grade school!
And even a battalion of grade schoolers can't beat high schoolers!
BUT!! With Sasago on our team, what level are we?
MA-KA-BE!!
YES, SIR!!
COL-LEGE LEVEL, SIR!!
DA DAANN
THAT IS RIGHT!!
YES, SIR!!
The observant among you should already know this, but...
Sasago is nearly at Pelé's level of skill.
But! Sasago is also easily injured ...
CLENCH
And so, I had an idea ...

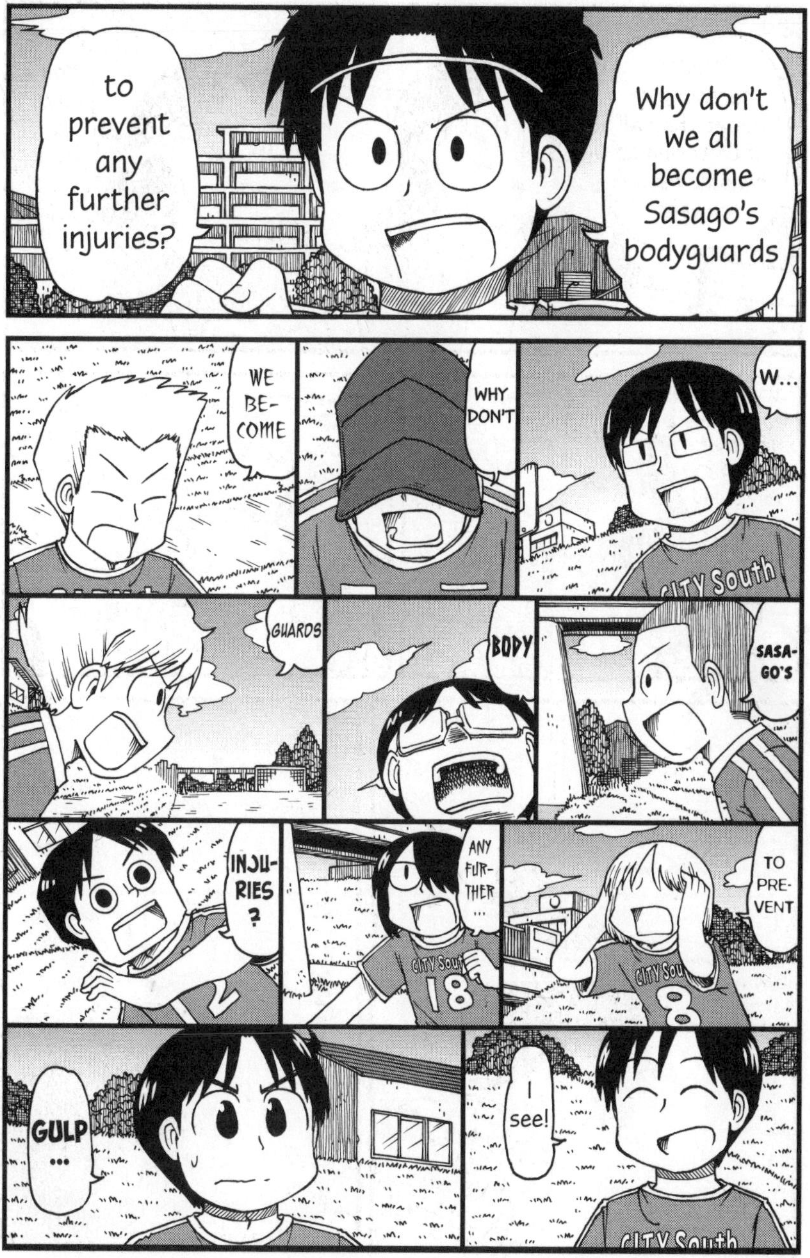
Why don't we all become Sasago's bodyguards
to prevent any further injuries?
W...
WHY DON'T
WE BE-COME
SASA-GO'S
BODY
GUARDS
TO PRE-VENT
ANY FUR-THER ...
INJU-RIES ?
I see!
GULP ...

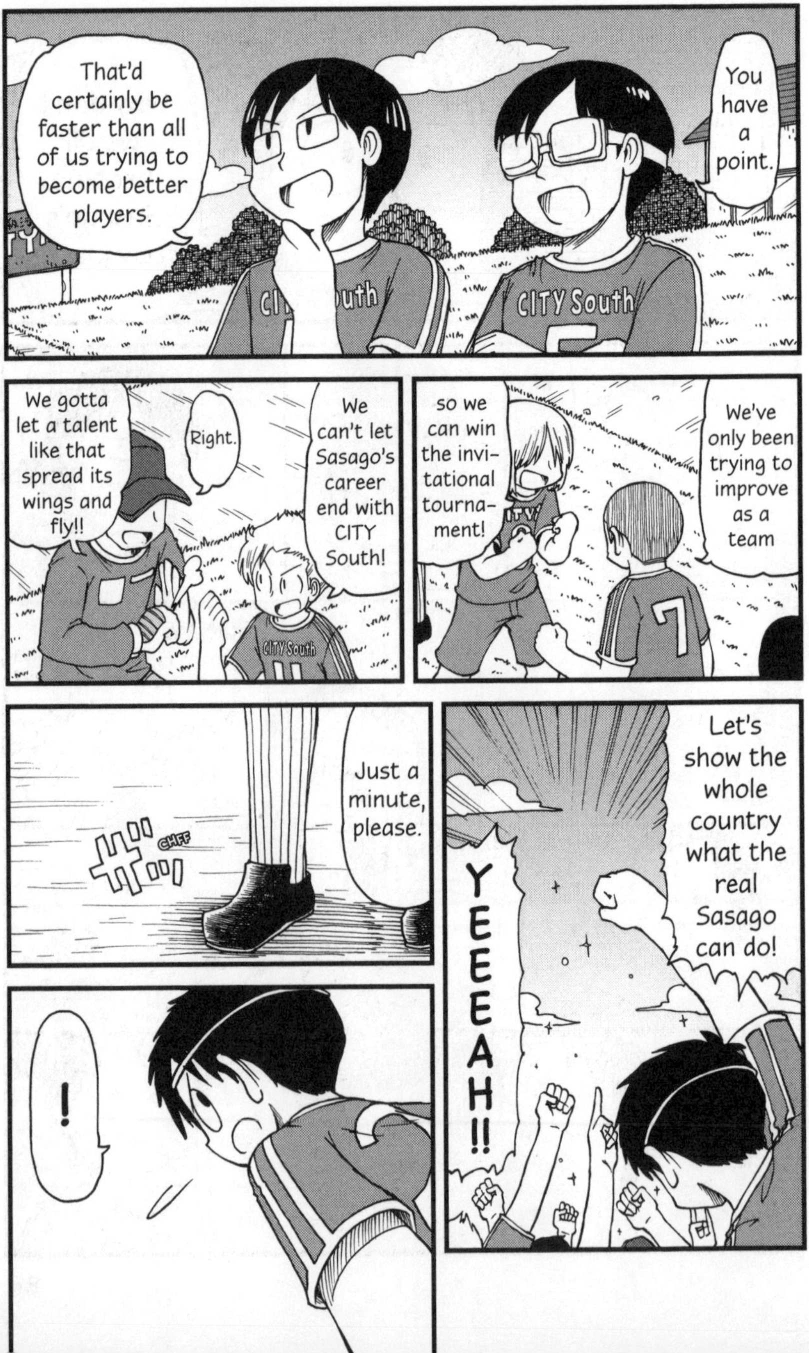
You have a point.
That'd certainly be faster than all of us trying to become better players.
CITY South
We've only been trying to improve as a team
so we can win the invitational tournament!
We can't let Sasago's career end with CITY South!
Right.
We gotta let a talent like that spread its wings and fly!!
CITY South
Let's show the whole country what the real Sasago can do!
YEEEAH!!
Just a minute, please.
CHFF
!

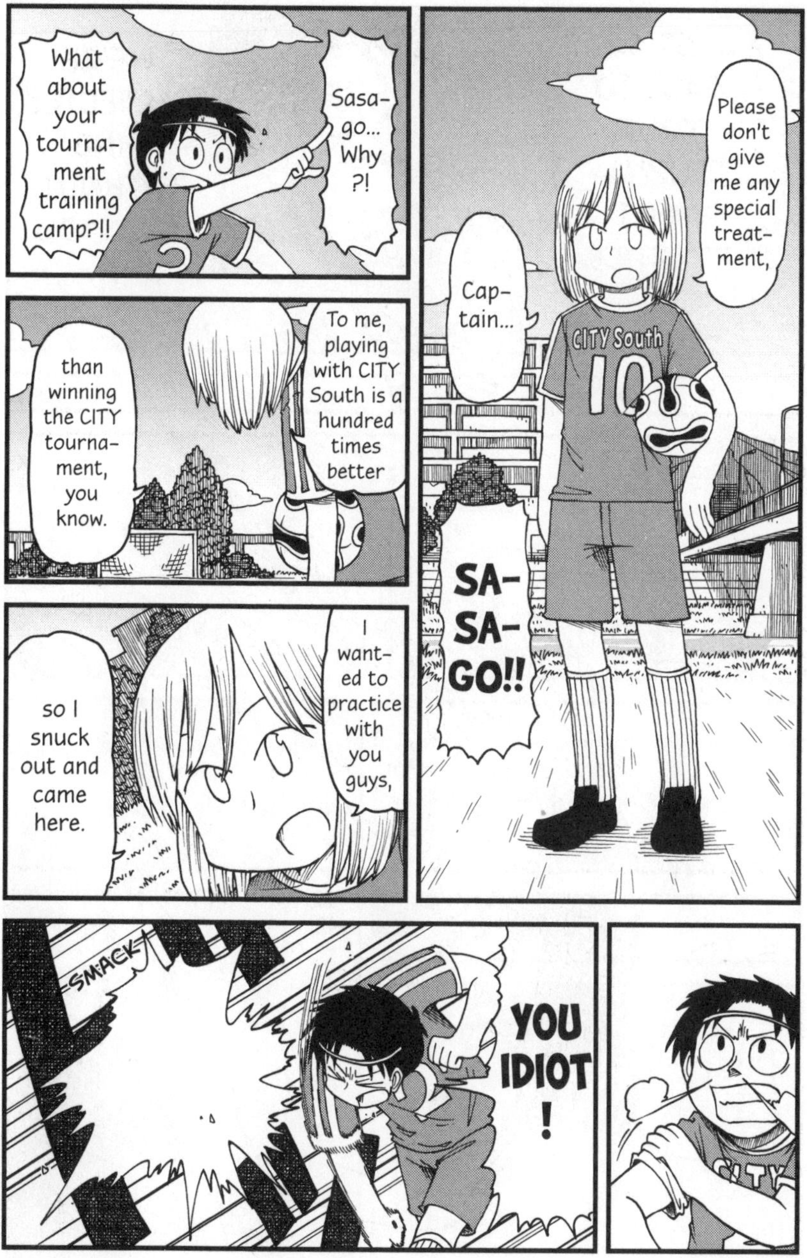
Please don't give me any special treatment,
Captain...
SA-SA-GO!!
Sasa-go... Why?!
What about your tournament training camp?!!
To me, playing with CITY South is a hundred times better
than winning the CITY tournament, you know.
I want-ed to practice with you guys,
so I snuck out and came here.
YOU IDIOT!
SMACK

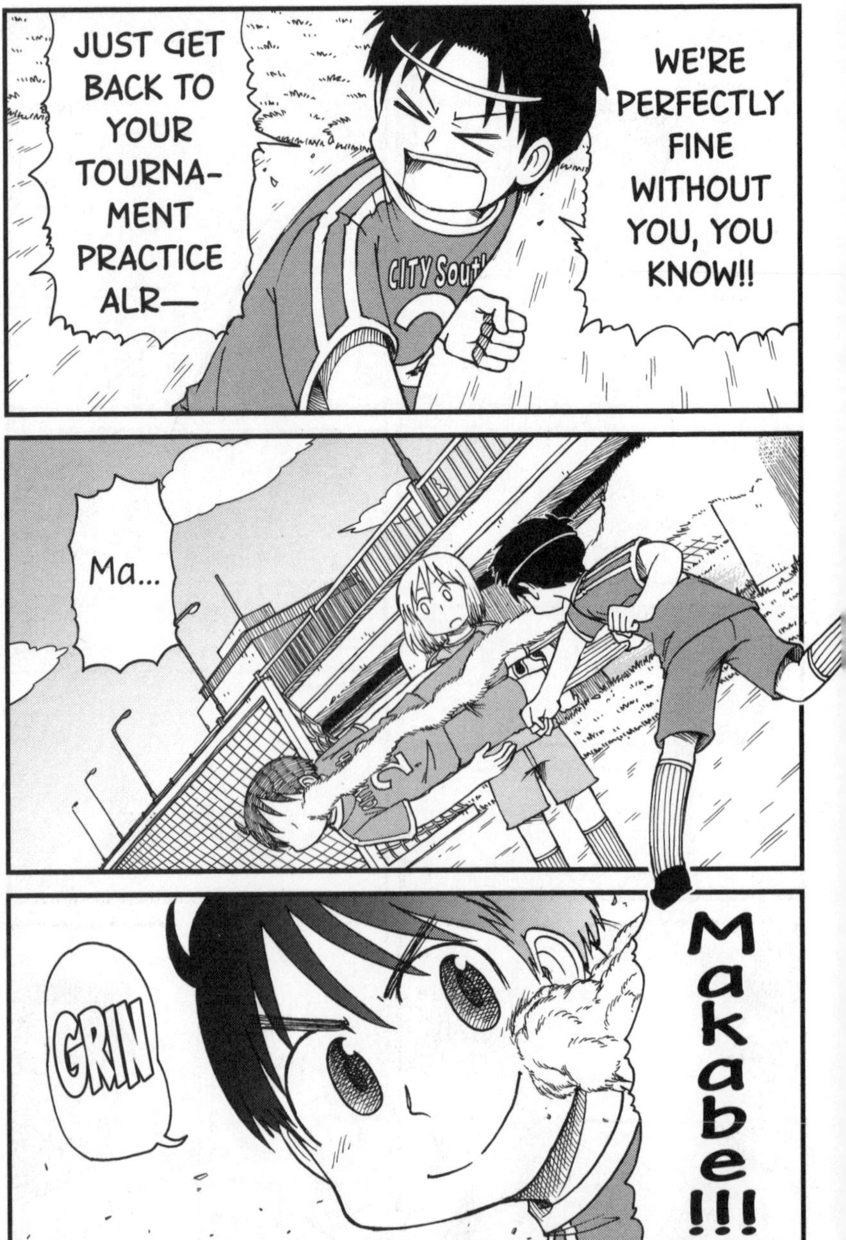
WE'RE PERFECTLY FINE WITHOUT YOU, YOU KNOW!!
JUST GET BACK TO YOUR TOURNAMENT PRACTICE ALR—
Ma...
Makabe!!!
GRIN

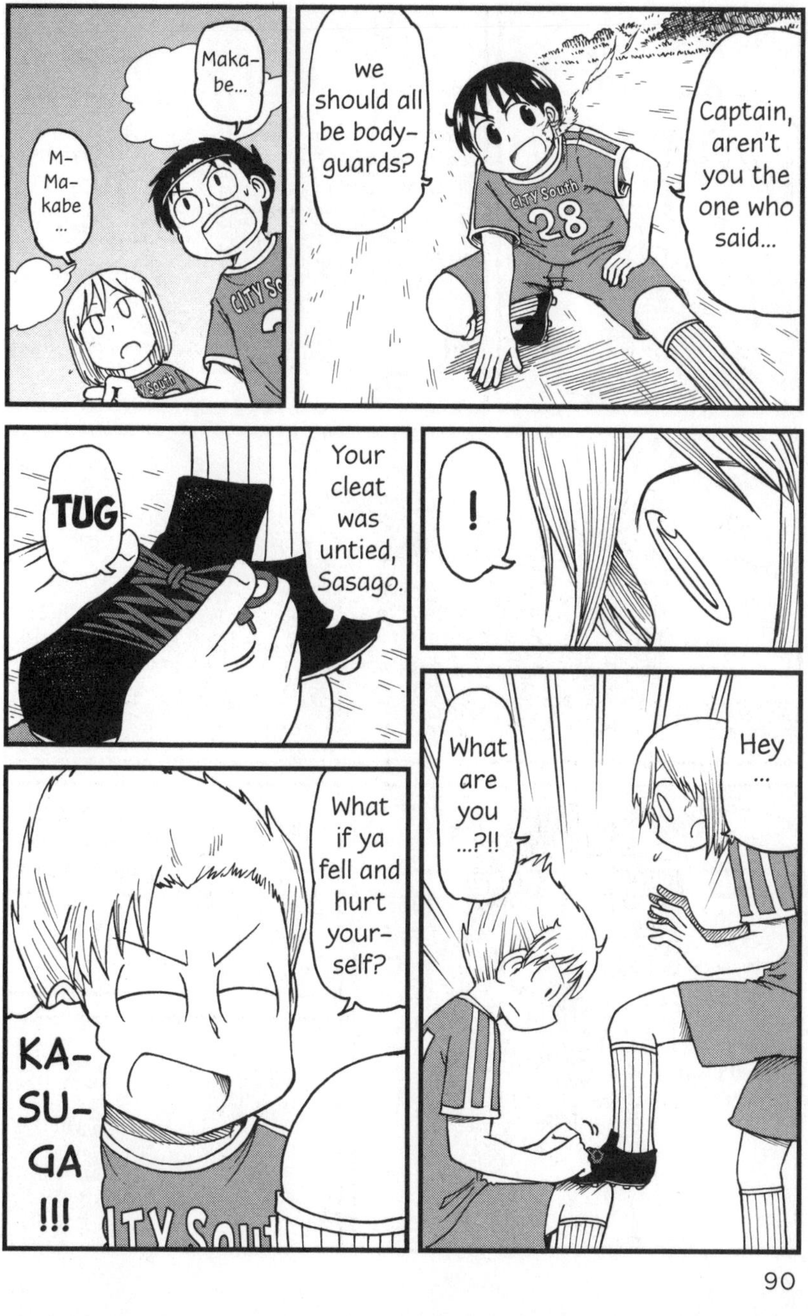
Captain, aren't you the one who said...
we should all be body-guards?
Maka-be...
M-Ma-kabe...
!
Your cleat was untied, Sasago.
TUG
Hey...
What are you...?!!
What if ya fell and hurt your-self?
KA-SU-GA!!!

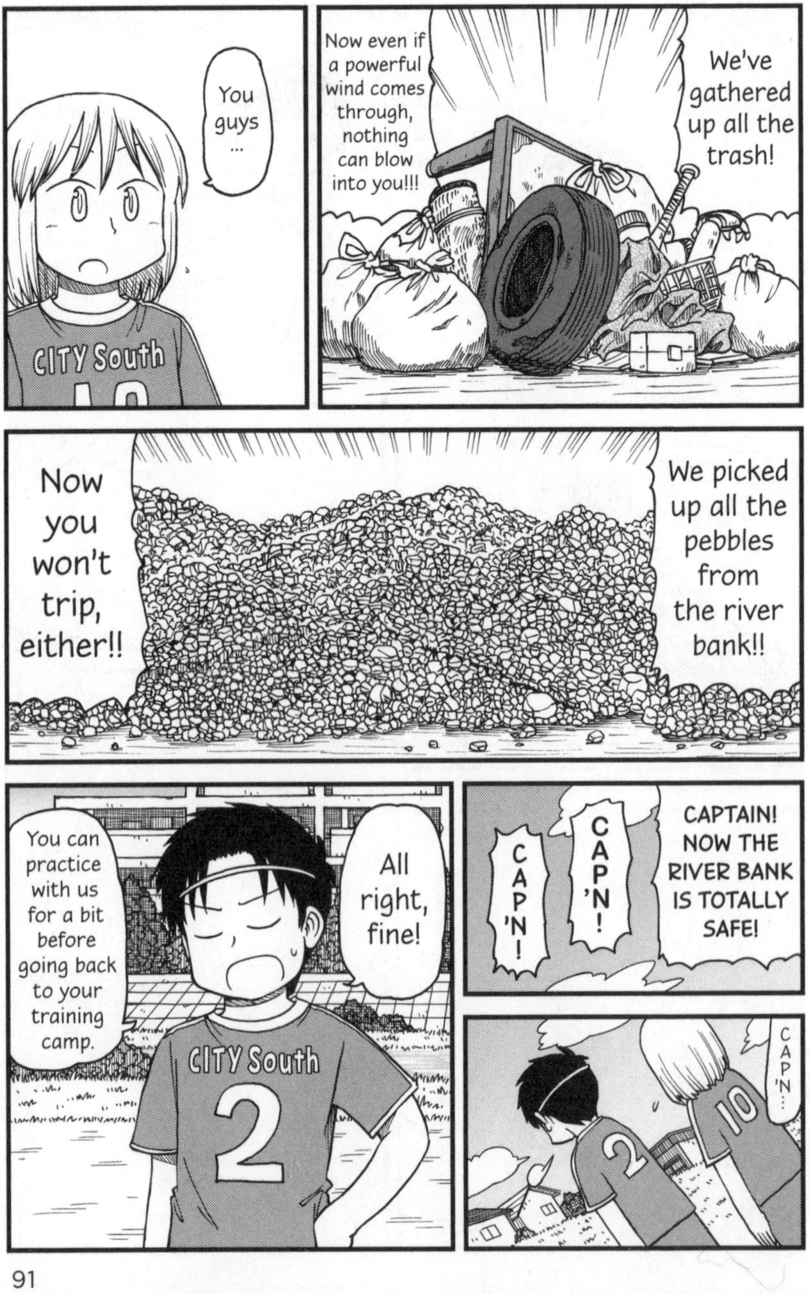
We've gathered up all the trash!
Now even if a powerful wind comes through, nothing can blow into you!!!
You guys ...
We picked up all the pebbles from the river bank!!
Now you won't trip, either!!
CAPTAIN! NOW THE RIVER BANK IS TOTALLY SAFE!
CAP'N!
CAP'N!
CAP'N...
All right, fine!
You can practice with us for a bit before going back to your training camp.

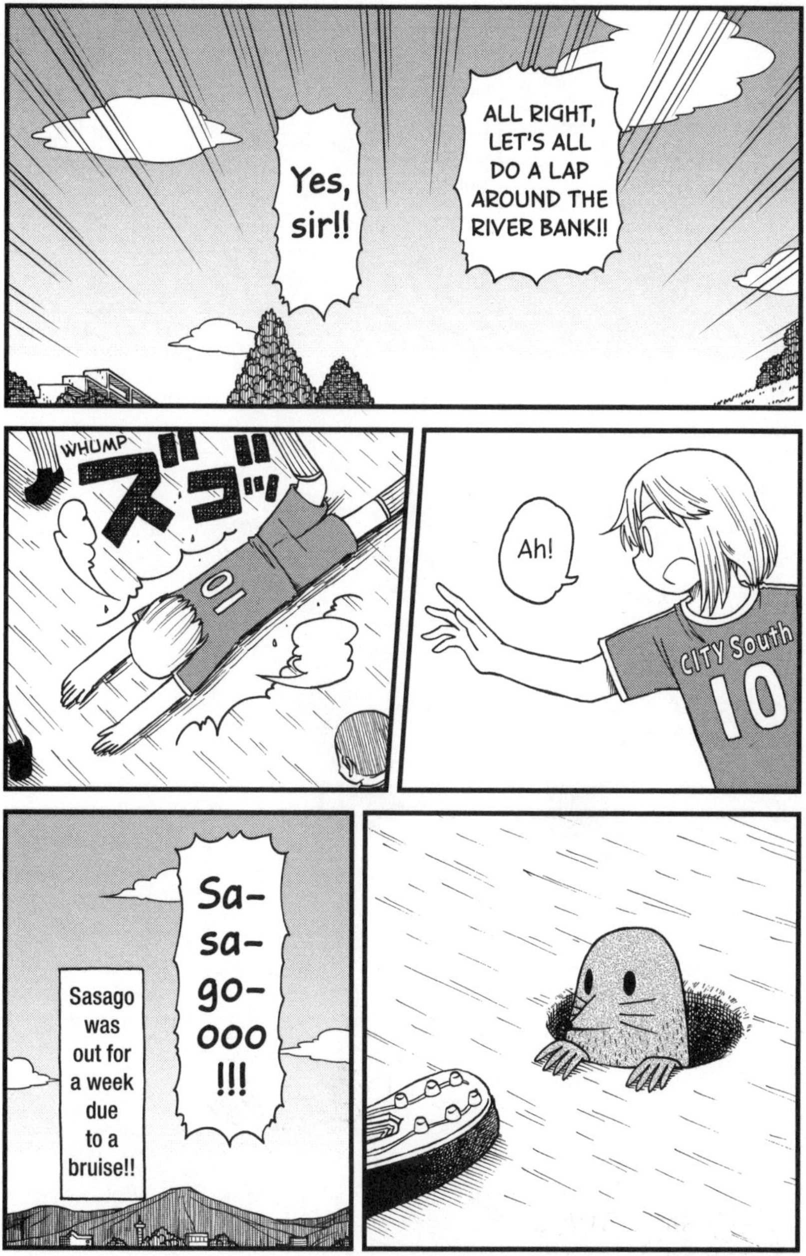
ALL RIGHT, LET'S ALL DO A LAP AROUND THE RIVER BANK!!
Yes, sir!!
Ah!
WHUMP
ズゴッ
Sa-sa-go-ooo!!!
Sasago was out for a week due to a bruise!!

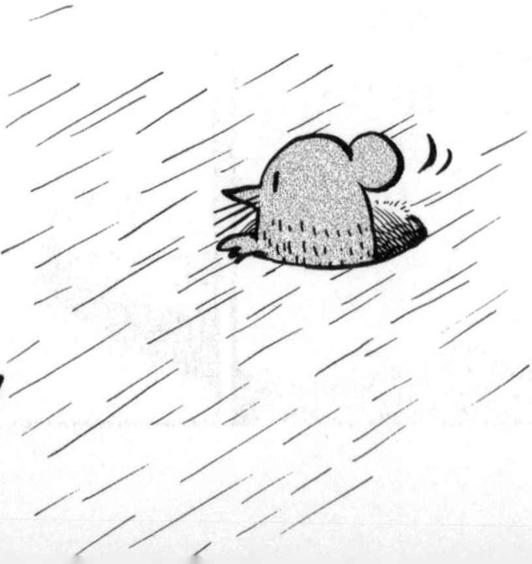

CITY

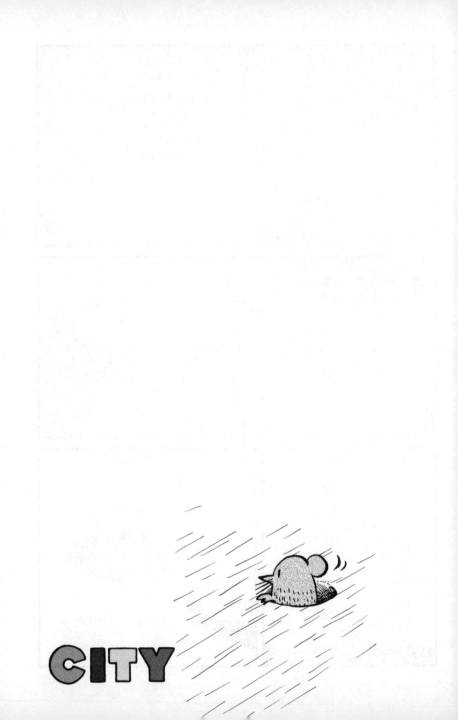

DRYER

乾
DRY

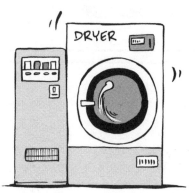

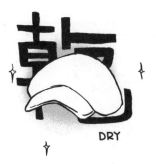

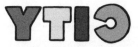

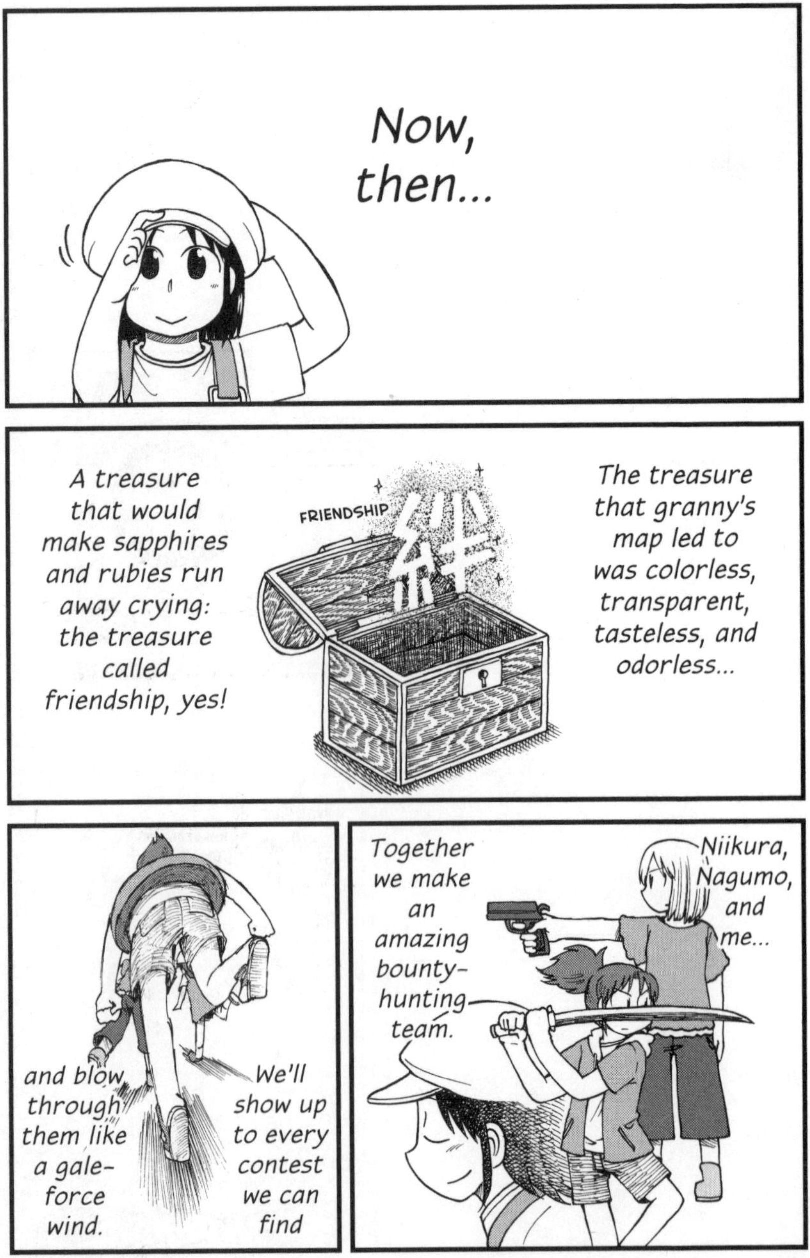
Now, then...
The treasure that granny's map led to was colorless, transparent, tasteless, and odorless...
FRIENDSHIP
A treasure that would make sapphires and rubies run away crying: the treasure called friendship, yes!
Niikura, Nagumo, and me...
Together we make an amazing bounty-hunting team.
We'll show up to every contest we can find
and blow through them like a gale-force wind.

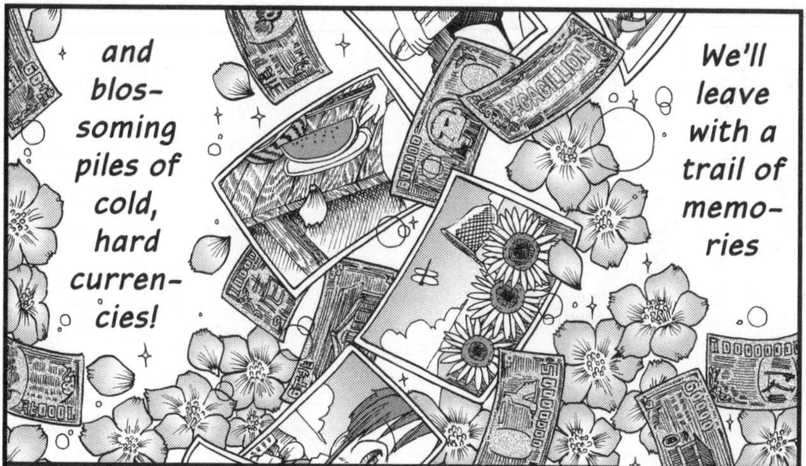
We'll leave with a trail of memories
and blossoming piles of cold, hard currencies!
YCAGILLION

Chapter 34 Wako Izumi's Poetic Community Stroll

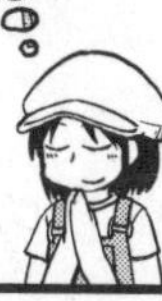

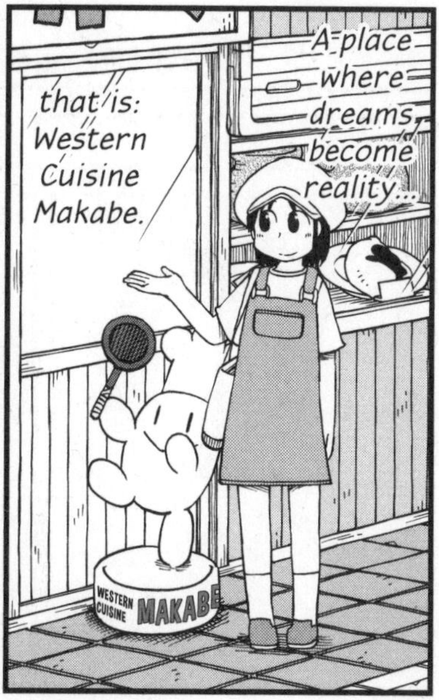
A place where dreams become reality...
that is: Western Cuisine Makabe.
WESTERN CUISINE MAKABE

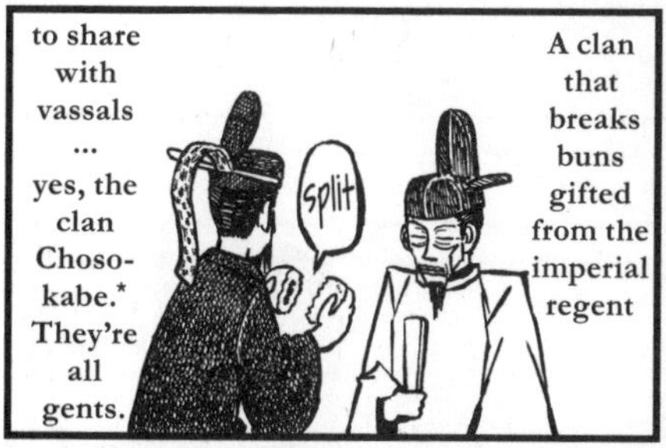
A clan that breaks buns gifted from the imperial regent
split
to share with vassals ... yes, the clan Chosokabe.* They're all gents.

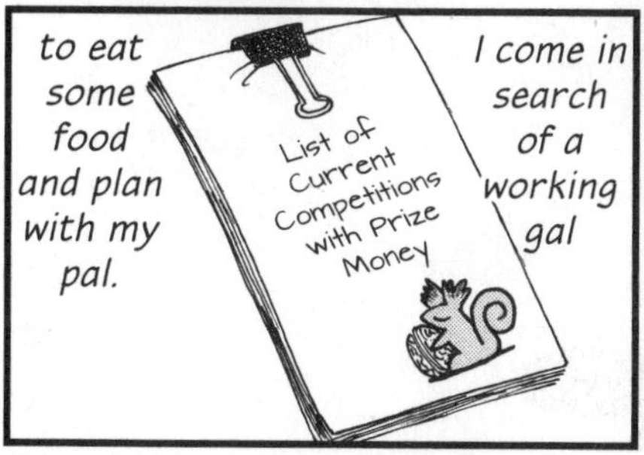
I come in search of a working gal
List of Current Competitions with Prize Money
to eat some food and plan with my pal.

*A samurai clan from the Warring States period (whose name rhymes with Makabe).

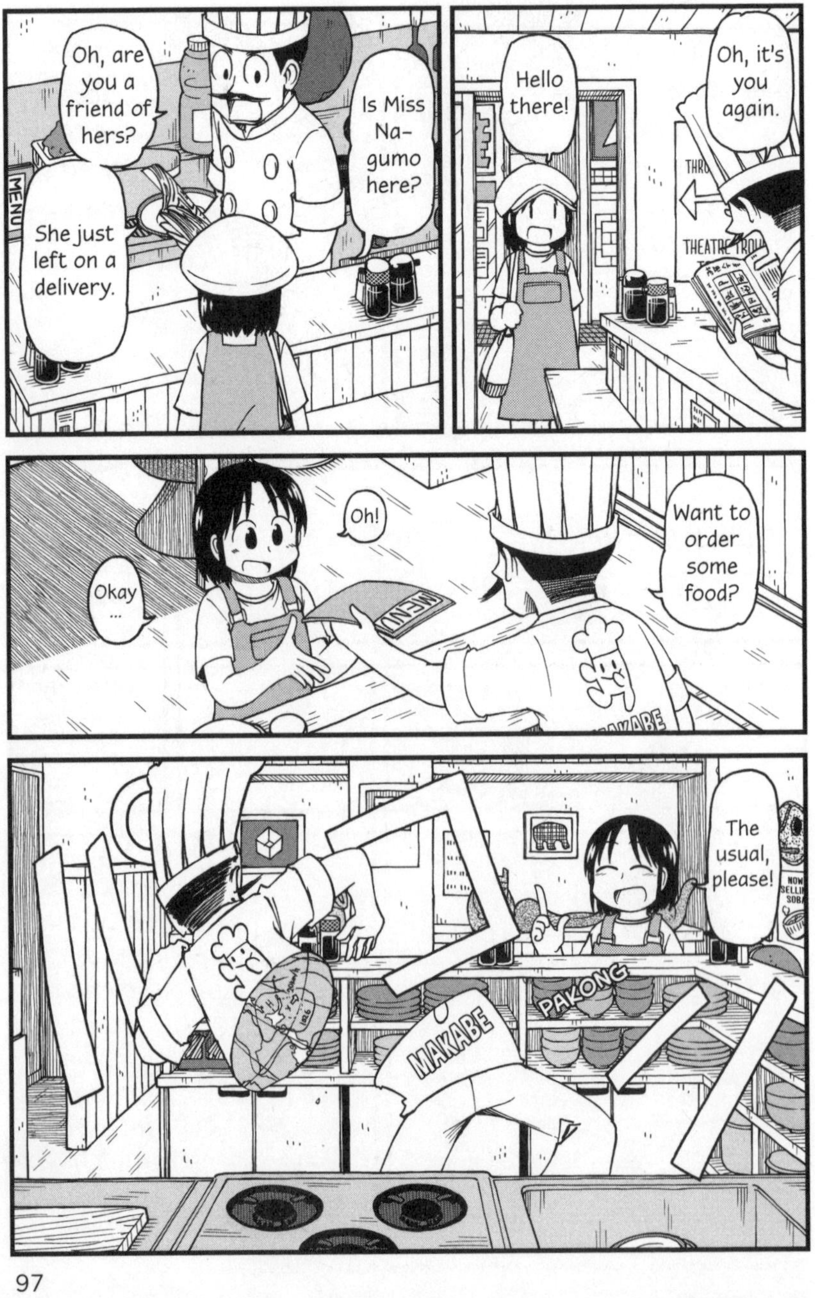
Oh, it's you again.
Hello there!
Is Miss Na-gumo here?
Oh, are you a friend of hers?
She just left on a delivery.
Want to order some food?
Oh!
Okay ...
The usual, please!
PAKONG

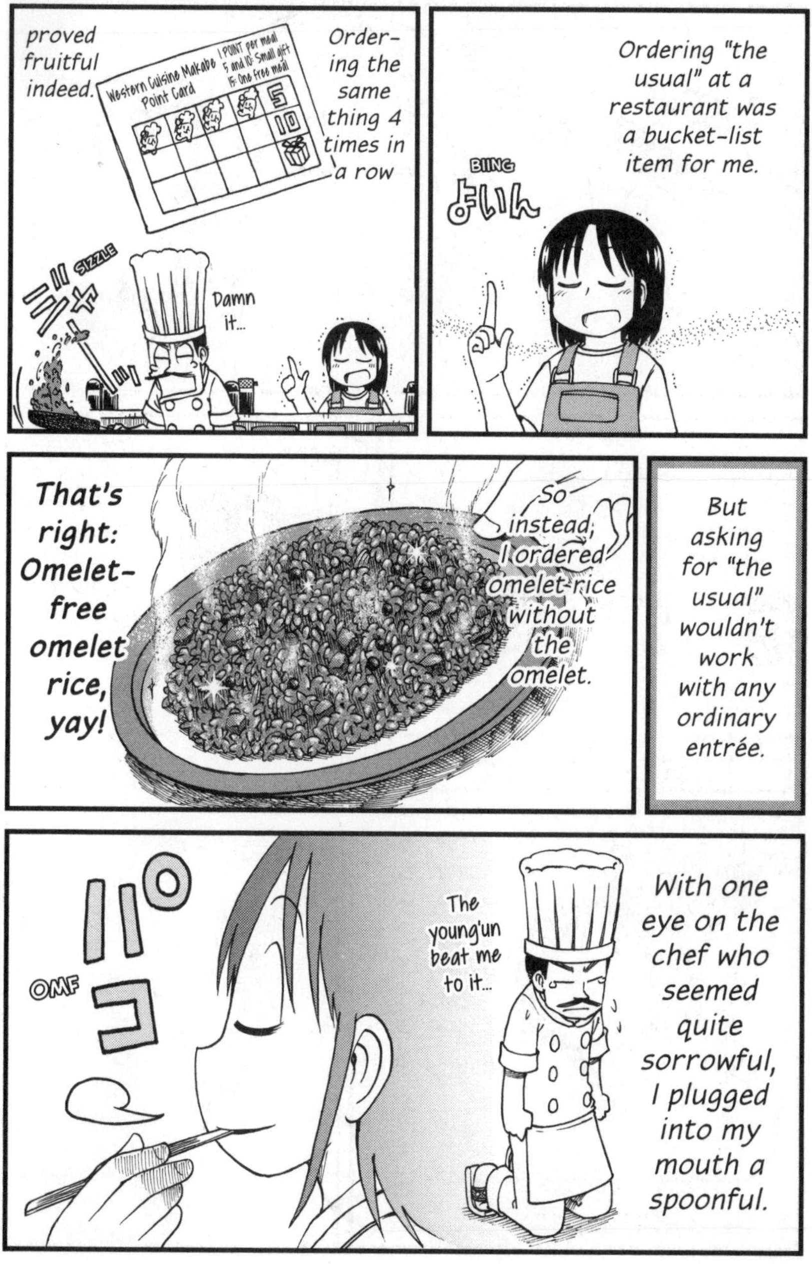
Ordering "the usual" at a restaurant was a bucket-list item for me.
BIING
よいん
Order-ing the same thing 4 times in a row
proved fruitful indeed.
Western Cuisine Makabe Point Card
1 POINT per meal
5 and 10: Small gift
15: One free meal
SIZZLE
Damn it...
But asking for "the usual" wouldn't work with any ordinary entrée.
So instead, I ordered omelet-rice without the omelet.
That's right: Omelet-free omelet rice, yay!
With one eye on the chef who seemed quite sorrowful, I plugged into my mouth a spoonful.
The young'un beat me to it...
OMF

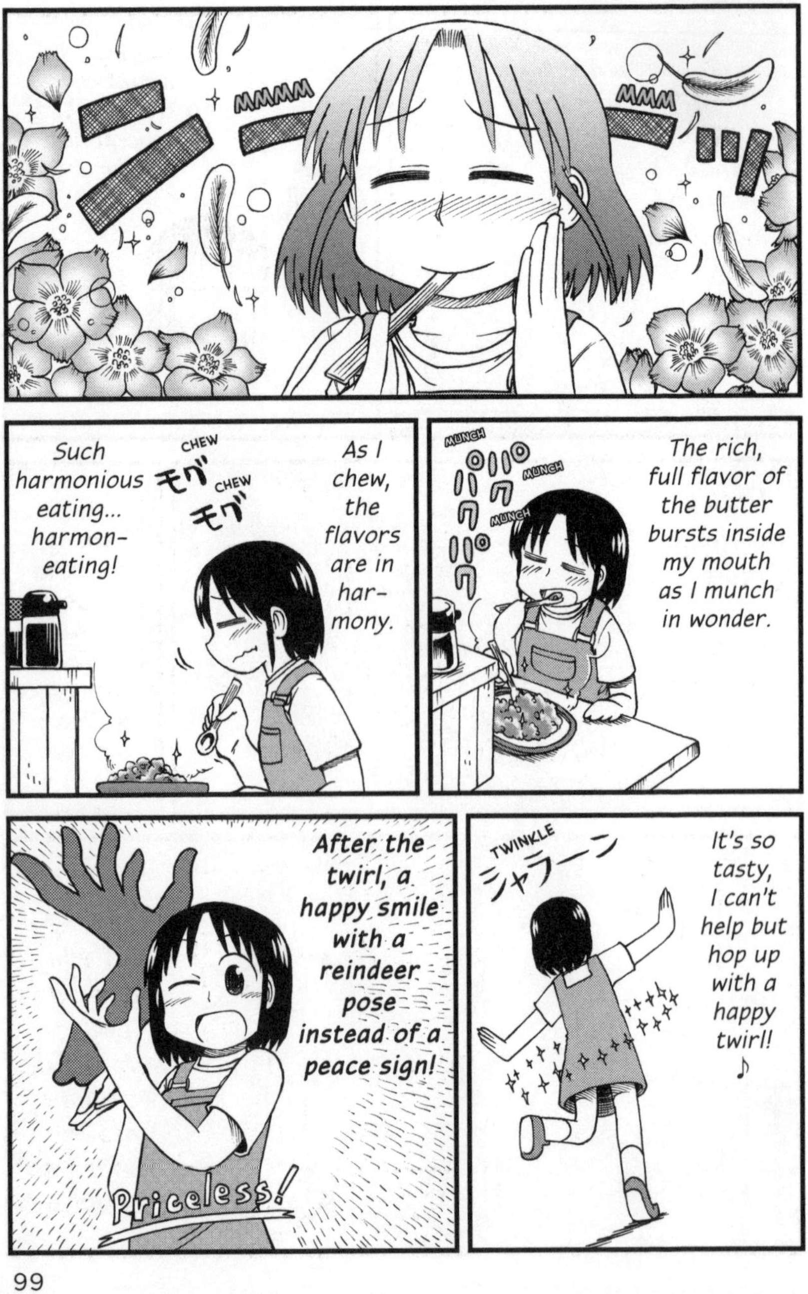
MMM
MMMM
The rich, full flavor of the butter bursts inside my mouth as I munch in wonder.
MUNCH
MUNCH
MUNCH
パクパク
As I chew, the flavors are in harmony.
CHEW
モグ
CHEW
モグ
Such harmonious eating... harmon-eating!
It's so tasty, I can't help but hop up with a happy twirl! ♪
TWINKLE
シャラーン
After the twirl, a happy smile with a reindeer pose instead of a peace sign!
Priceless!

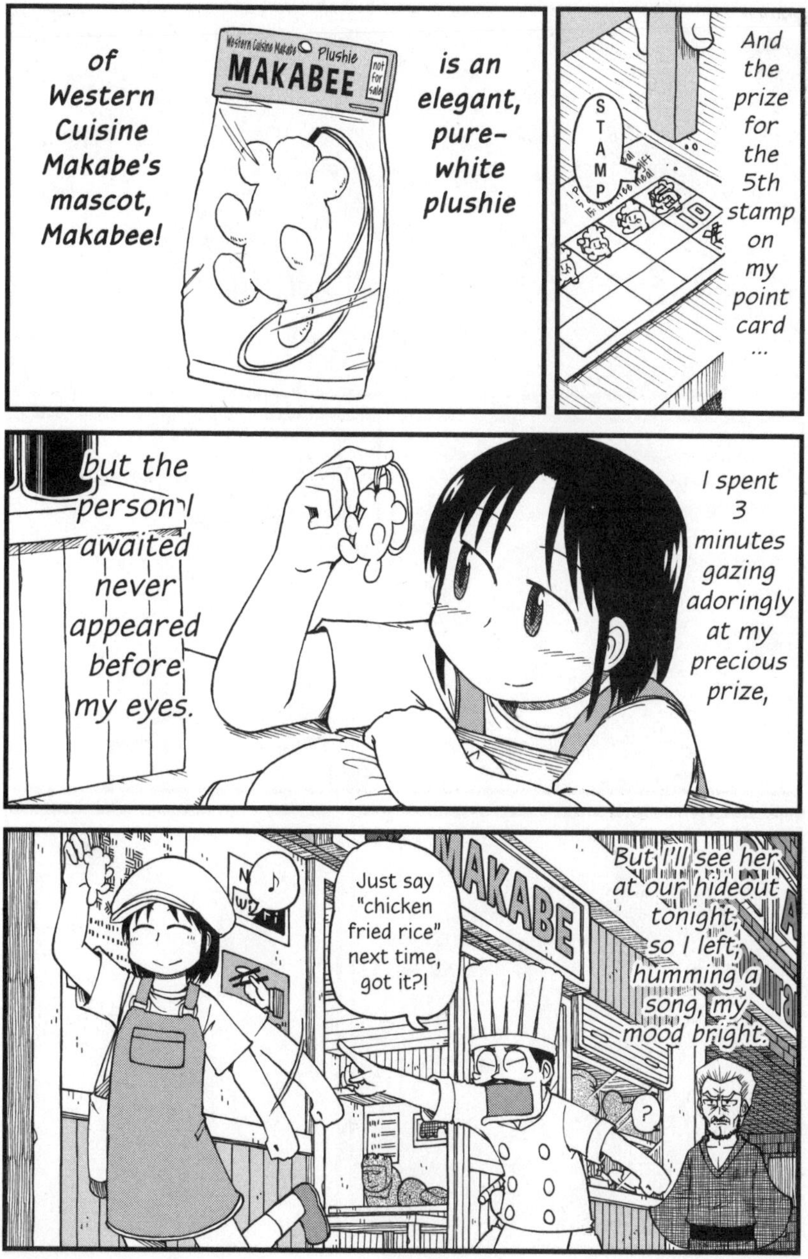
STAMP
And the prize for the 5th stamp on my point card ...
is an elegant, pure-white plushie
Western Cuisine Makabe Plushie
MAKABEE
not for sale
of Western Cuisine Makabe's mascot, Makabee!
I spent 3 minutes gazing adoringly at my precious prize,
but the person I awaited never appeared before my eyes.
But I'll see her at our hideout tonight, so I left, humming a song, my mood bright.
?
MAKABE
Just say "chicken fried rice" next time, got it?!
♪

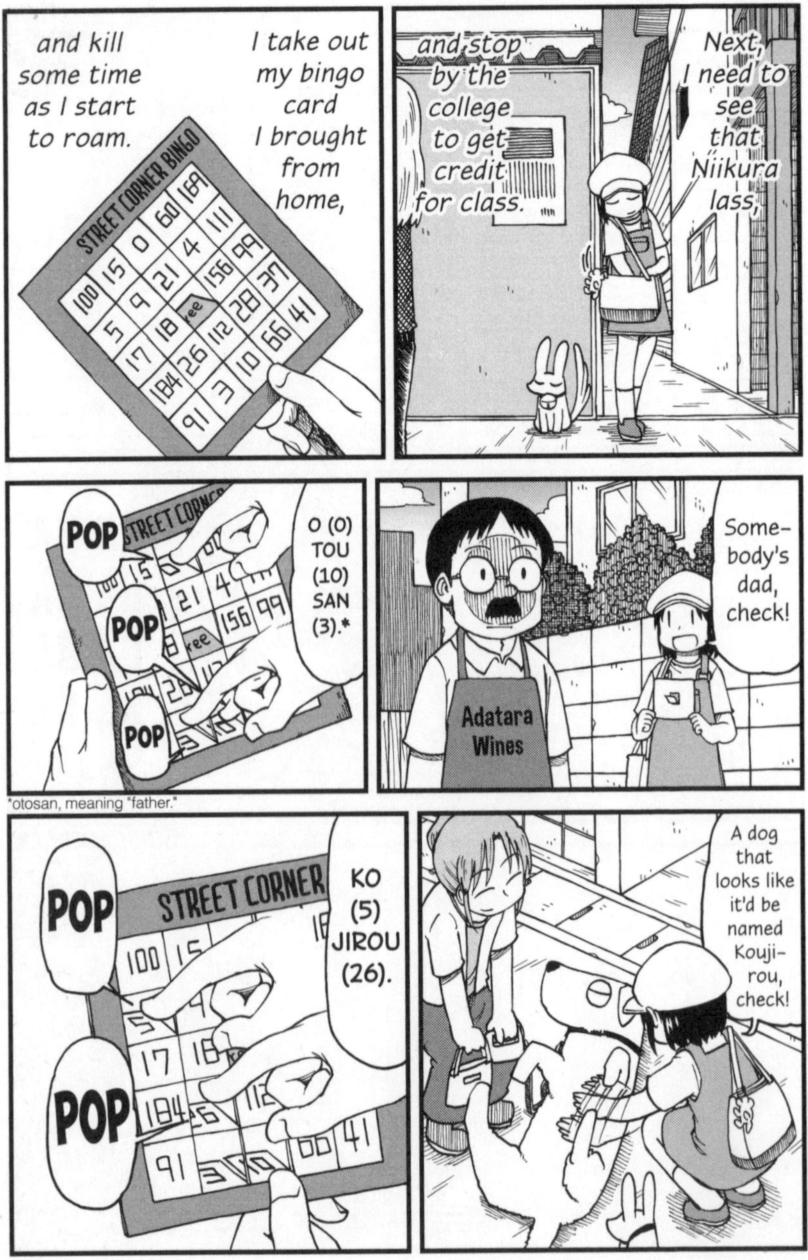
Next, I need to see that Niikura lass,
and stop by the college to get credit for class.
I take out my bingo card I brought from home,
and kill some time as I start to roam.
STREET CORNER BINGO
Some-body's dad, check!
Adatara Wines
O (0) TOU (10) SAN (3).*
POP
POP
POP
STREET CORNER
A dog that looks like it'd be named Kouji-rou, check!
KO (5) JIROU (26).
POP
POP
STREET CORNER

*otosan, meaning "father."

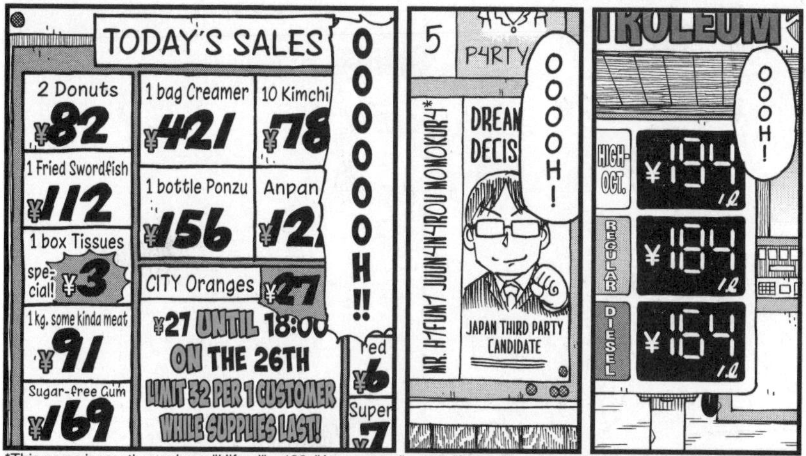
IROLEUM
OOOH!
HIGH-OCT.
¥194 1ℓ
REGULAR
¥184 1ℓ
DIESEL
¥164 1ℓ
5
P4RTY
OOOOH!
MR. H1FUM1 JUUN4N4ROU MOMOKUR4*
DREAM
DECIS
JAPAN THIRD PARTY CANDIDATE
TODAY'S SALES
OOOOOOOH!!
2 Donuts ¥82
1 bag Creamer ¥421
10 Kimchi ¥78
1 Fried Swordfish ¥112
1 bottle Ponzu ¥156
Anpan ¥12
1 box Tissues special! ¥3
CITY Oranges ¥27
1 kg. some kinda meat ¥91
¥27 UNTIL 18:00 ON THE 26TH
LIMIT 32 PER 1 CUSTOMER
WHILE SUPPLIES LAST!
Red ¥6
Sugar-free Gum ¥169
Super ¥7

*This name is mostly numbers: "Hifumi" = 123, "Juunanarou" = 176, "Momo" is written with the kanji for 100.

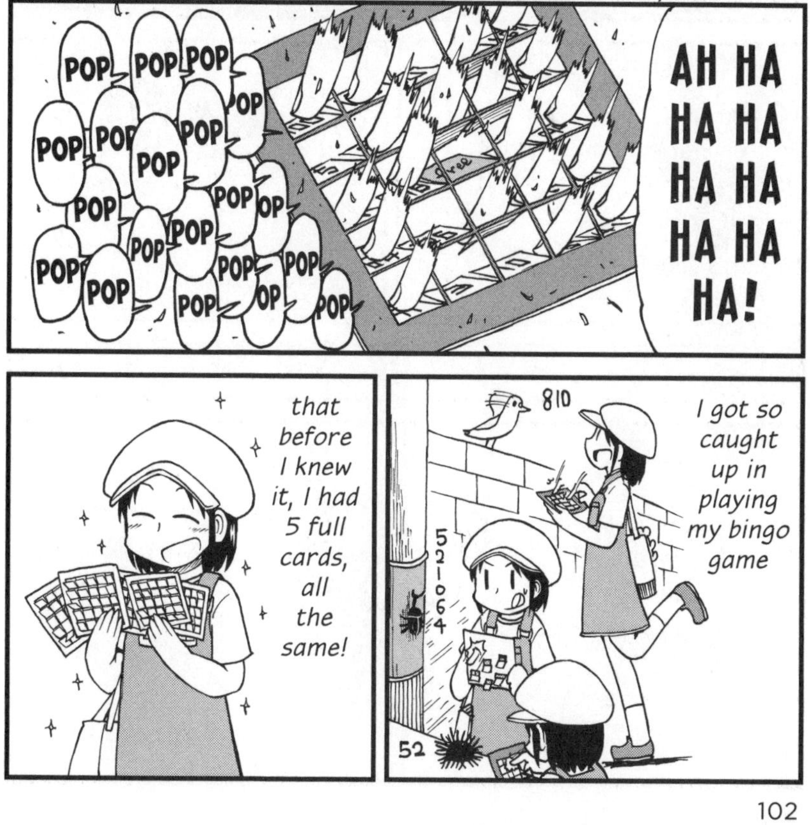
AH HA HA HA HA HA HA HA HA!
POP POP POP POP POP POP POP POP POP POP POP POP POP POP POP POP POP POP POP POP POP POP
810
I got so caught up in playing my bingo game
52-1064
52
that before I knew it, I had 5 full cards, all the same!

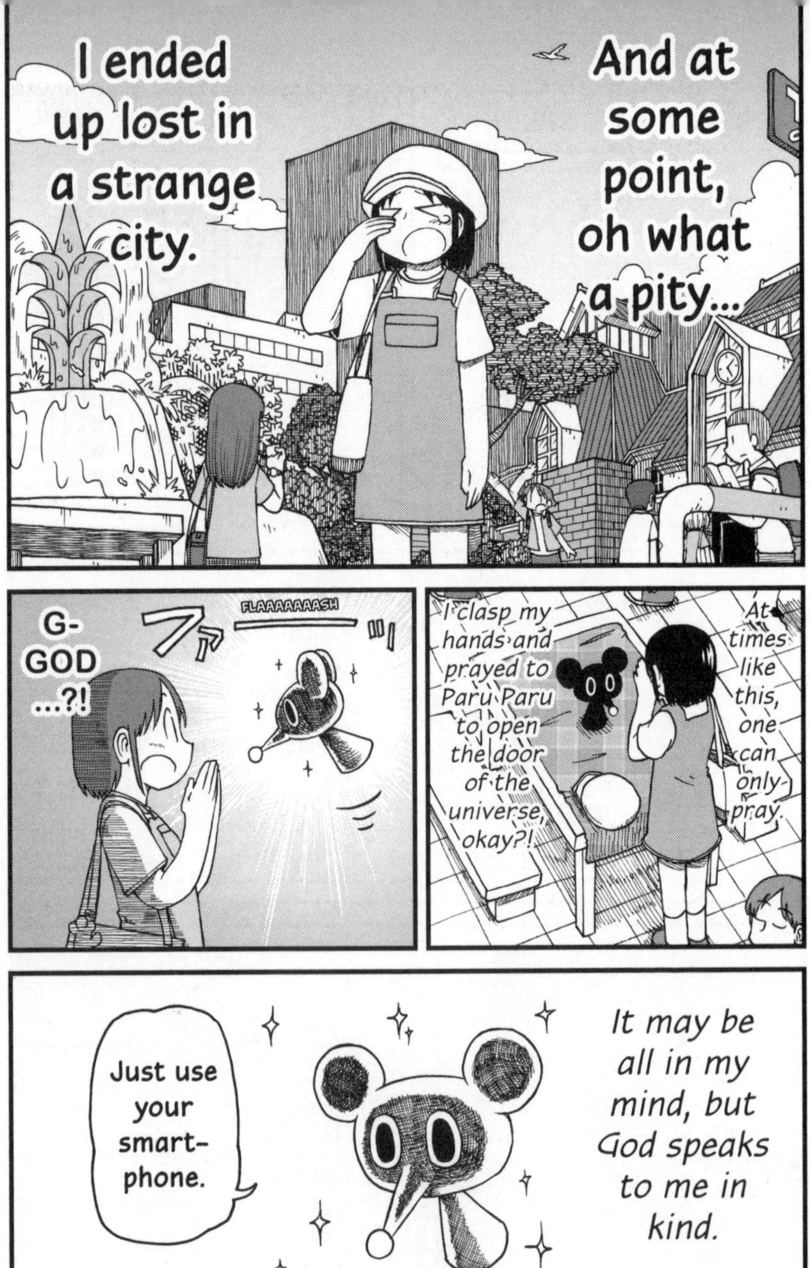

And at some point, oh what a pity...
I ended up lost in a strange city.
At times like this, one can only pray.
I clasp my hands and prayed to Paru Paru to open the door of the universe, okay?!
FLAAAAAAASH
G-GOD ...?!
It may be all in my mind, but God speaks to me in kind.
Just use your smart-phone.

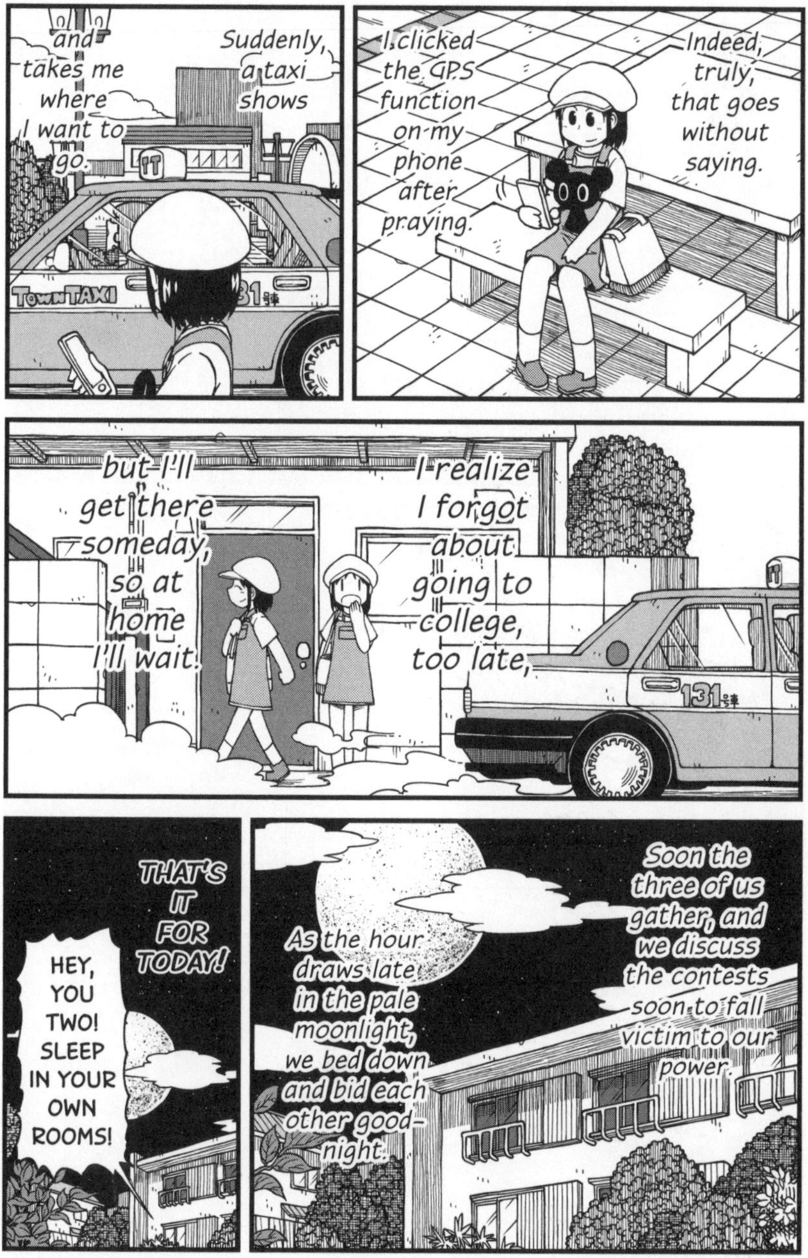
Indeed, truly, that goes without saying.
I clicked the GPS function on my phone after praying.
Suddenly, a taxi shows
and takes me where I want to go.
TOWN TAXI
I realize I forgot about going to college, too late,
but I'll get there someday, so at home I'll wait.
Soon the three of us gather, and we discuss the contests soon to fall victim to our power.
As the hour draws late in the pale moonlight, we bed down and bid each other good-night.
THAT'S IT FOR TODAY!
HEY, YOU TWO! SLEEP IN YOUR OWN ROOMS!

Western Cuisine Makabe
Plushie
not for sale
MAKABEE
Western
Makabe
Point Card

CITY

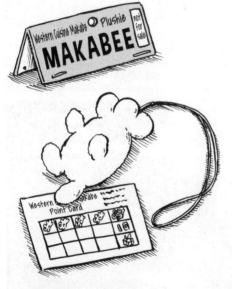

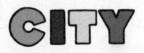

WEDNESDAY
12:26

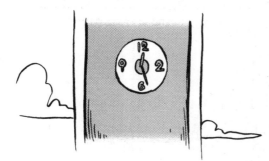

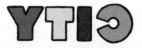

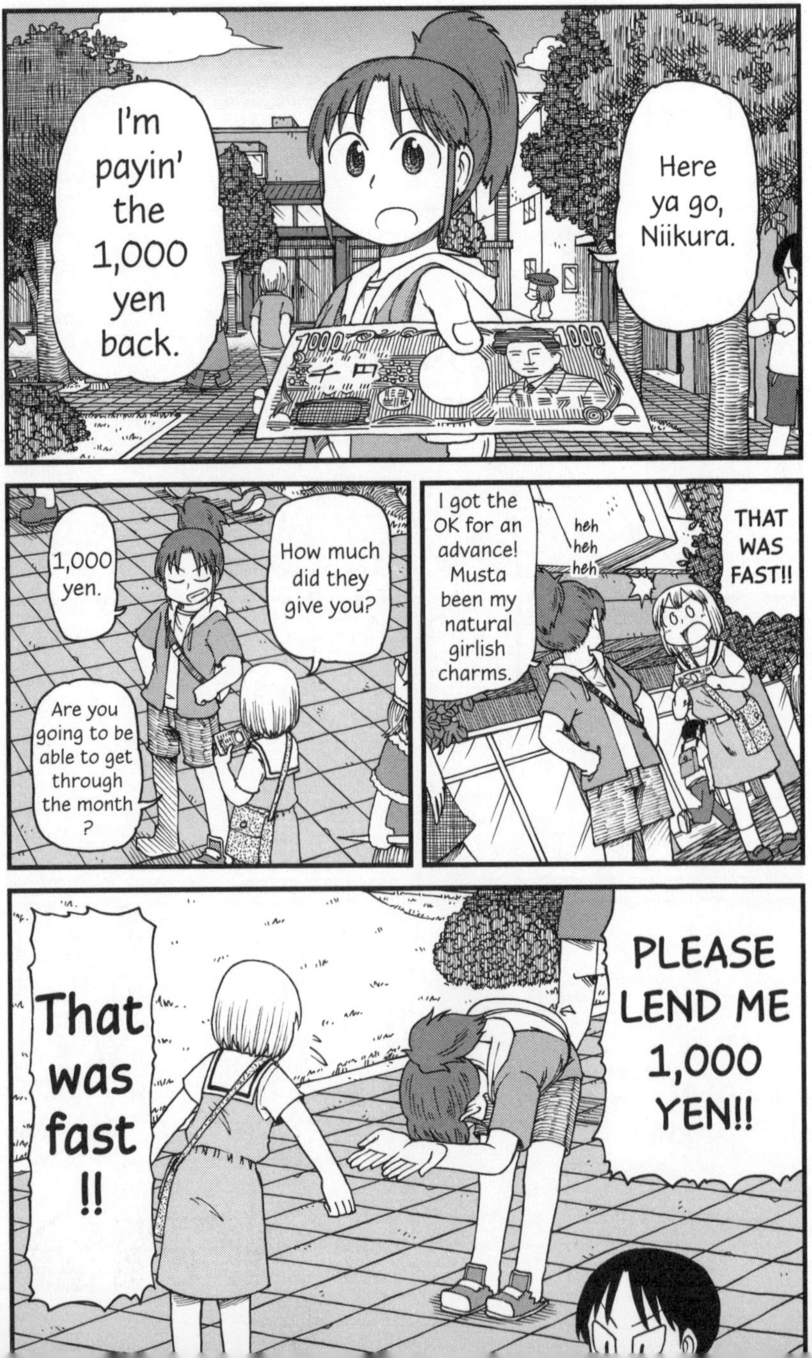

Here ya go, Niikura.
I'm payin' the 1,000 yen back.
I got the OK for an advance! Musta been my natural girlish charms.
heh heh heh
THAT WAS FAST!!
How much did they give you?
1,000 yen.
Are you going to be able to get through the month?
PLEASE LEND ME 1,000 YEN!!
That was fast!!

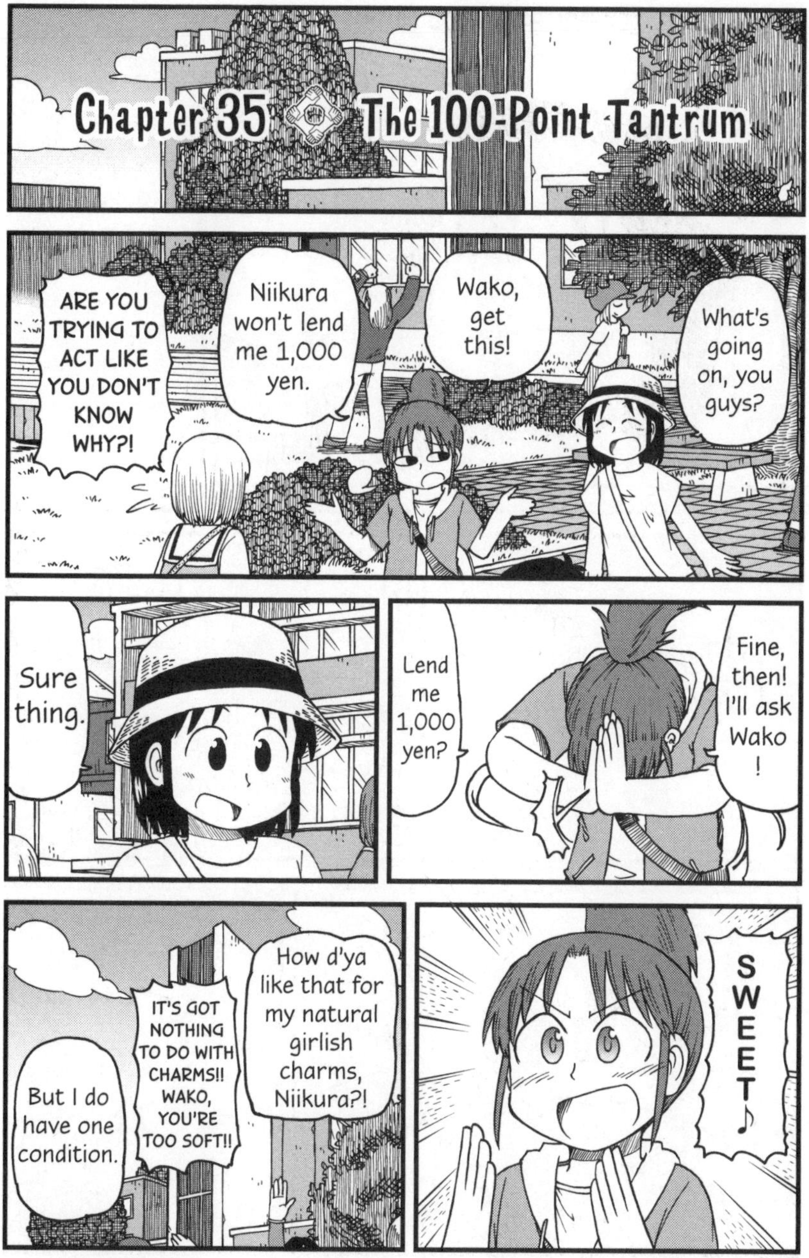
Chapter 35 The 100-Point Tantrum
What's going on, you guys?
Wako, get this!
Niikura won't lend me 1,000 yen.
ARE YOU TRYING TO ACT LIKE YOU DON'T KNOW WHY?!
Fine, then! I'll ask Wako!
Lend me 1,000 yen?
Sure thing.
SWEET♪
How d'ya like that for my natural girlish charms, Niikura?!
IT'S GOT NOTHING TO DO WITH CHARMS!! WAKO, YOU'RE TOO SOFT!!
But I do have one condition.

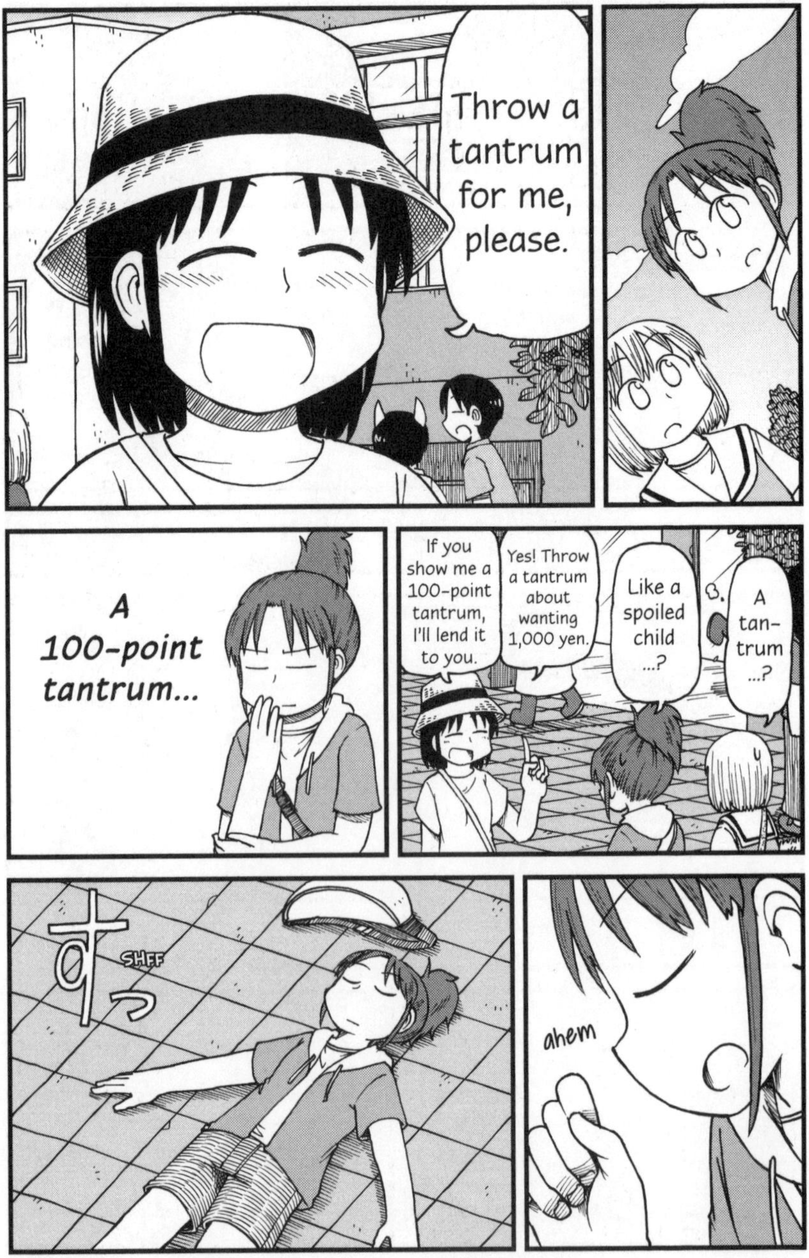
Throw a tantrum for me, please.
A tan-trum ...?
Like a spoiled child ...?
Yes! Throw a tantrum about wanting 1,000 yen.
If you show me a 100-point tantrum, I'll lend it to you.
A 100-point tantrum...
ahem
すっ
SHFF

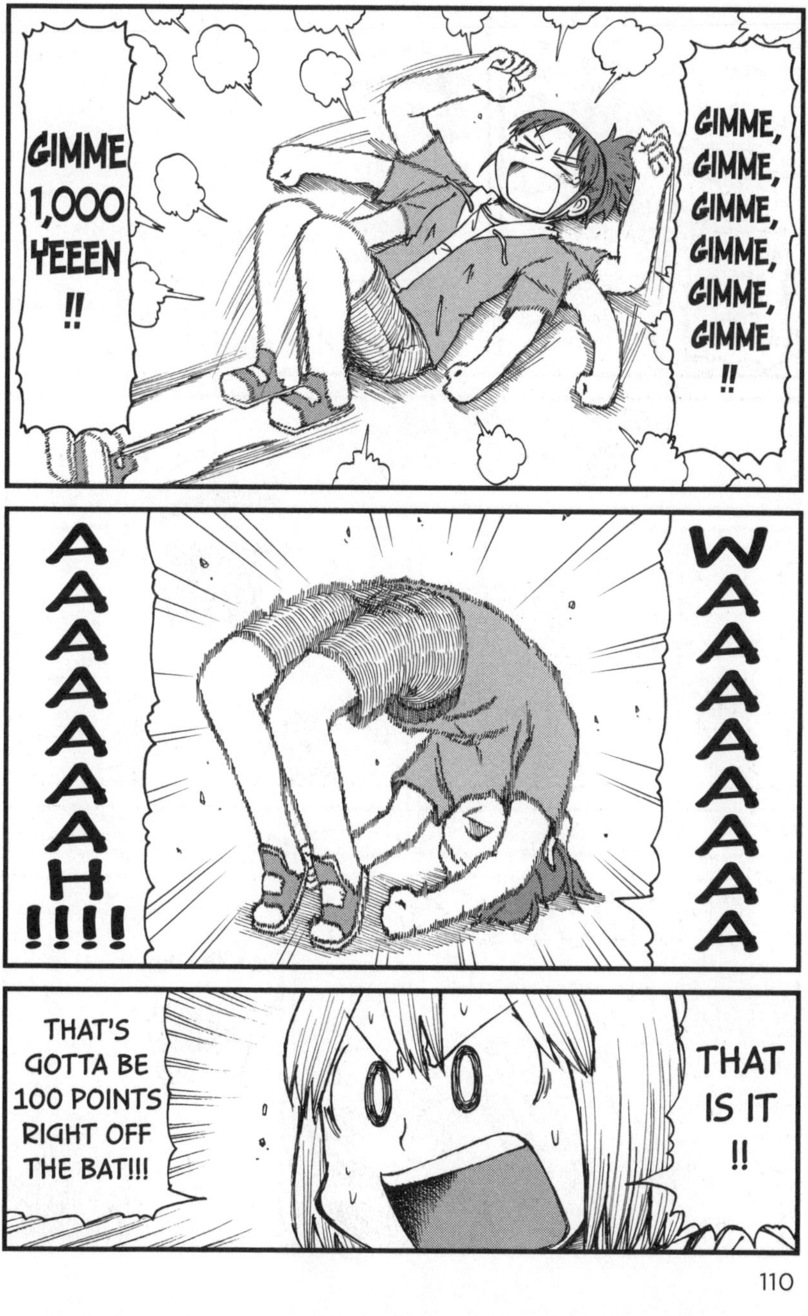
GIMME, GIMME, GIMME, GIMME, GIMME, GIMME!!
GIMME 1,000 YEEEN!!
WAAAAAAAAA
AAAAAAAH!!!!
THAT IS IT!!
THAT'S GOTTA BE 100 POINTS RIGHT OFF THE BAT!!!

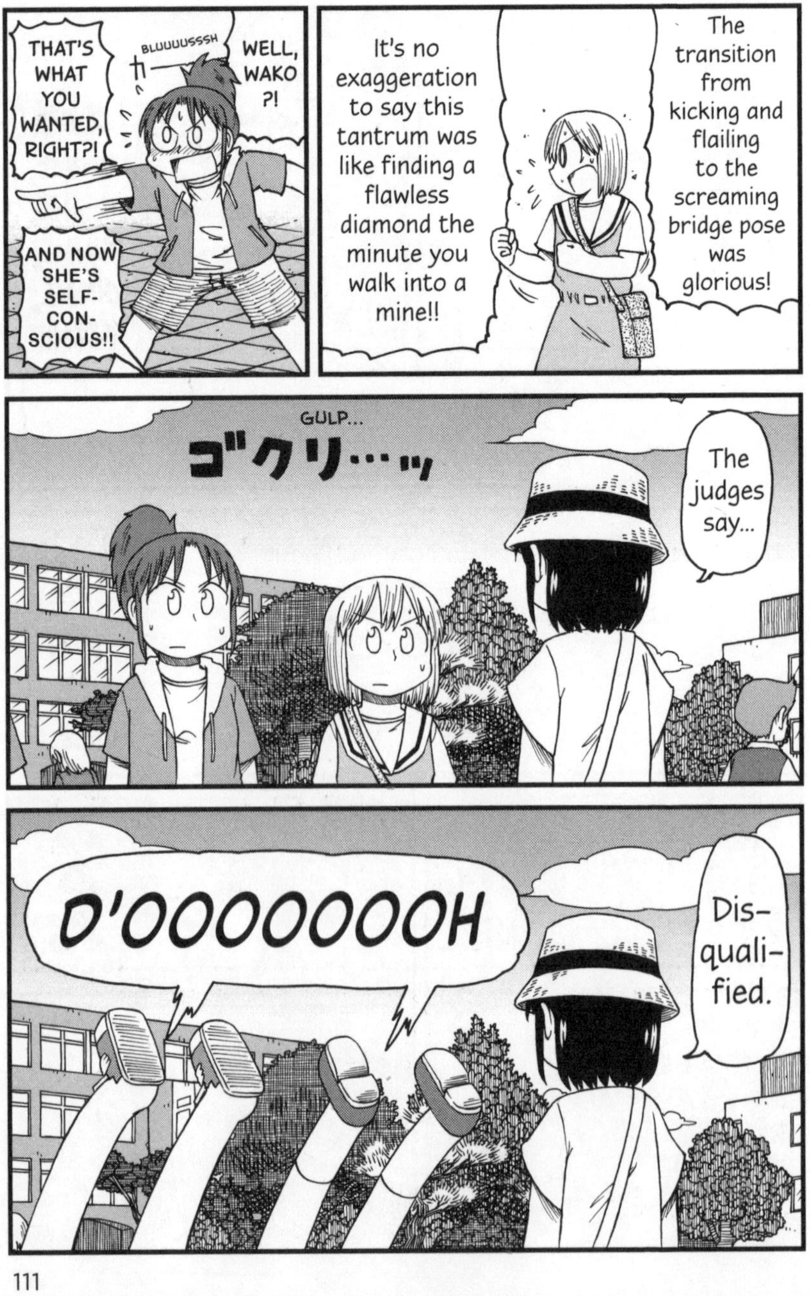
The transition from kicking and flailing to the screaming bridge pose was glorious!
It's no exaggeration to say this tantrum was like finding a flawless diamond the minute you walk into a mine!!
WELL, WAKO?!
BLUUUUSSSH
THAT'S WHAT YOU WANTED, RIGHT?!
AND NOW SHE'S SELF-CONSCIOUS!!
The judges say...
GULP...
ゴクリ…ッ
Dis-qualified.
D'OOOOOOOH

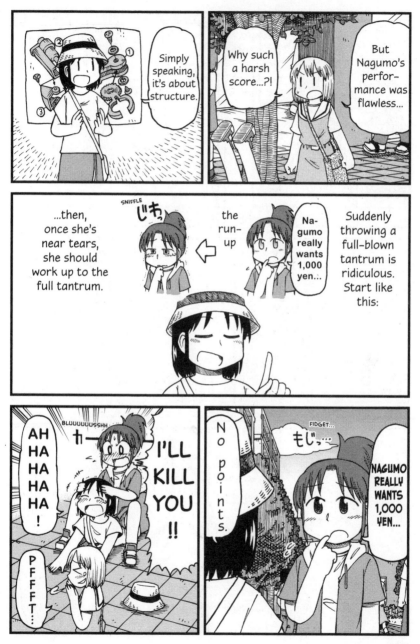

But Nagumo's perfor-mance was flawless...
Why such a harsh score...?!
Simply speaking, it's about structure.
Suddenly throwing a full-blown tantrum is ridiculous. Start like this:
Na-gumo really wants 1,000 yen...
the run-up
SNIFFLE
じわっ
...then, once she's near tears, she should work up to the full tantrum.
FIDGET...
もじっ...
NAGUMO REALLY WANTS 1,000 YEN...
No points.
I'LL KILL YOU !!
BLUUUUUUSSHH
カー
AH HA HA HA HA!
PFFFT...

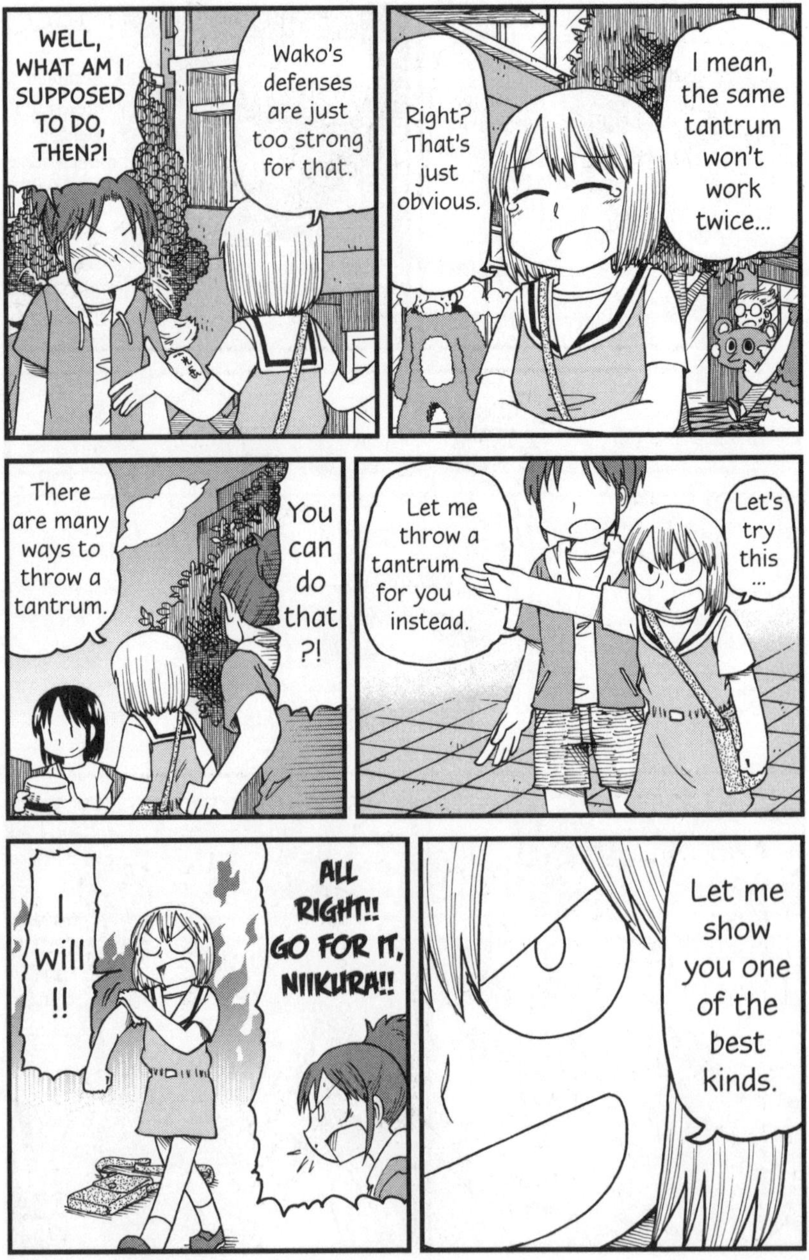
I mean, the same tantrum won't work twice...
Right? That's just obvious.
Wako's defenses are just too strong for that.
WELL, WHAT AM I SUPPOSED TO DO, THEN?!
Let's try this ...
Let me throw a tantrum for you instead.
You can do that ?!
There are many ways to throw a tantrum.
Let me show you one of the best kinds.
ALL RIGHT!! GO FOR IT, NIIKURA!!
I will !!

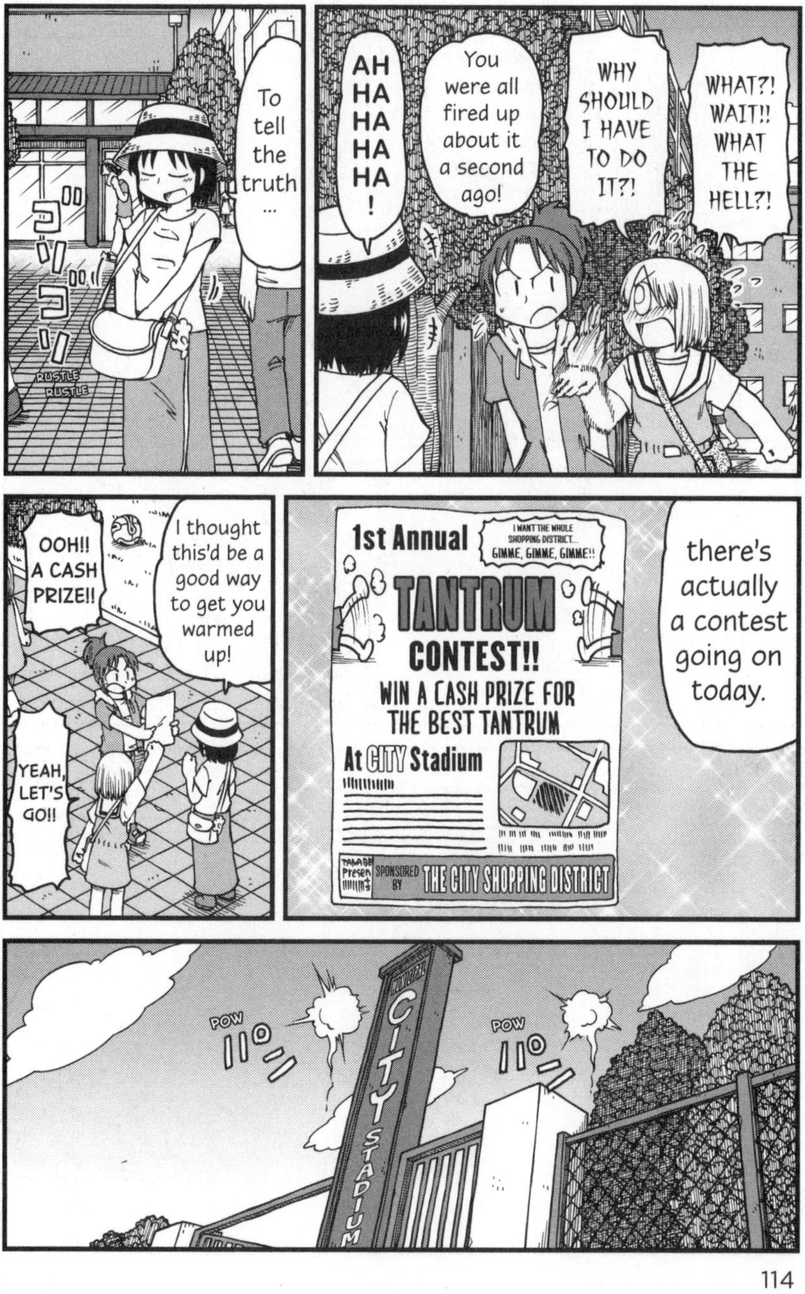
WHAT?! WAIT!! WHAT THE HELL?!
WHY SHOULD I HAVE TO DO IT?!
You were all fired up about it a second ago!
AH HA HA HA HA!
To tell the truth ...
RUSTLE RUSTLE
there's actually a contest going on today.
1st Annual
I WANT THE WHOLE SHOPPING DISTRICT... GIMME, GIMME, GIMME!!
TANTRUM CONTEST!!
WIN A CASH PRIZE FOR THE BEST TANTRUM
At CITY Stadium
SPONSORED BY THE CITY SHOPPING DISTRICT
I thought this'd be a good way to get you warmed up!
OOH!! A CASH PRIZE!!
YEAH, LET'S GO!!
POW
POW
CITY STADIUM

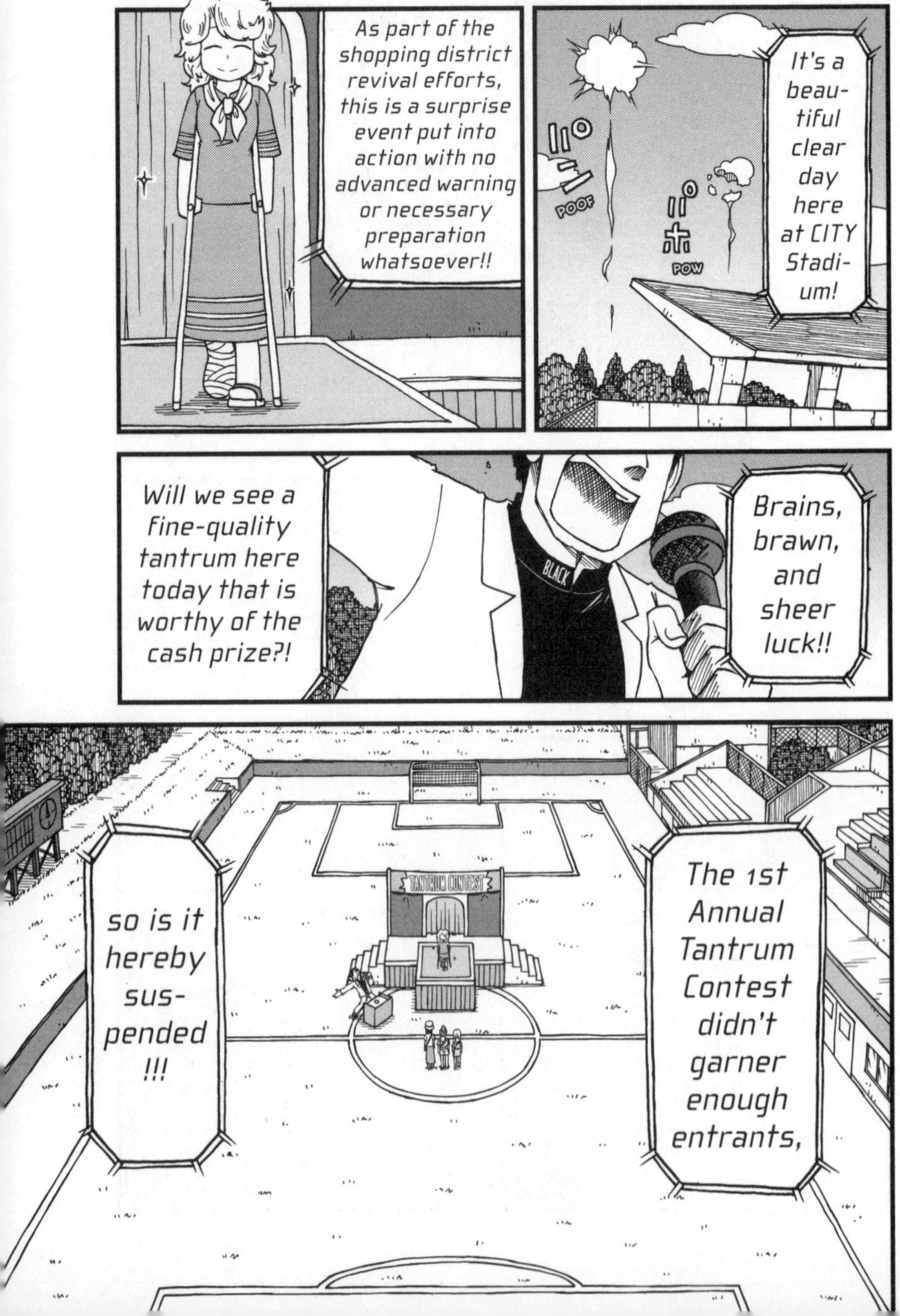
It's a beau-tiful clear day here at CITY Stadi-um!
POW
POOF
As part of the shopping district revival efforts, this is a surprise event put into action with no advanced warning or necessary preparation whatsoever!!
Brains, brawn, and sheer luck!!
BLACK
Will we see a fine-quality tantrum here today that is worthy of the cash prize?!
The 1st Annual Tantrum Contest didn't garner enough entrants,
TANTRUM CONTEST
so is it hereby sus-pended !!!

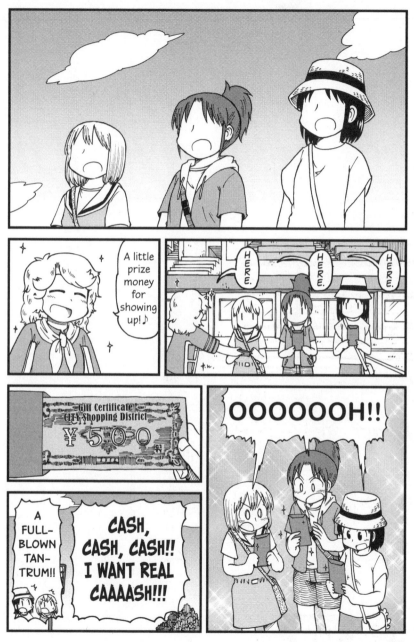

HERE.
HERE.
HERE.
A little prize money for showing up!♪
OOOOOOH!!
Gift Certificate
CITY Shopping District
¥500
CASH, CASH, CASH!! I WANT REAL CAAAASH!!!
A FULL-BLOWN TAN-TRUM!!

6
20

CITY

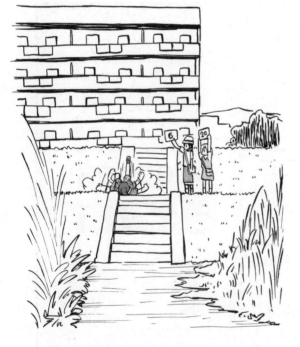

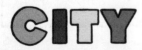

Gift Certificate
CITY Shopping District
¥500

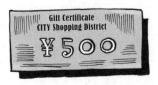

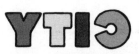

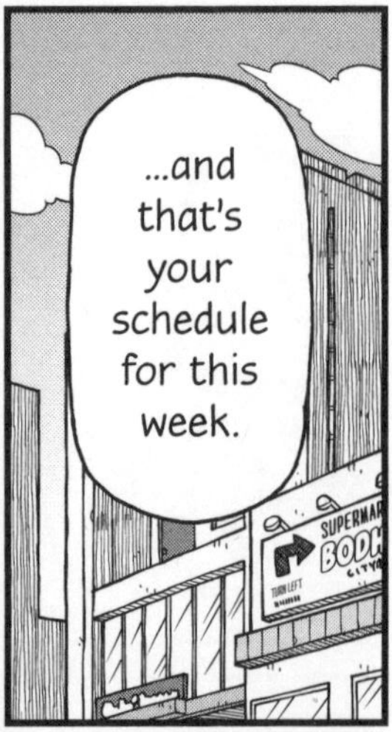
...and that's your schedule for this week.

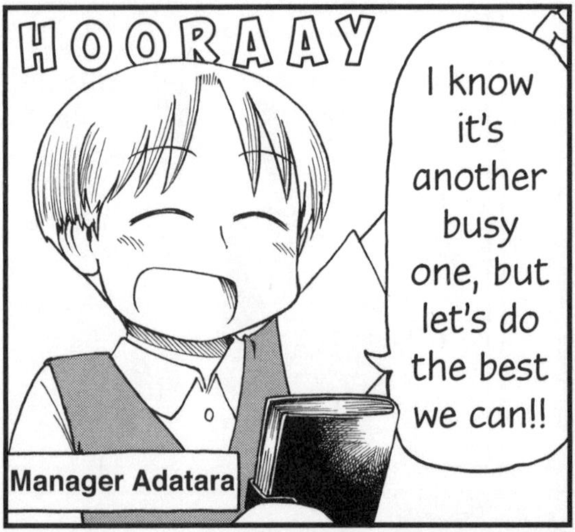
HOORAAY
I know it's another busy one, but let's do the best we can!!
Manager Adatara

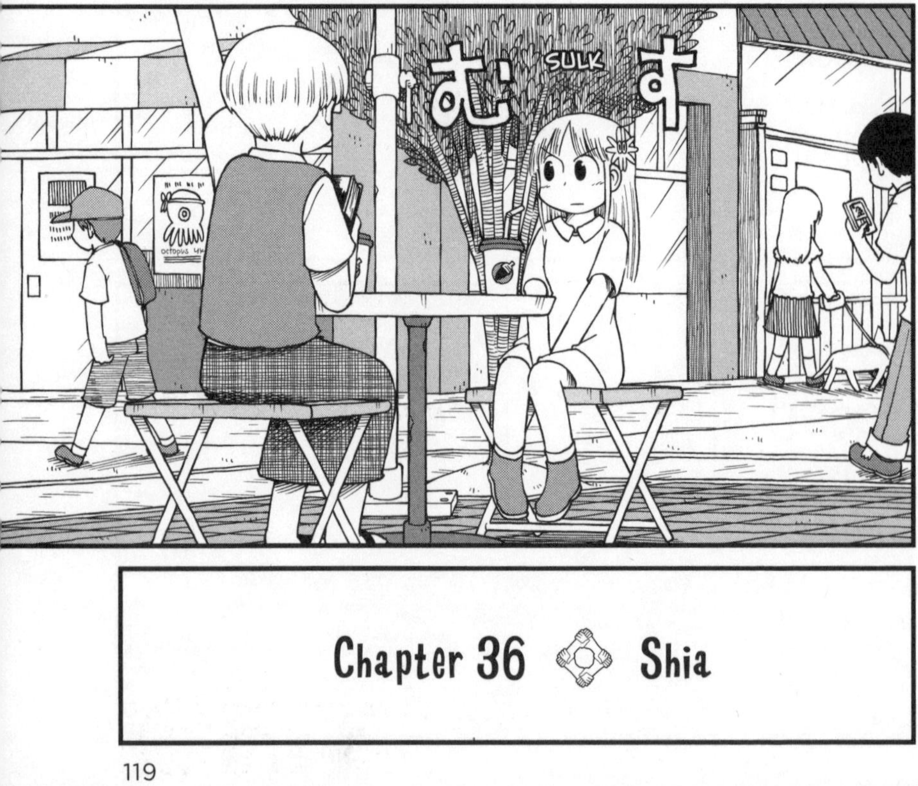
むす
SULK

Chapter 36 ◇ Shia

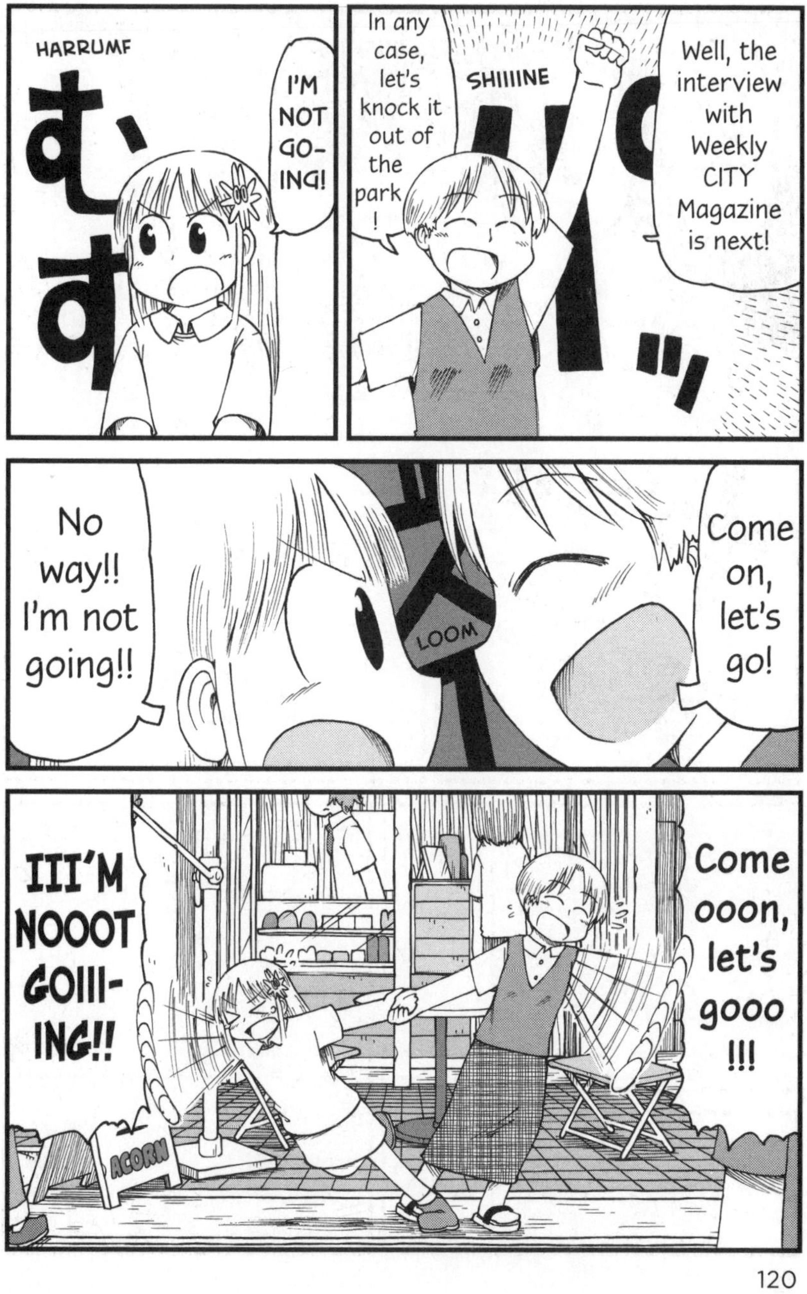

Well, the interview with Weekly CITY Magazine is next!
SHIIIINE
In any case, let's knock it out of the park!
I'M NOT GO-ING!
HARRUMF
むす
Come on, let's go!
LOOM
No way!! I'm not going!!
Come ooon, let's gooo!!!
III'M NOOOT GOIIII-ING!!
ACORN

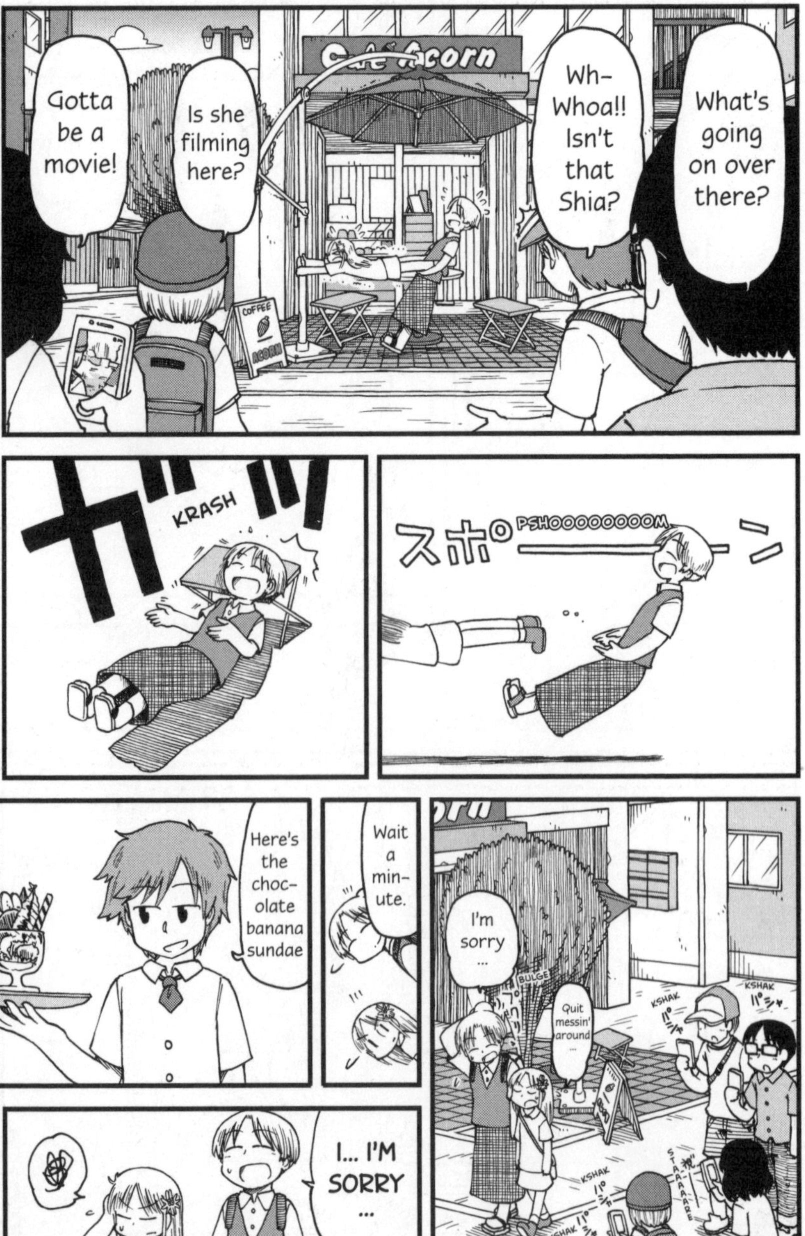
What's going on over there?
Wh- Whoa!! Isn't that Shia?
Is she filming here?
Gotta be a movie!
スポーーン
PSHOOOOOOOOOM
ガッ
KRASH
I'm sorry ...
BULGE
Quit messin' around ...
KSHAK
パシャ
KSHAK
パシャ
KSHAK
パシャ
KSHAK
パシャ
STAAAAARE
Wait a min-ute.
Here's the chocolate banana sundae
that you or-dered.
I... I'M SORRY ...

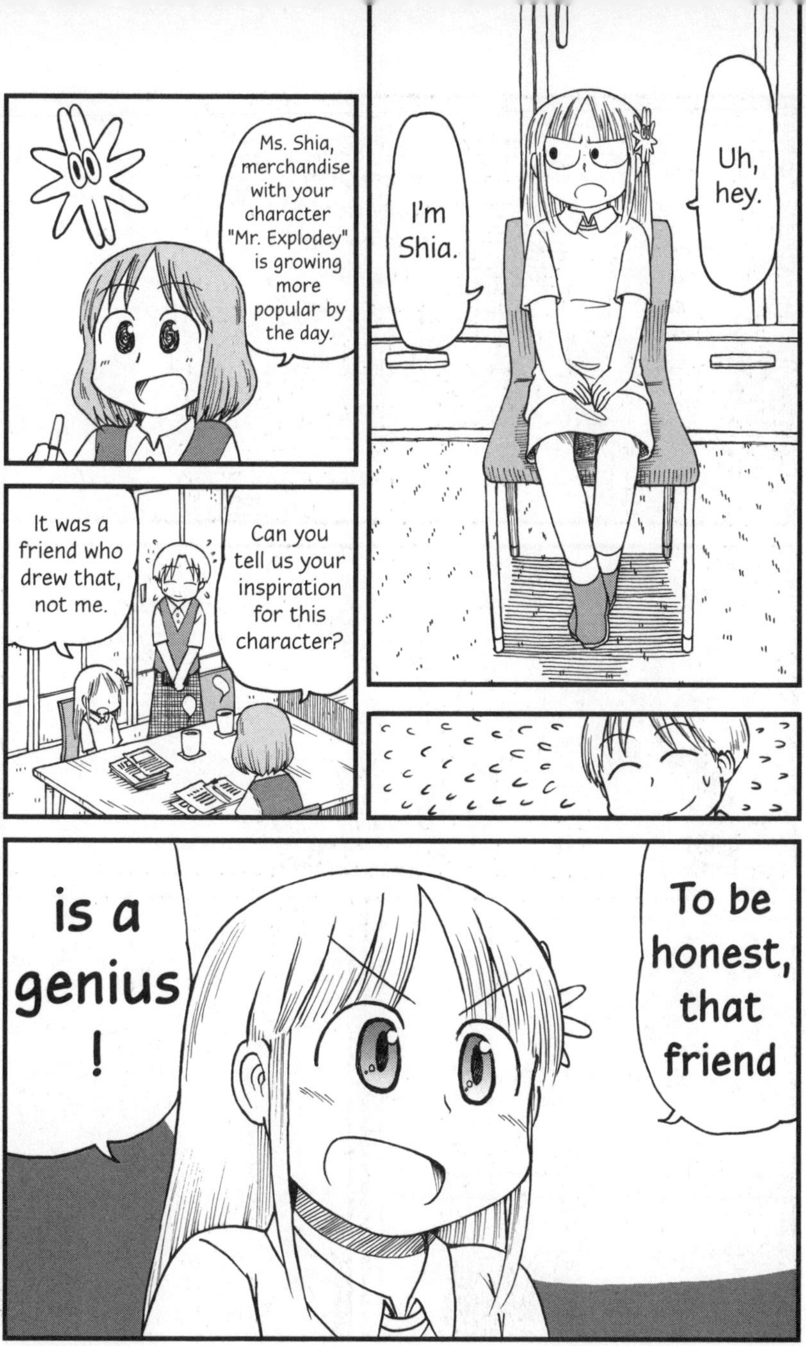
Uh, hey.
I'm Shia.
Ms. Shia, merchandise with your character "Mr. Explodey" is growing more popular by the day.
Can you tell us your inspiration for this character?
It was a friend who drew that, not me.
To be honest, that friend
is a genius !

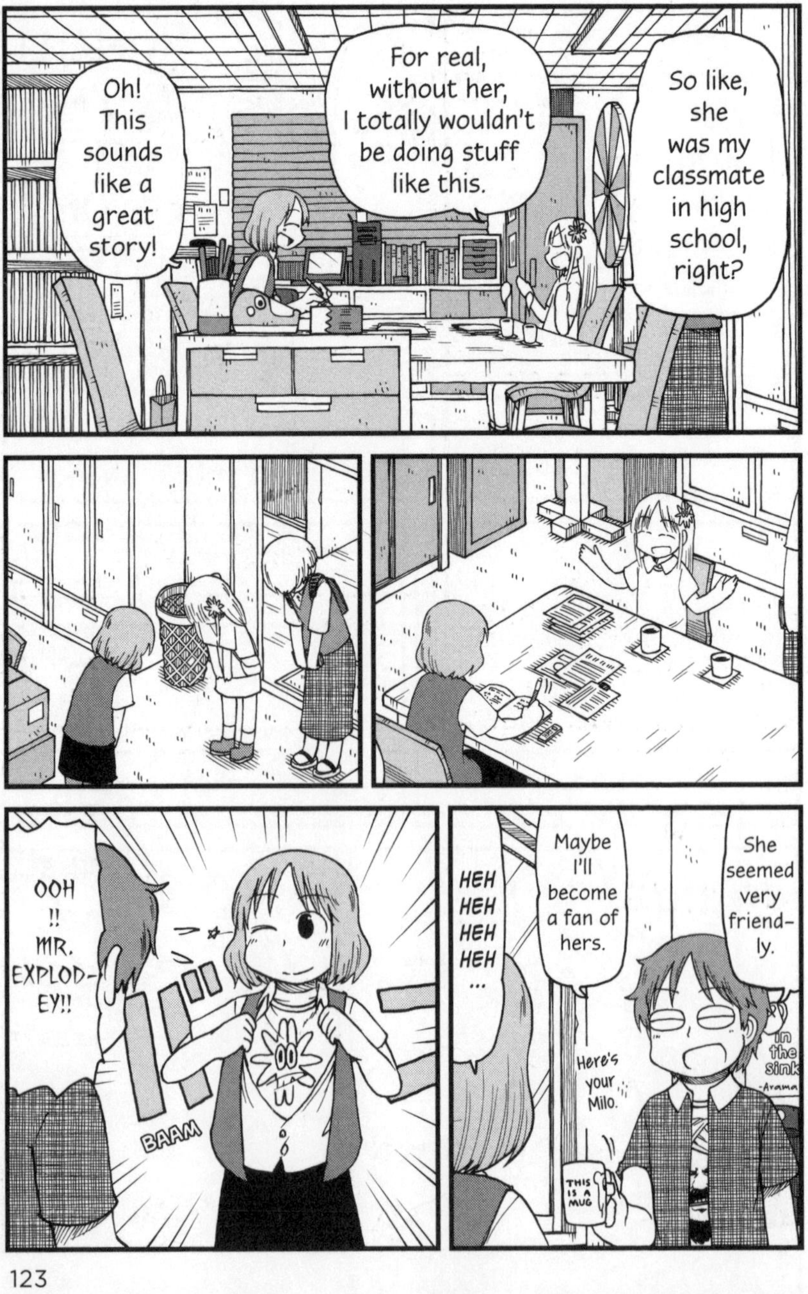
So like, she was my classmate in high school, right?
For real, without her, I totally wouldn't be doing stuff like this.
Oh! This sounds like a great story!
She seemed very friend-ly.
In the sink -Arama
Maybe I'll become a fan of hers.
HEH HEH HEH HEH ...
Here's your Milo.
THIS IS A MUG
OOH !! MR. EXPLOD-EY!!
BAAM

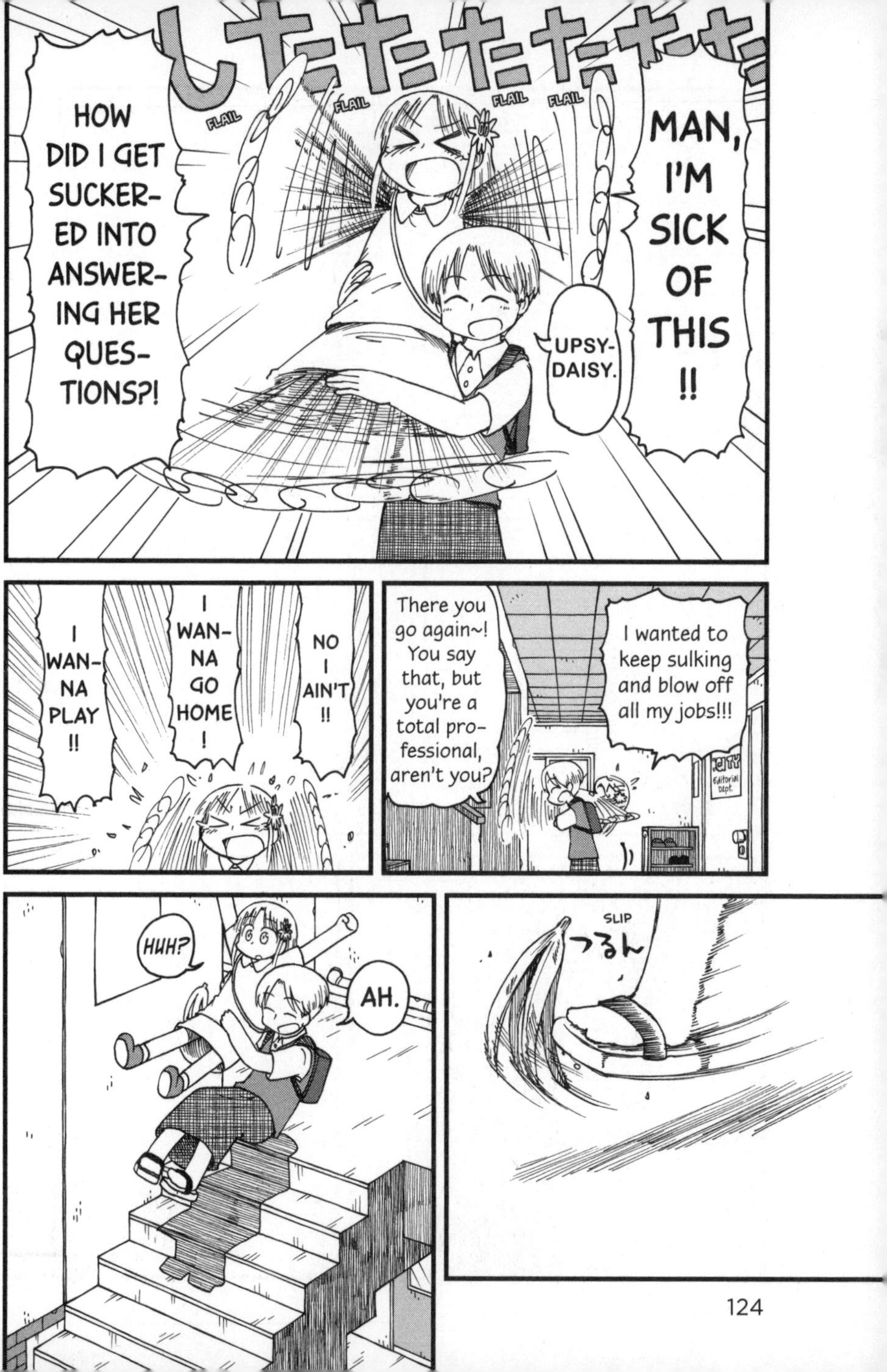
FLAIL
FLAIL
FLAIL
FLAIL
MAN, I'M SICK OF THIS!!
UPSY-DAISY.
HOW DID I GET SUCKERED INTO ANSWERING HER QUESTIONS?!
I wanted to keep sulking and blow off all my jobs!!!
Editorial Dept.
There you go again~! You say that, but you're a total professional, aren't you?
NO I AIN'T!!
I WANNA GO HOME!
I WANNA PLAY!!
SLIP
つるん
AH.
HUH?

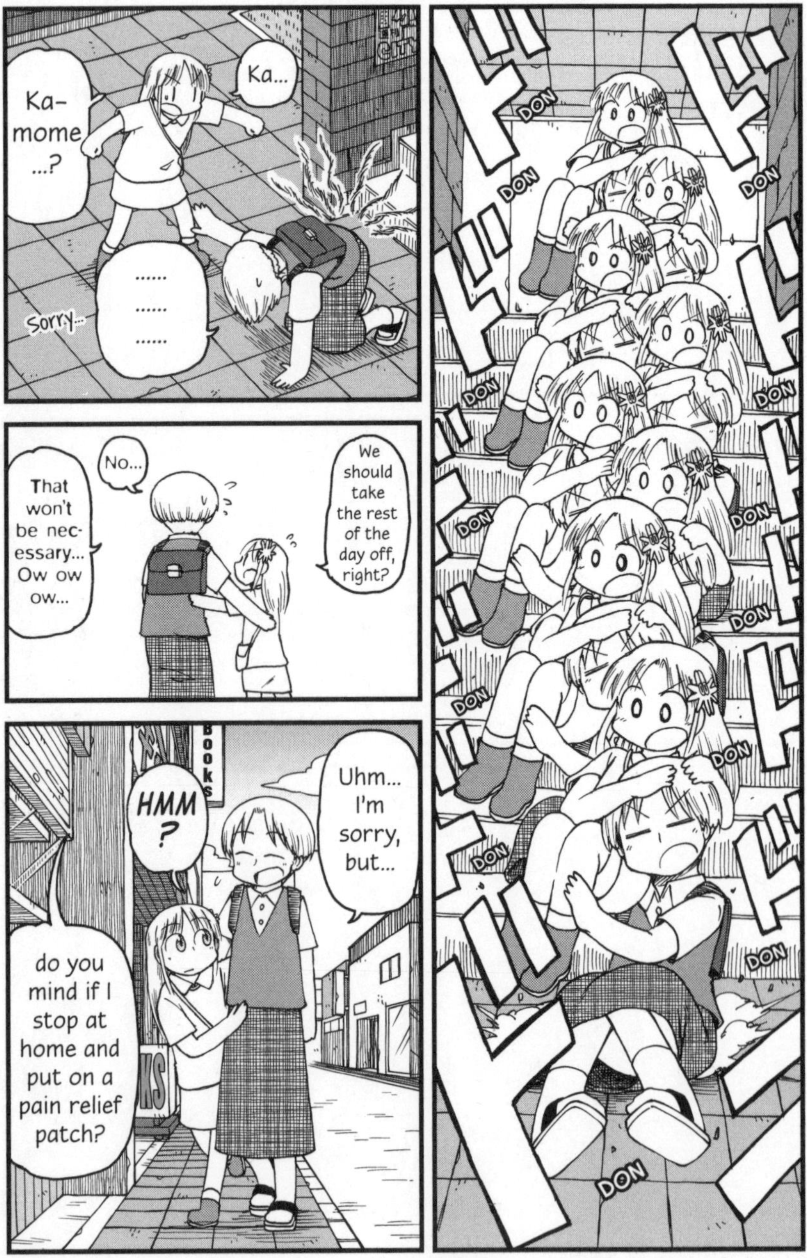
DON
DON
DON
DON
DON
DON
DON
DON
DON
DON
DON
DON
DON
Ka...
Ka-mome ...?
....
Sorry...
We should take the rest of the day off, right?
No...
That won't be necessary... Ow ow ow...
Uhm... I'm sorry, but...
BOOKS
HMM ?
do you mind if I stop at home and put on a pain relief patch?

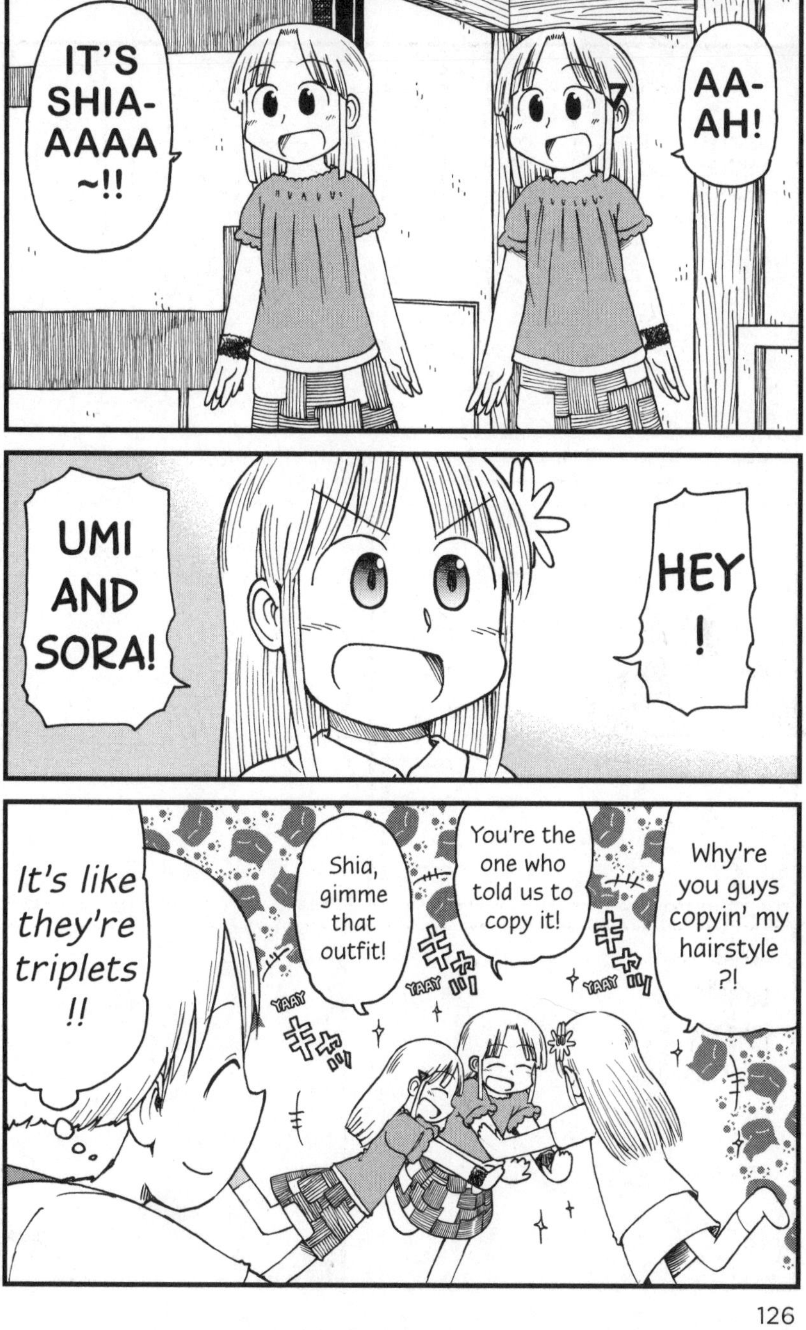
AA-AH!
IT'S SHIA-AAAA~!!
HEY!
UMI AND SORA!
Why're you guys copyin' my hairstyle?!
You're the one who told us to copy it!
Shia, gimme that outfit!
YAAY
YAAY
YAAY
It's like they're triplets!!

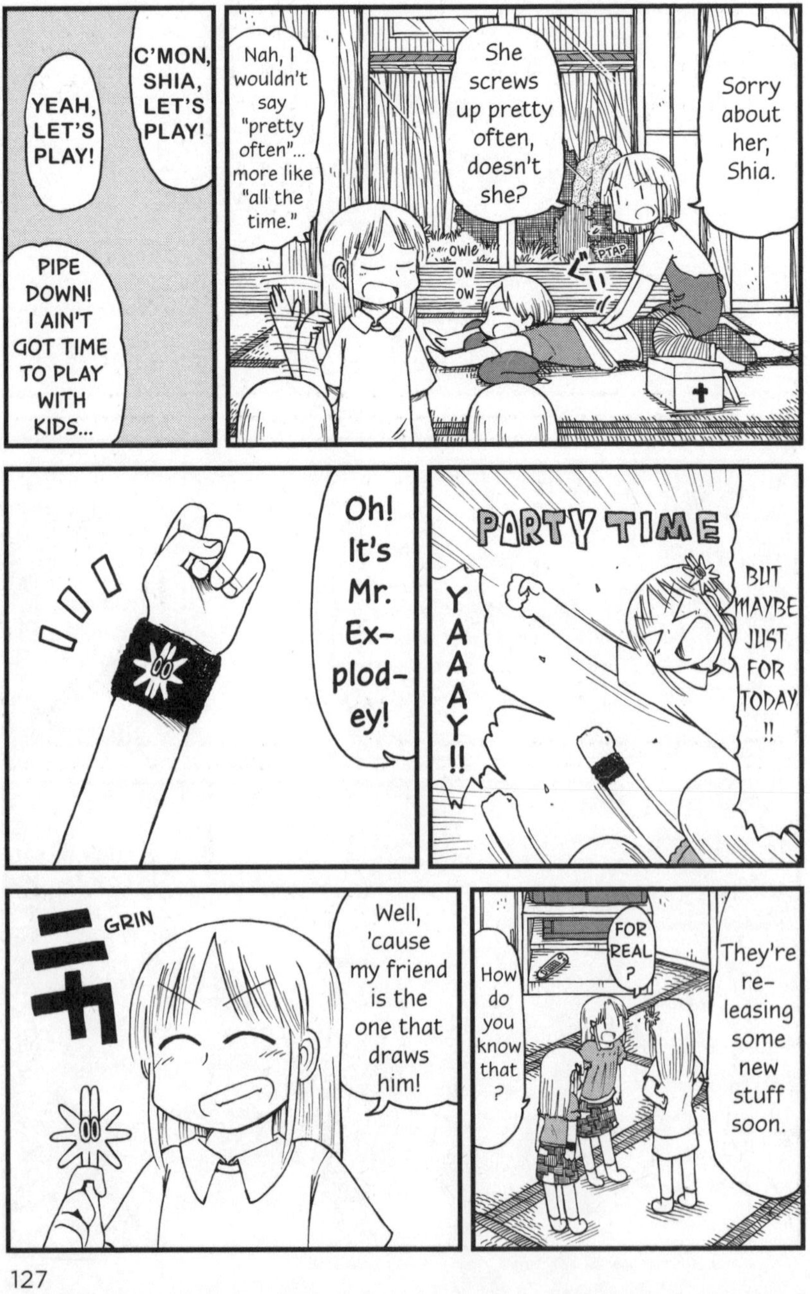
Sorry about her, Shia.
She screws up pretty often, doesn't she?
PTAP
OWIE OW OW
Nah, I wouldn't say "pretty often"... more like "all the time."
C'MON, SHIA, LET'S PLAY!
YEAH, LET'S PLAY!
PIPE DOWN! I AIN'T GOT TIME TO PLAY WITH KIDS...
PARTY TIME
BUT MAYBE JUST FOR TODAY !!
YAAAAY!!
Oh! It's Mr. Ex-plod-ey!
They're re-leasing some new stuff soon.
FOR REAL ?
How do you know that ?
Well, 'cause my friend is the one that draws him!
ニカ
GRIN

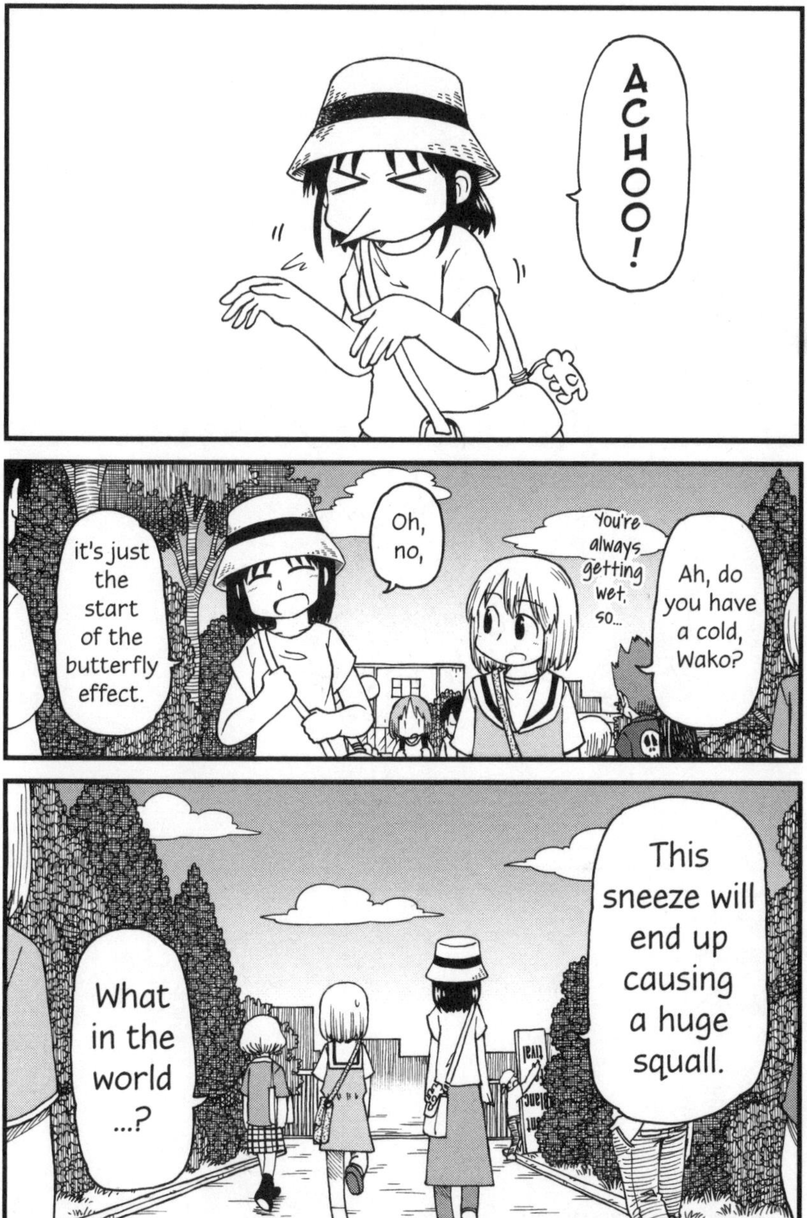
ACHOO!
Ah, do you have a cold, Wako?
You're always getting wet, so...
Oh, no,
it's just the start of the butterfly effect.
This sneeze will end up causing a huge squall.
What in the world ...?

*A trope in Japan is that a person will sneeze if someone is talking about them.

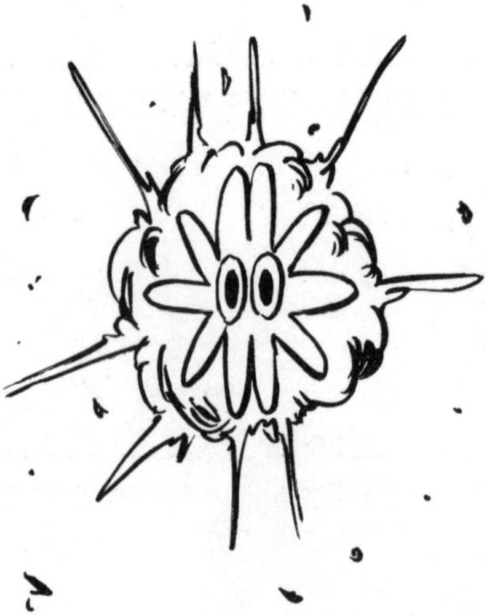

CITY

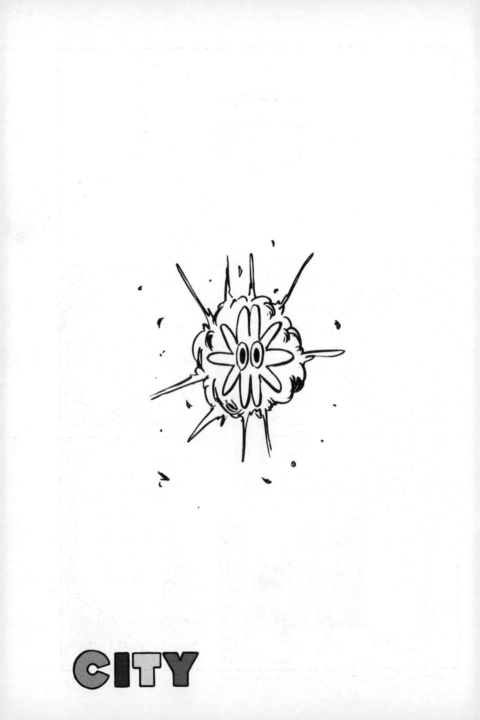

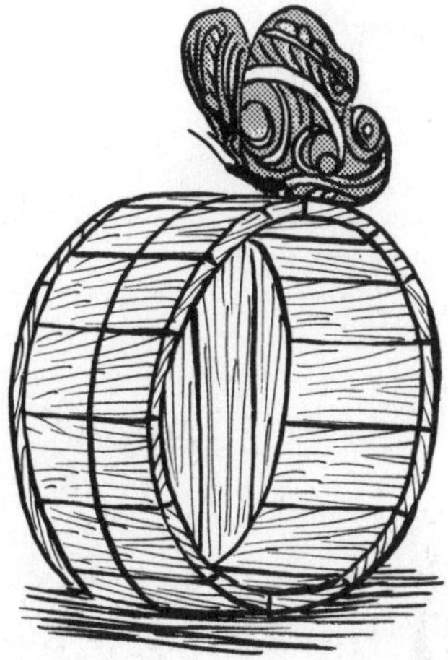

CITY

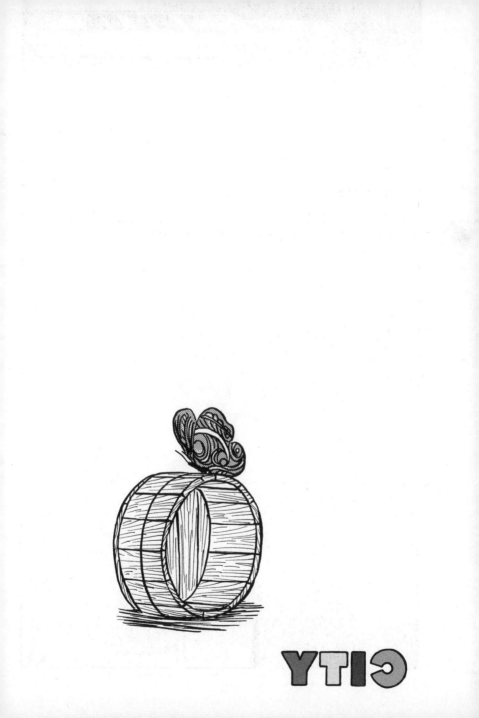

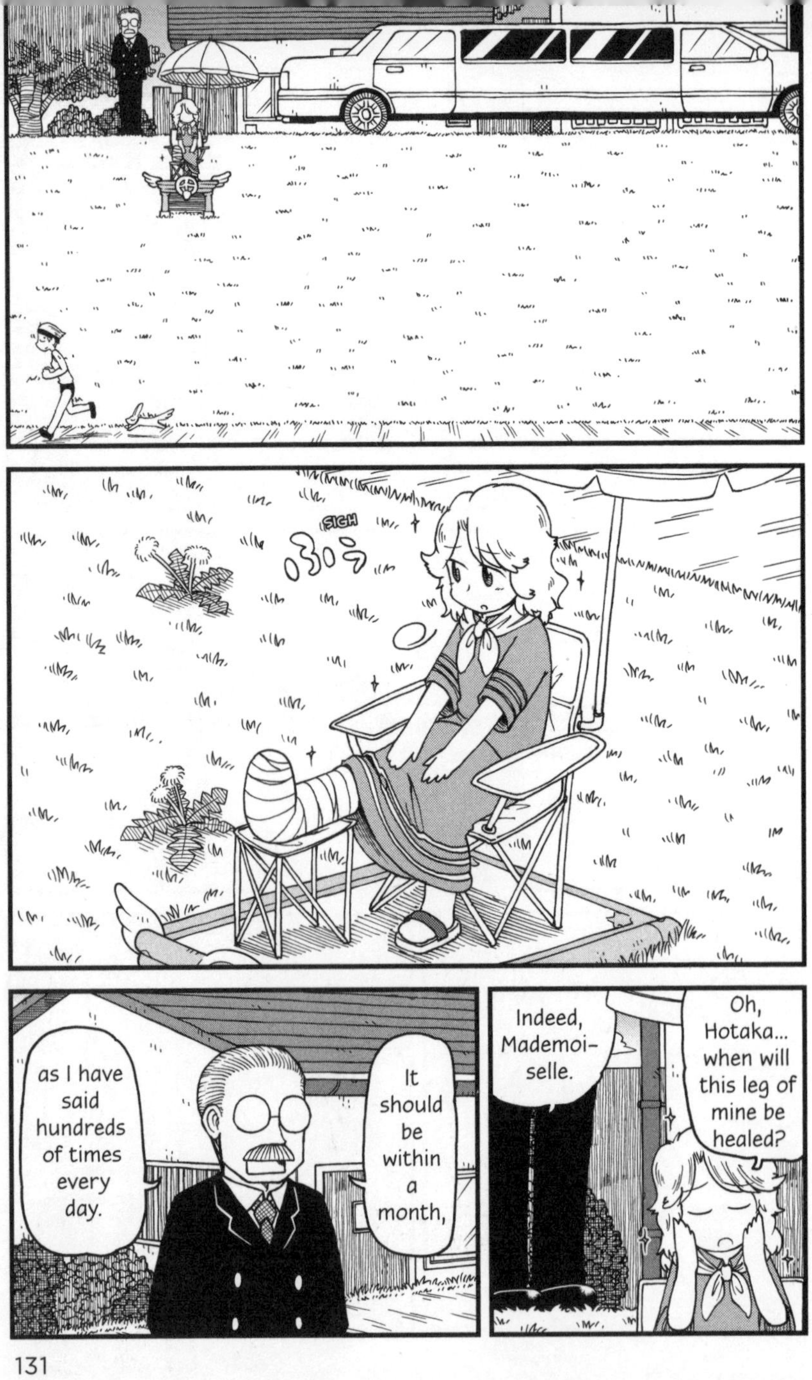
SIGH
Oh, Hotaka... when will this leg of mine be healed?
Indeed, Mademoiselle.
It should be within a month,
as I have said hundreds of times every day.

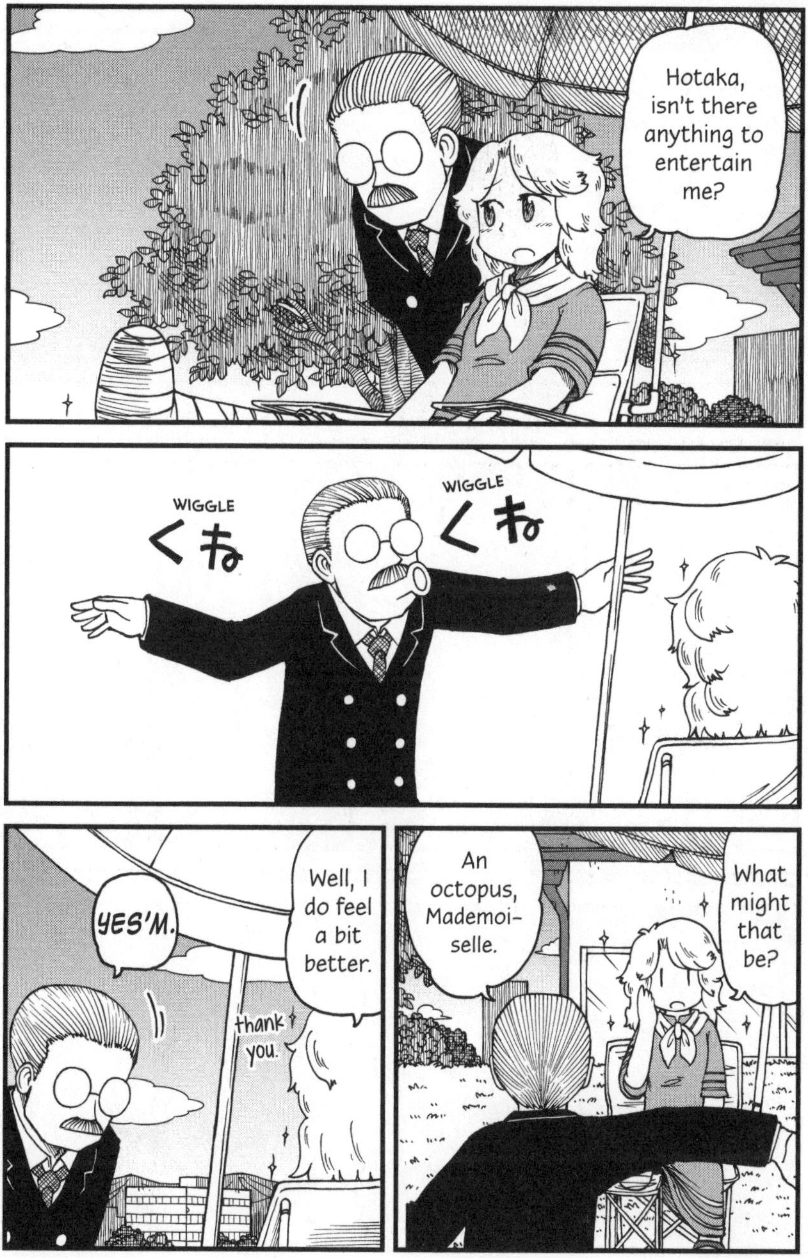

Hotaka, isn't there anything to entertain me?
WIGGLE
くね
WIGGLE
くね
What might that be?
An octopus, Mademoiselle.
Well, I do feel a bit better.
thank you.
YES'M.

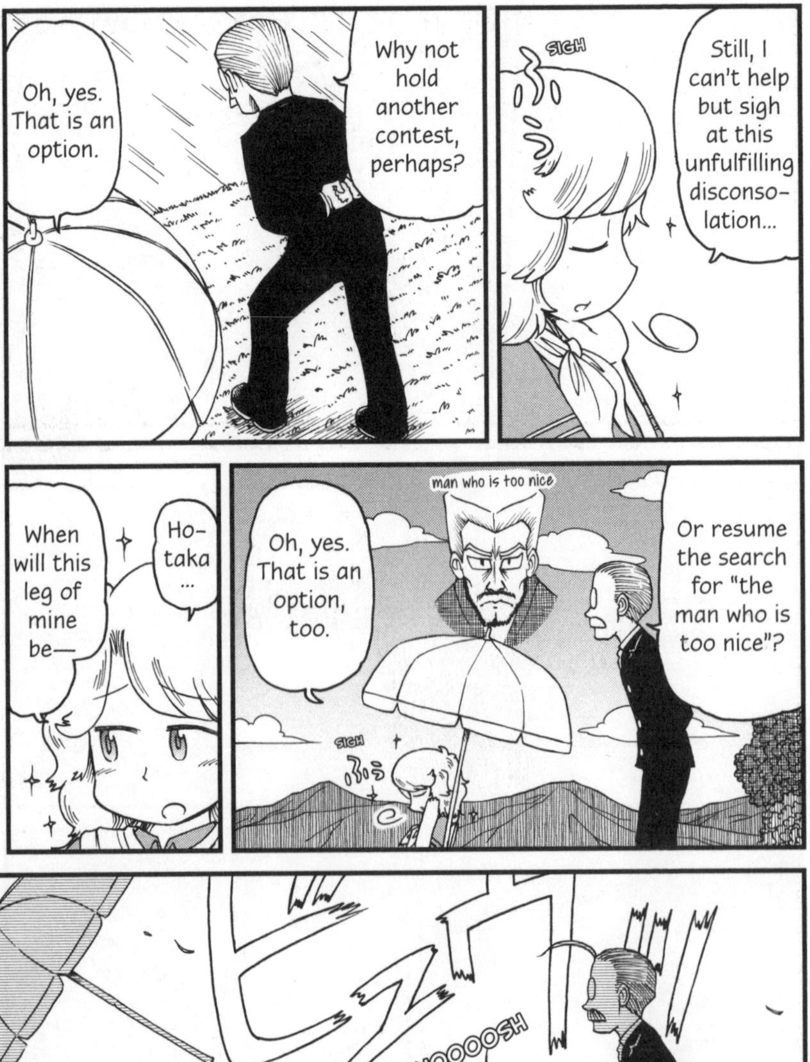
SIGH
Still, I can't help but sigh at this unfulfilling disconso-lation...
Why not hold another contest, perhaps?
Oh, yes. That is an option.
Or resume the search for "the man who is too nice"?
man who is too nice
Oh, yes. That is an option, too.
SIGH
Ho-taka ...
When will this leg of mine be—
ZWOOOOSH

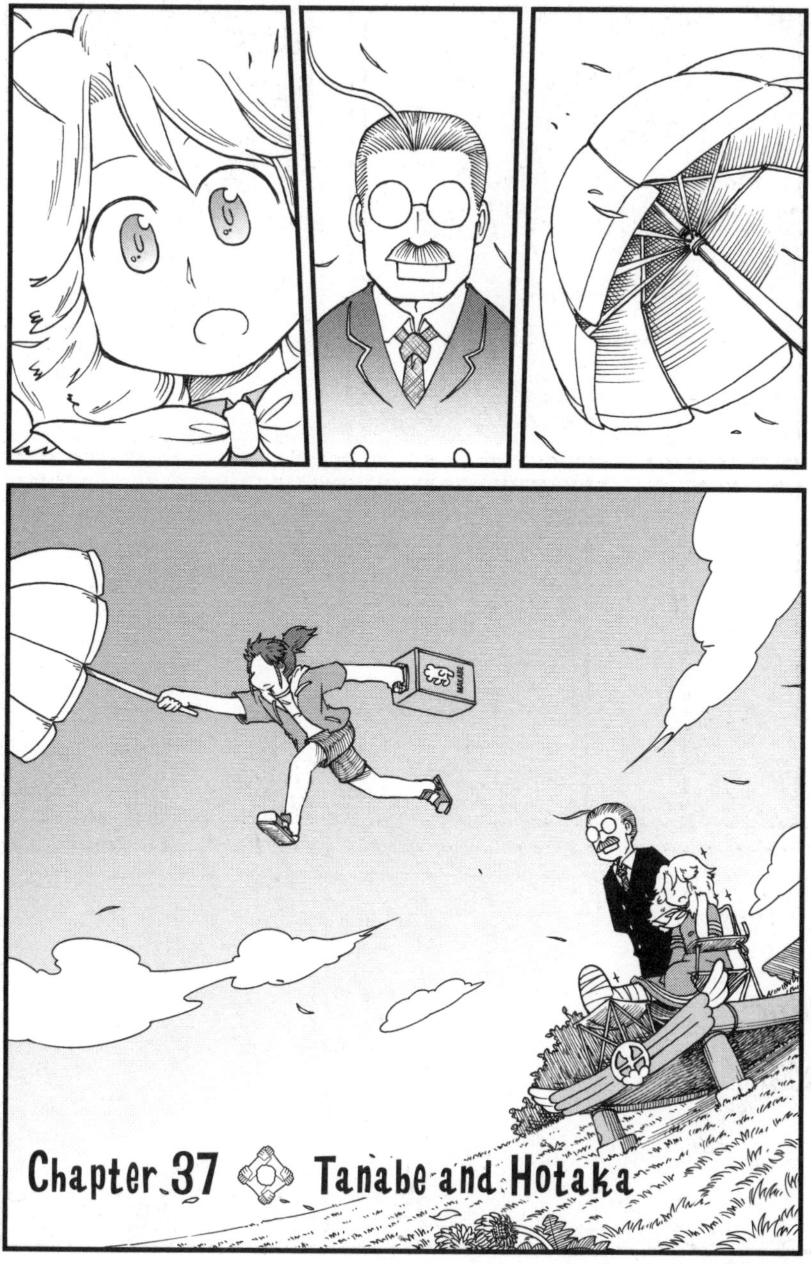
MAKABE
Chapter 37 Tanabe and Hotaka

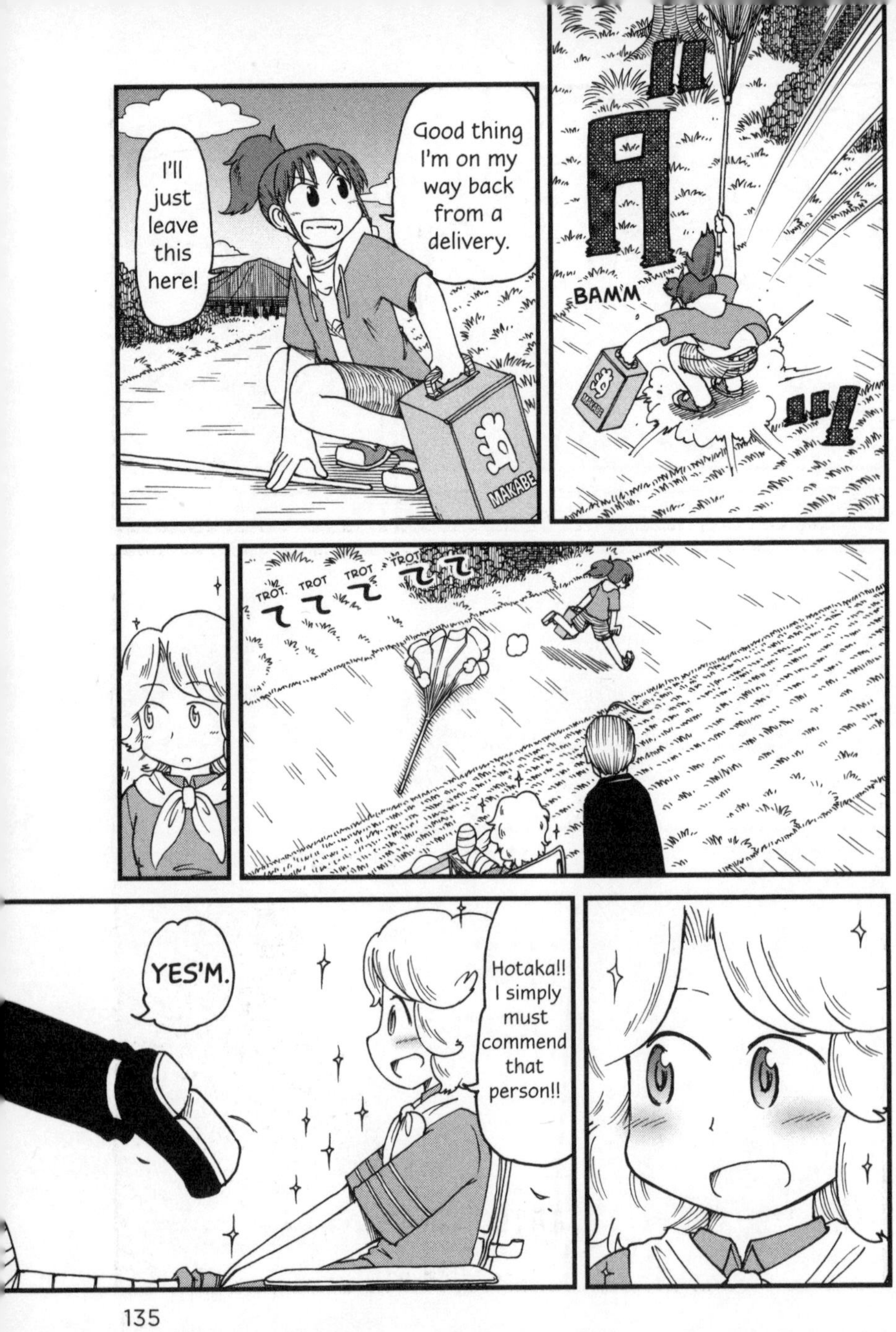
BAMM
Good thing I'm on my way back from a delivery.
I'll just leave this here!
MAKABE
TROT. TROT TROT TROT
Hotaka!! I simply must commend that person!!
YES'M.

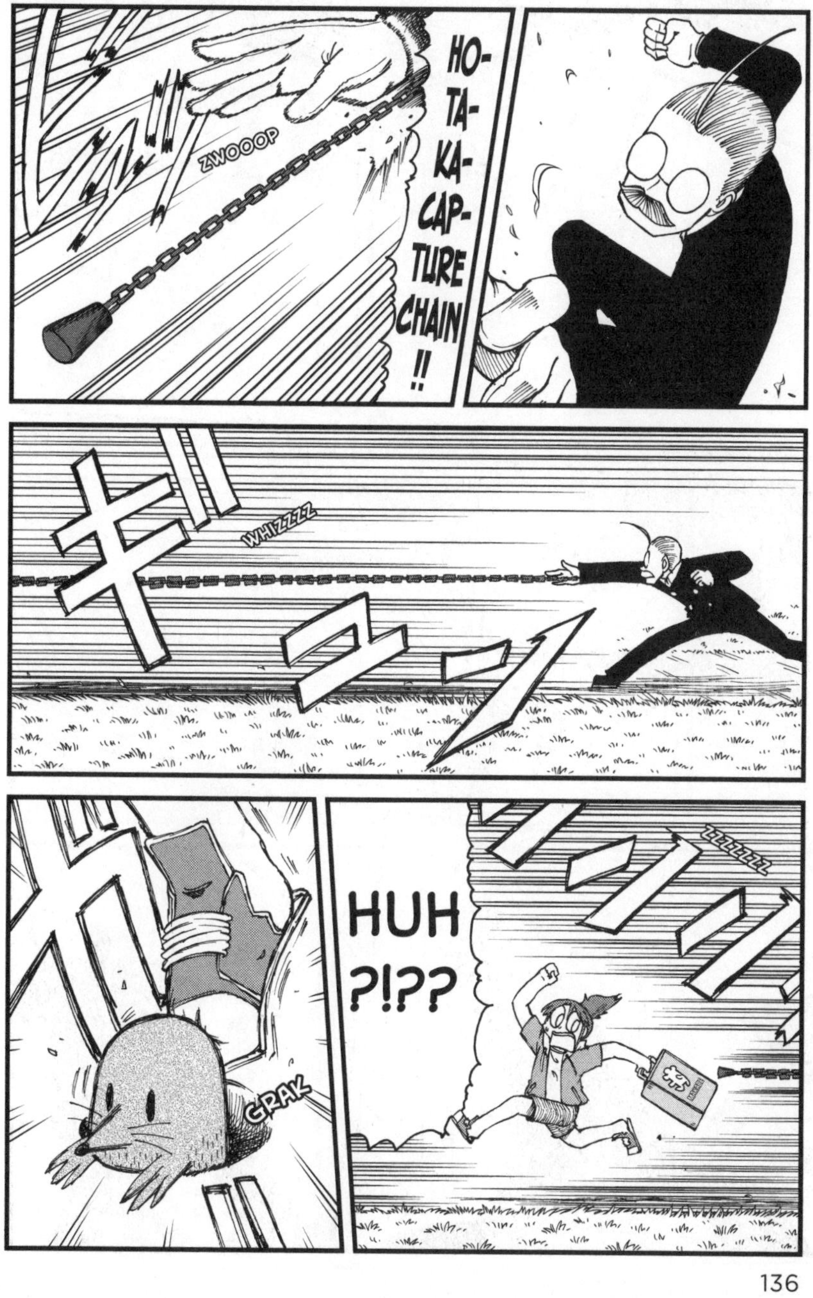
HO-TA-KA-CAP-TURE CHAIN!!
ZWOOOP
WHIZZZZ
ZZZZZZZ
HUH ?!??
GRAK

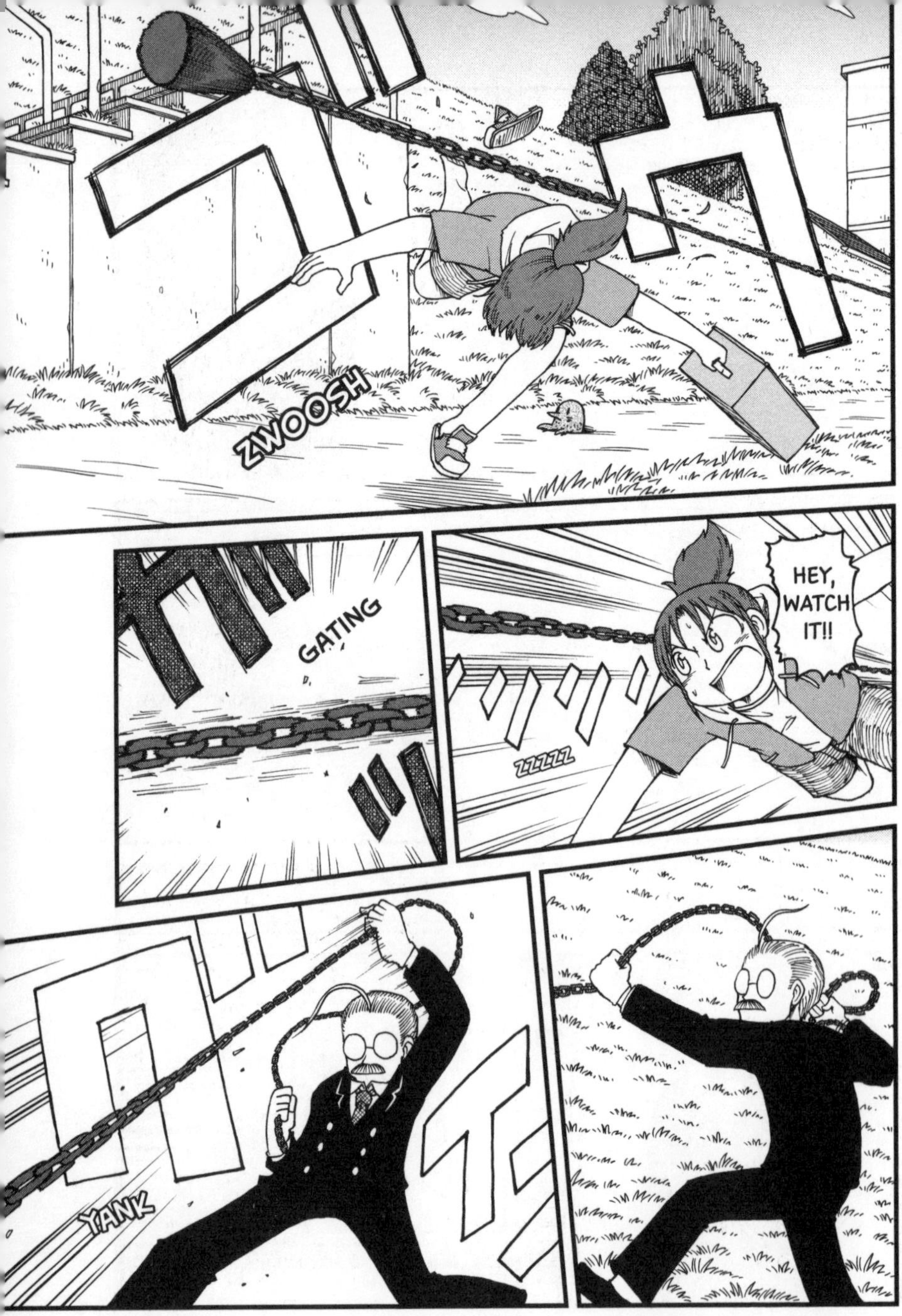
ZWOOSH
HEY, WATCH IT!!
ZZZZZ
GATING
YANK

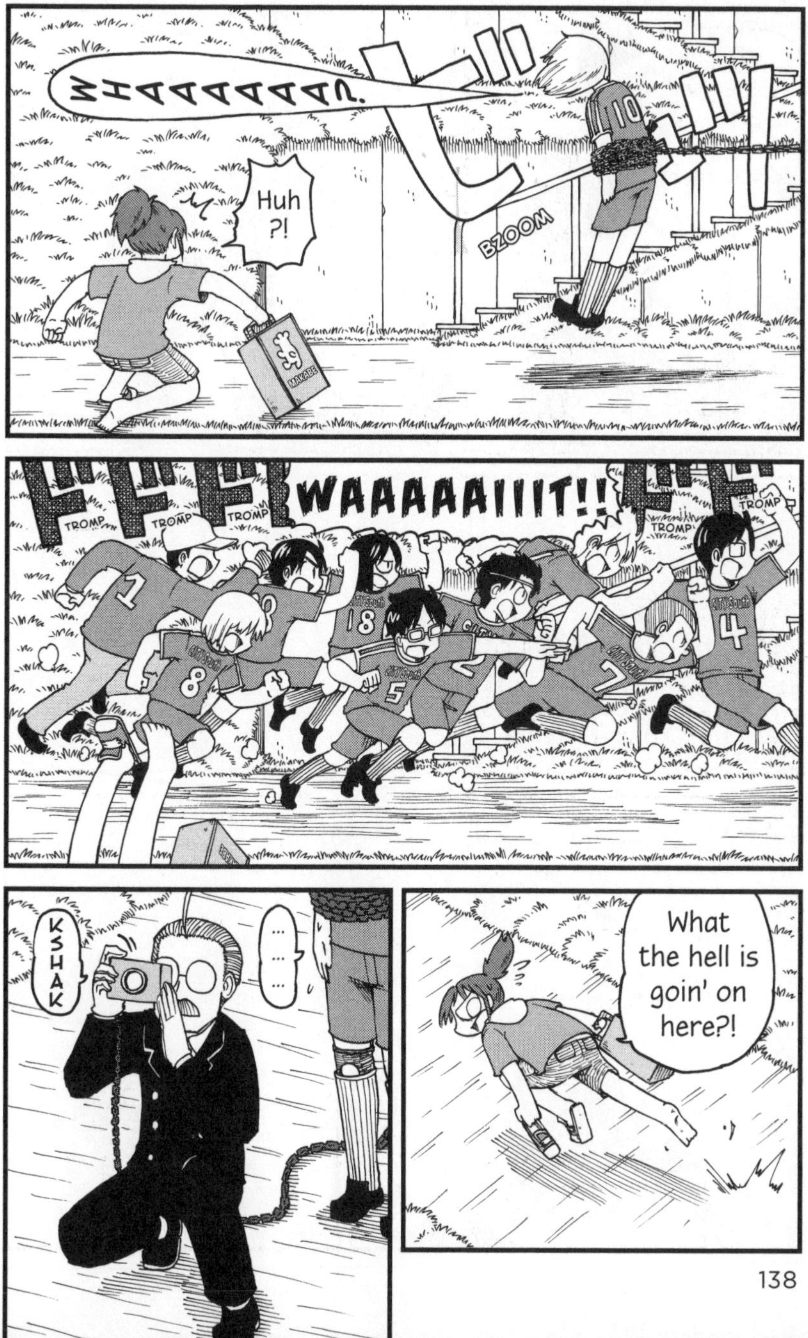
Huh ?!
BZOOM
MAKABE
WAAAAAIIIT!!
TROMP
TROMP
TROMP
TROMP
TROMP
What the hell is goin' on here?!
......
KSHAK

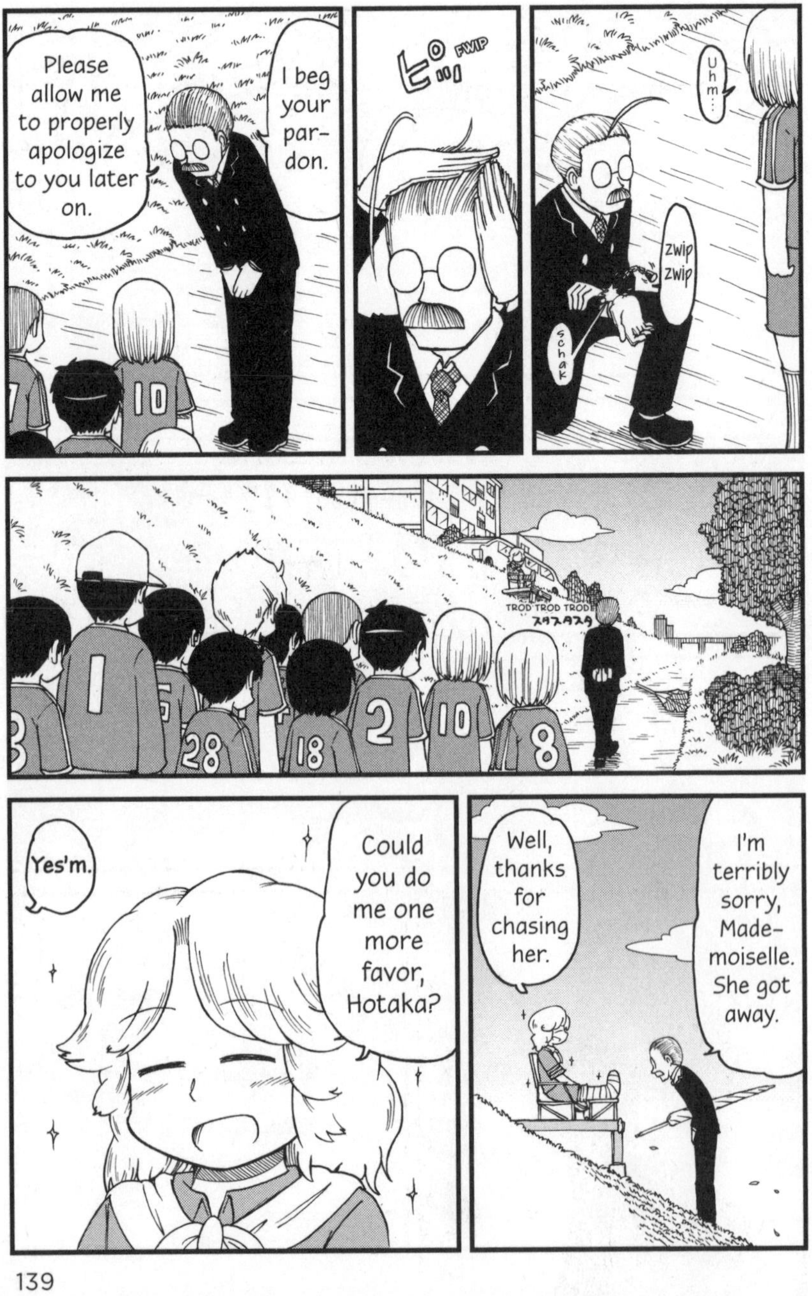
Uhm...
zwip zwip
schak
FWIP
I beg your pardon.
Please allow me to properly apologize to you later on.
TROD TROD TROD
スタスタ
I'm terribly sorry, Mademoiselle. She got away.
Well, thanks for chasing her.
Could you do me one more favor, Hotaka?
Yes'm.

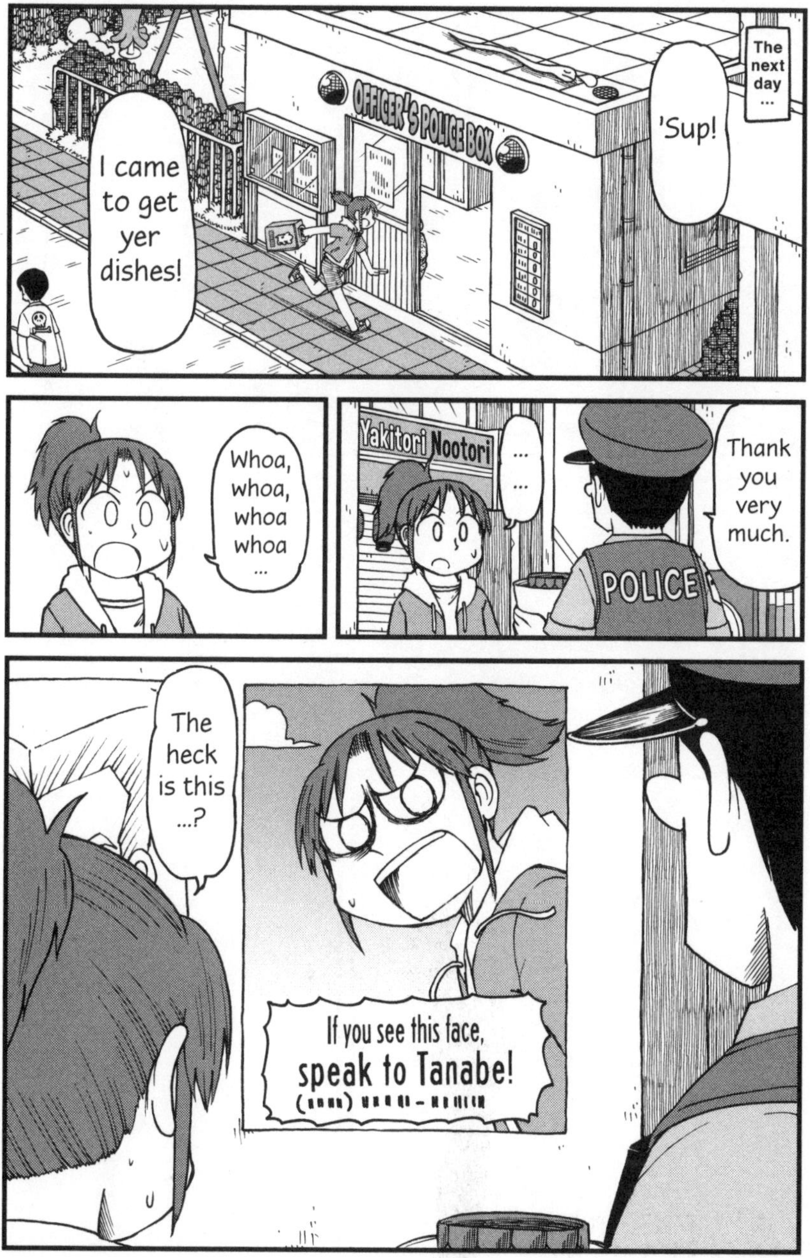
The next day ...
'Sup!
OFFICER'S POLICE BOX
I came to get yer dishes!
Thank you very much.
POLICE
... ...
Yakitori Nootori
Whoa, whoa, whoa whoa ...
The heck is this ...?
If you see this face, speak to Tanabe!

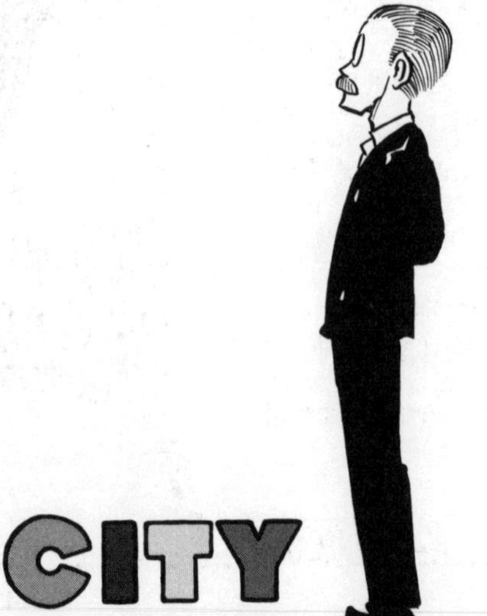
CITY

THURSDAY
23:00

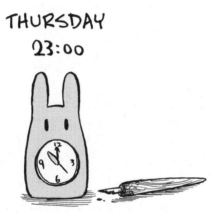

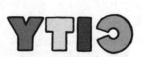

Miss Jump 1

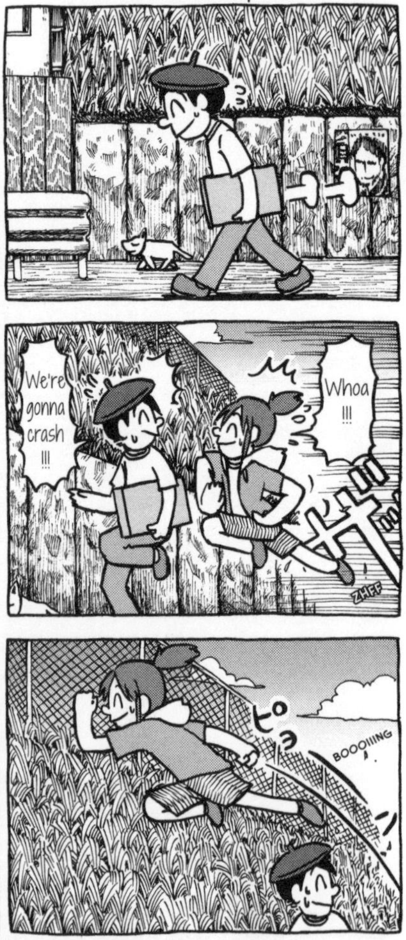
Whoa !!!
We're gonna crash !!!
ZHFF
BOOOIIING
Watch it, pal!!
She jumped ?!

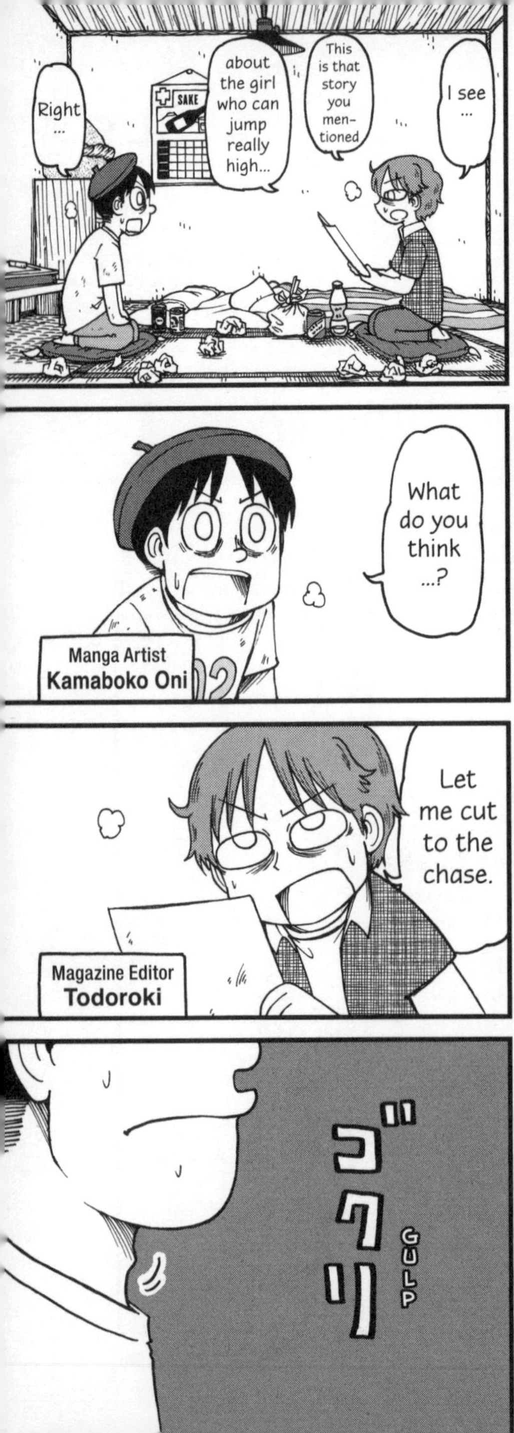
I see ...
This is that story you mentioned
about the girl who can jump really high...
Right ...
What do you think ...?
Manga Artist
Kamaboko Oni
Let me cut to the chase.
Magazine Editor
Todoroki
ゴクリ
GULP

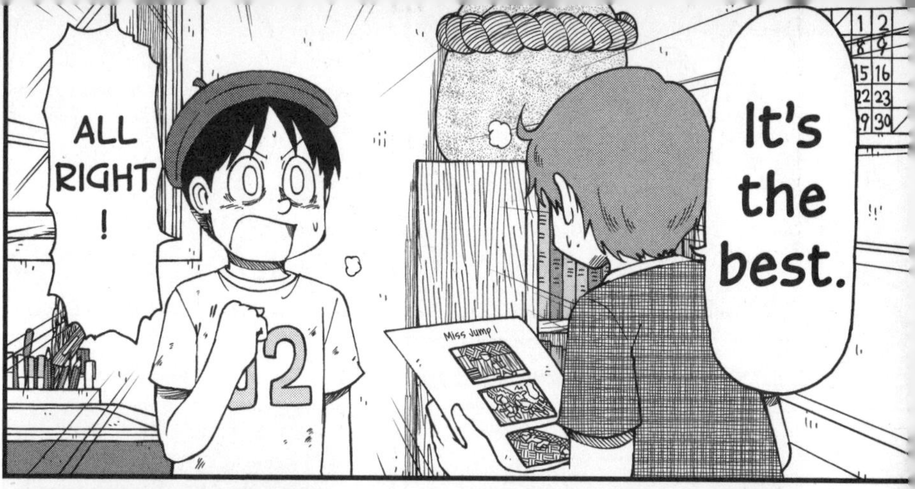
It's the best.
ALL RIGHT!
Miss Jump!

Chapter 38 A Manga Artist's TRAGIC Tale

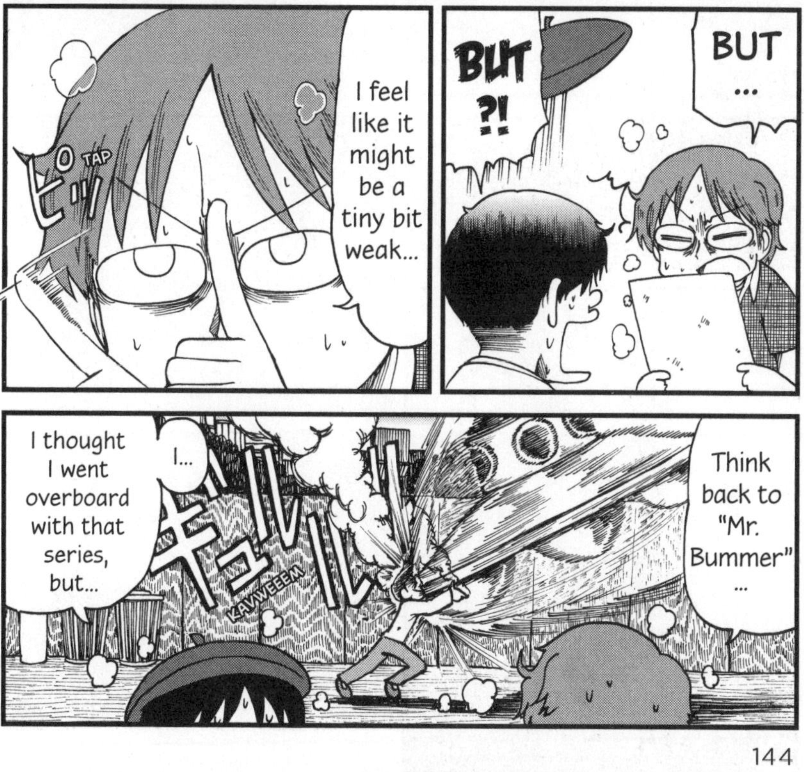
BUT...
BUT?!
I feel like it might be a tiny bit weak...
TAP
Think back to "Mr. Bummer"...
I...
KAVWEEEM
I thought I went overboard with that series, but...

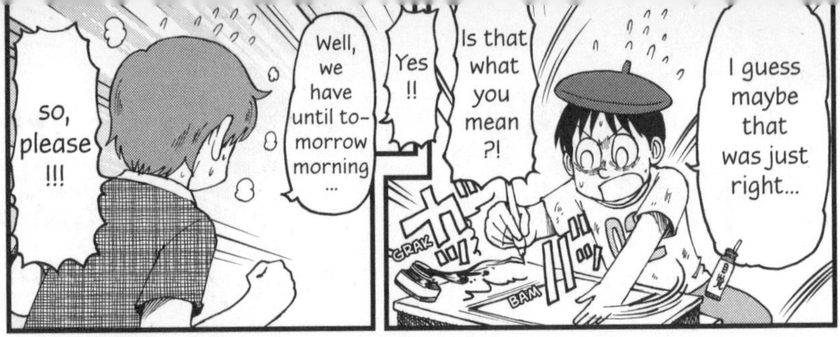
I guess maybe that was just right...
Is that what you mean ?!
GRAK
BAM
Yes !!
Well, we have until to-morrow morning ...
so, please !!!

Miss Jump 1

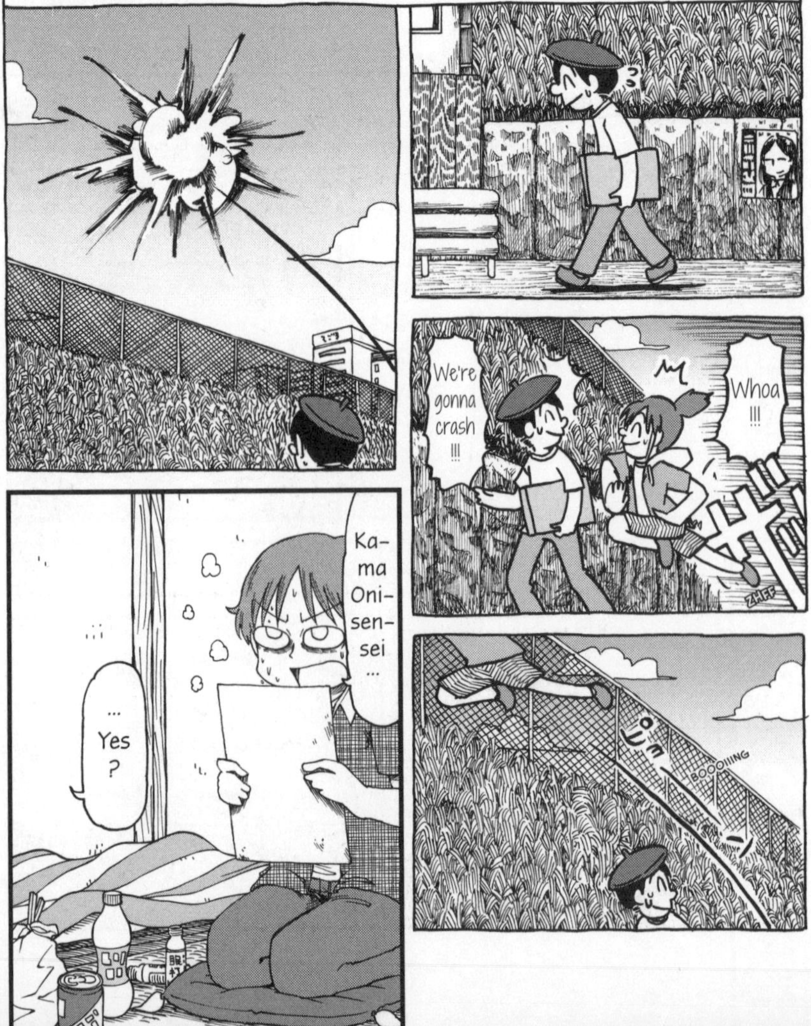
Whoa !!!
We're gonna crash !!!
ZHFF
BOOOIIING
Kama-Oni-sensei ...
... Yes ?

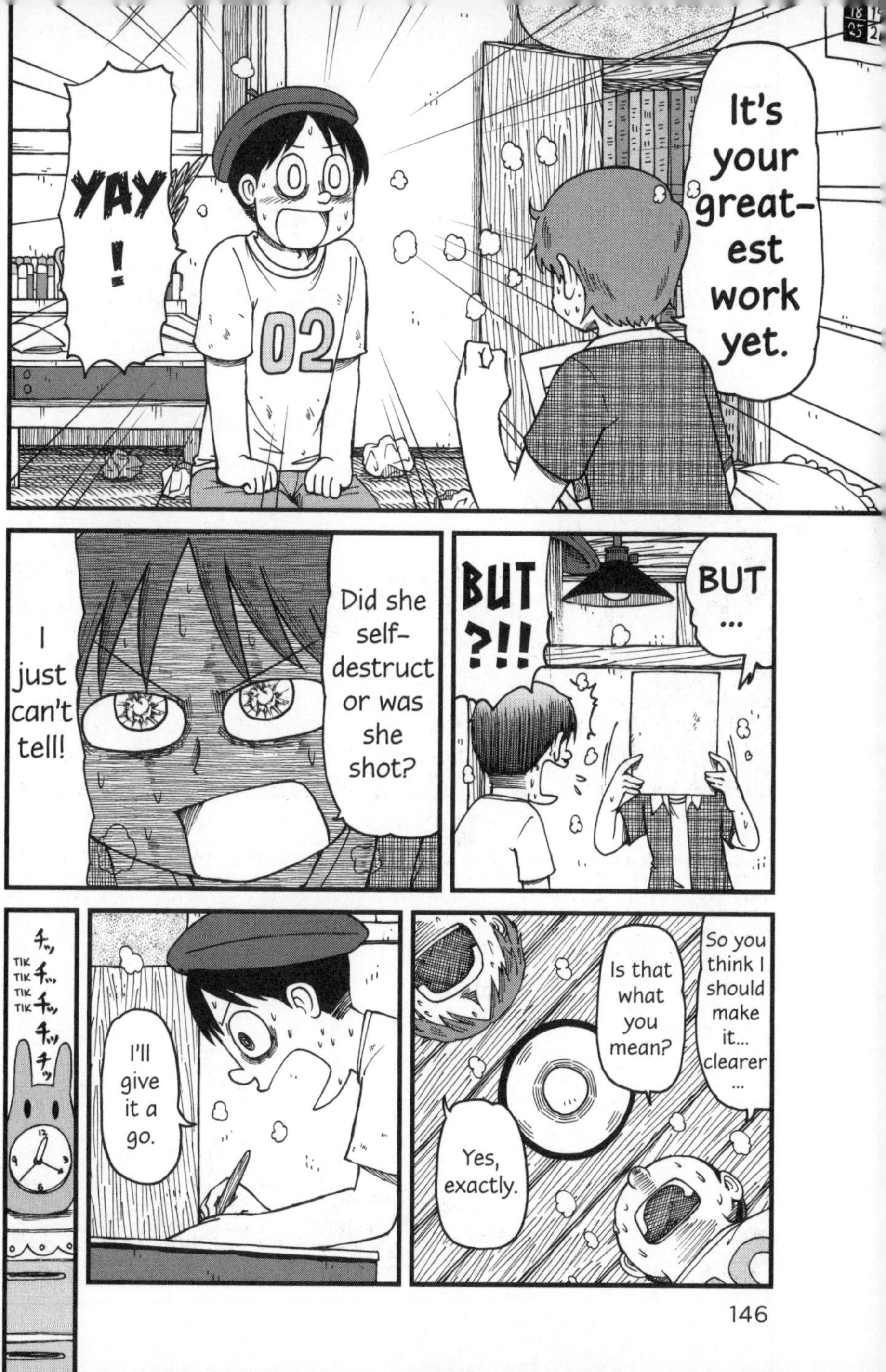
It's your great-est work yet.
YAY!
BUT ...
BUT ?!!
Did she self-destruct or was she shot?
I just can't tell!
So you think I should make it... clearer ...
Is that what you mean?
Yes, exactly.
I'll give it a go.
チッ チッ チッ チッ チッ
TIK TIK TIK TIK

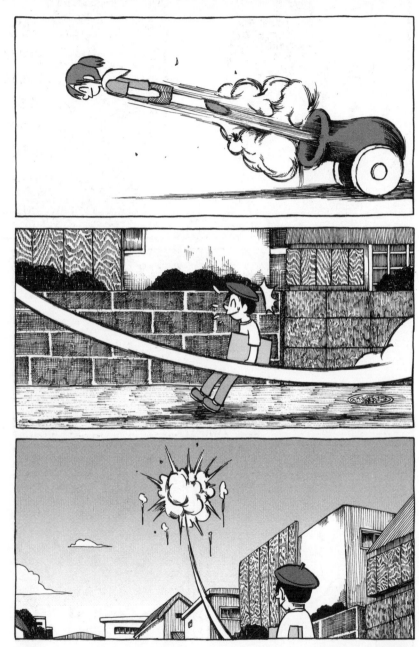

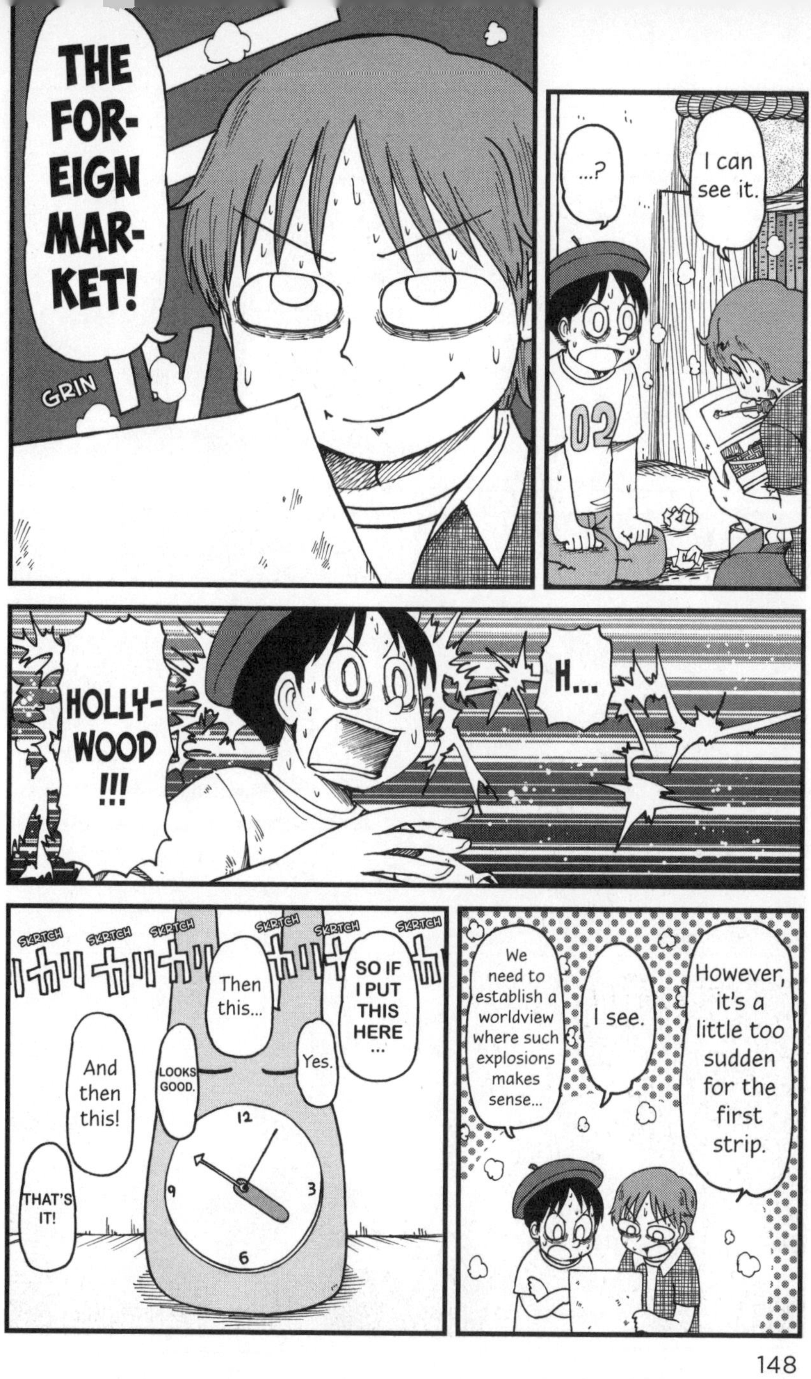
I can see it.
...?
THE FOR-EIGN MAR-KET!
GRIN
H...
HOLLY-WOOD !!!
However, it's a little too sudden for the first strip.
I see.
We need to establish a worldview where such explosions makes sense...
SKRTCH SKRTCH SKRTCH SKRTCH SKRTCH SKRTCH
SO IF I PUT THIS HERE ...
Then this...
Yes.
LOOKS GOOD.
And then this!
THAT'S IT!

Miss Jump 1

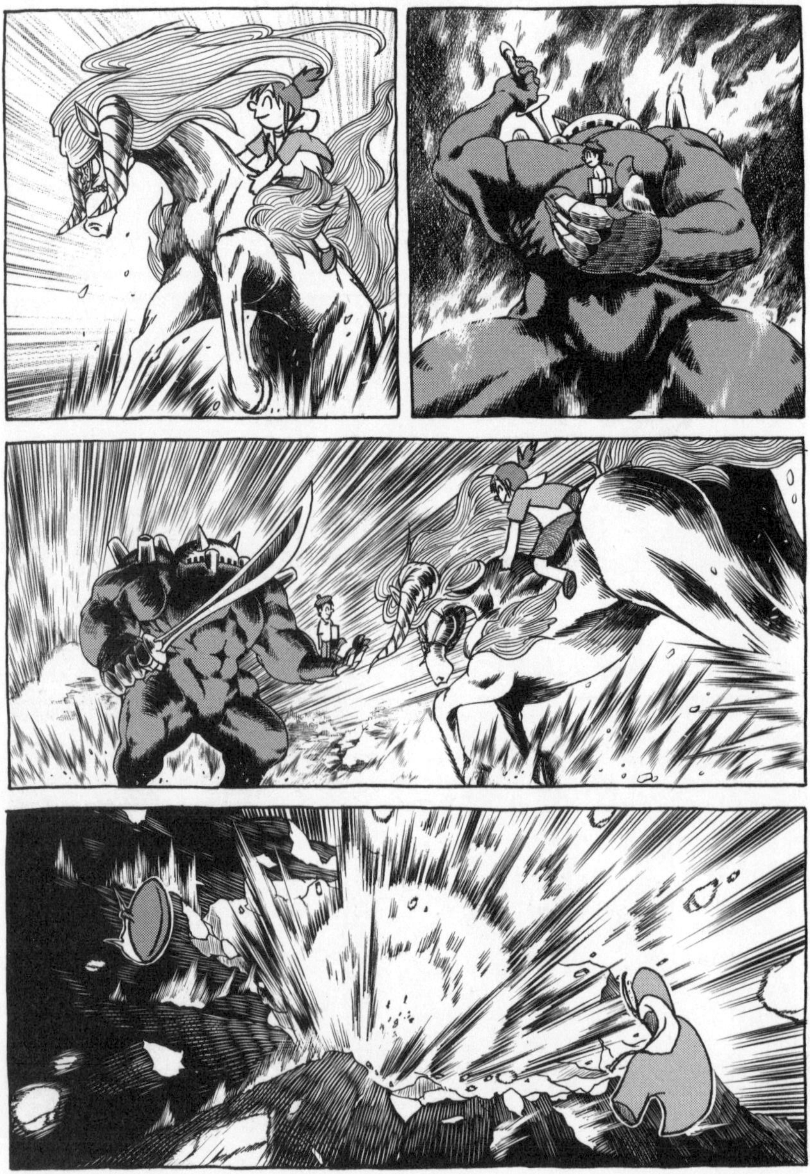

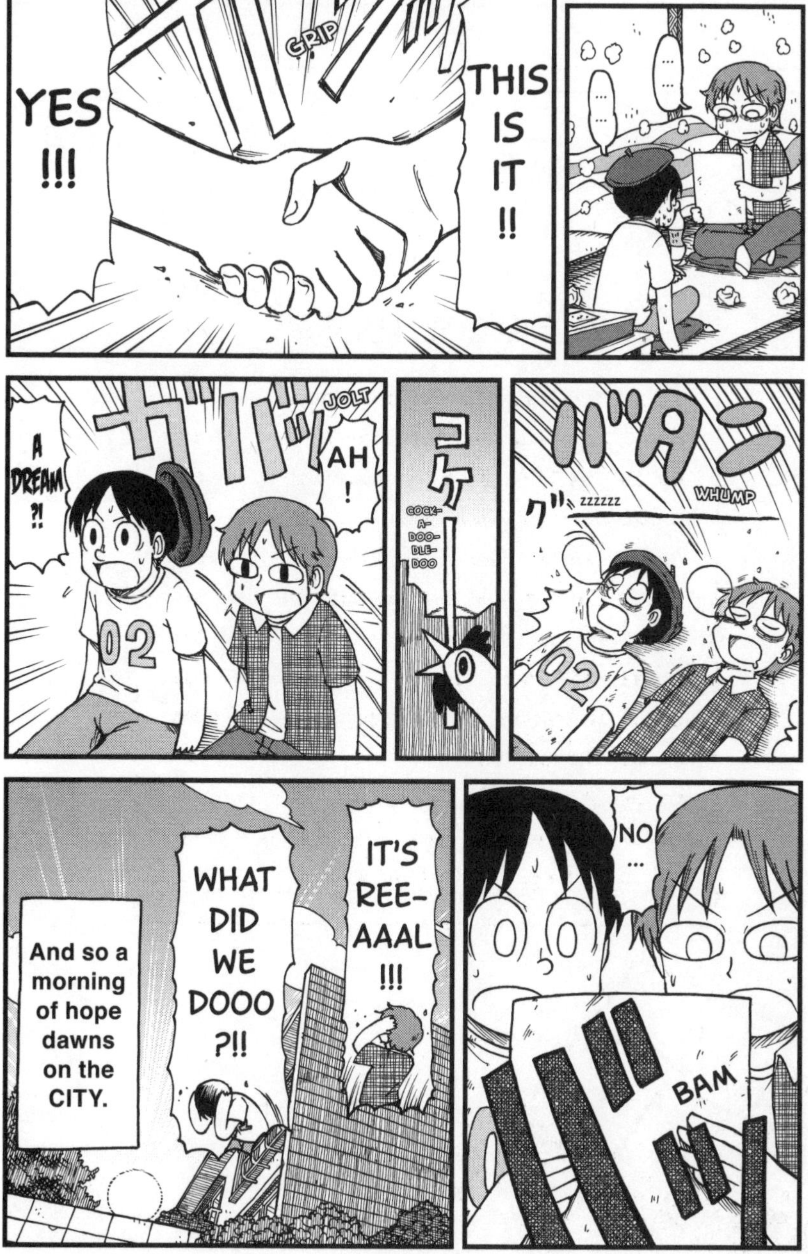
…
…
THIS IS IT!!
GRIP
YES!!!
WHUMP
zzzzzz
COCK-A-DOODLE-DOO
JOLT
AH!
A DREAM?!
NO…
BAM
IT'S REE-AAAL!!!
WHAT DID WE DOOO?!!
And so a morning of hope dawns on the CITY.

CONTENTS

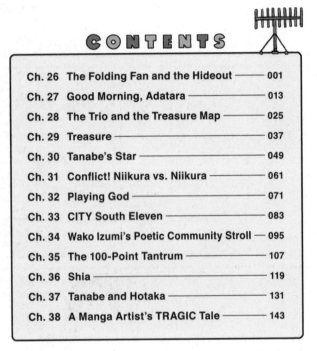

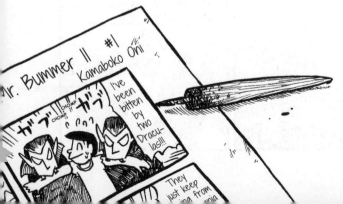

Mr. Bummer || #1 Kamaboko Oni

I've been bitten by two Draculas!!!

CHOMP!! ガブ ガブ CHOMP!!

They just keep

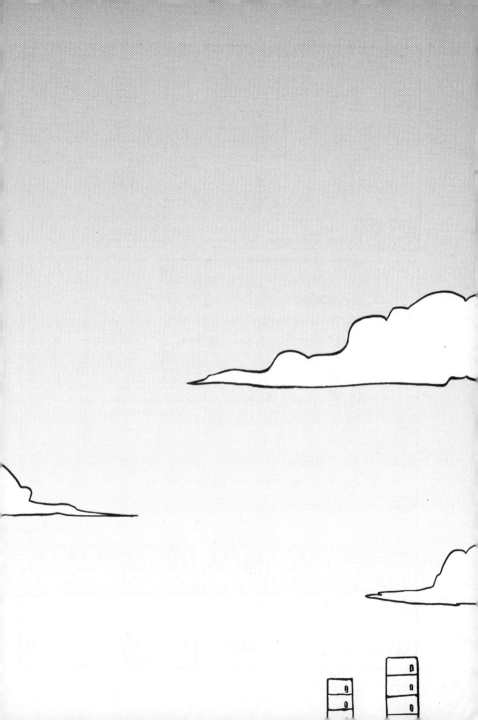

SWEET OLIVE MANOR
101
FRI
Ah!
!!!
I fell asleep.
Huh?
Where's Nagumo?
SLIDE
スス
And Wako?
I guess they left.
YAAAWN~
Chapter 39 To Be Continued

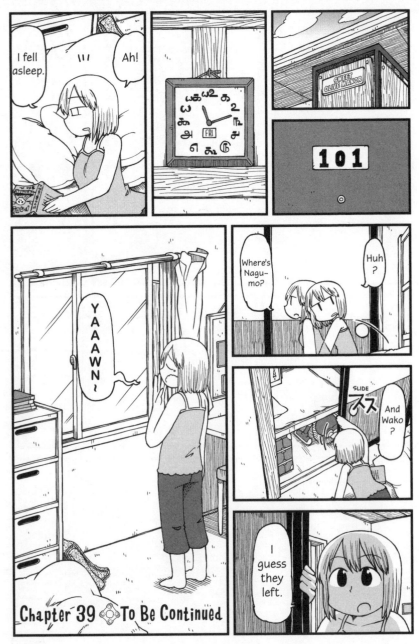

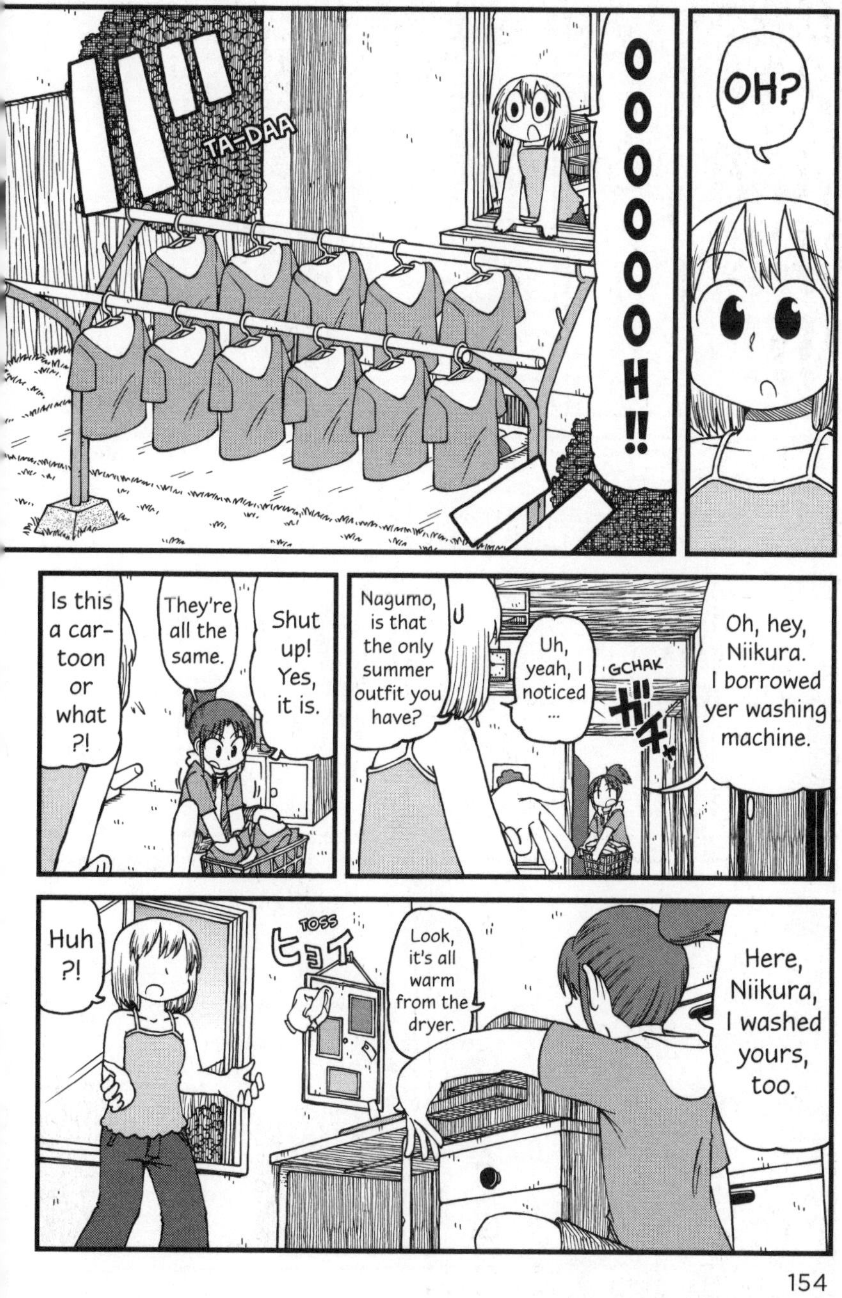
OH?
OOOOOOOH!!
TA-DAA
Oh, hey, Niikura. I borrowed yer washing machine.
GCHAK
ガチャ
Uh, yeah, I noticed ...
Nagumo, is that the only summer outfit you have?
Shut up! Yes, it is.
They're all the same.
Is this a cartoon or what?!
Here, Niikura, I washed yours, too.
Look, it's all warm from the dryer.
TOSS
ヒョイ
Huh?!

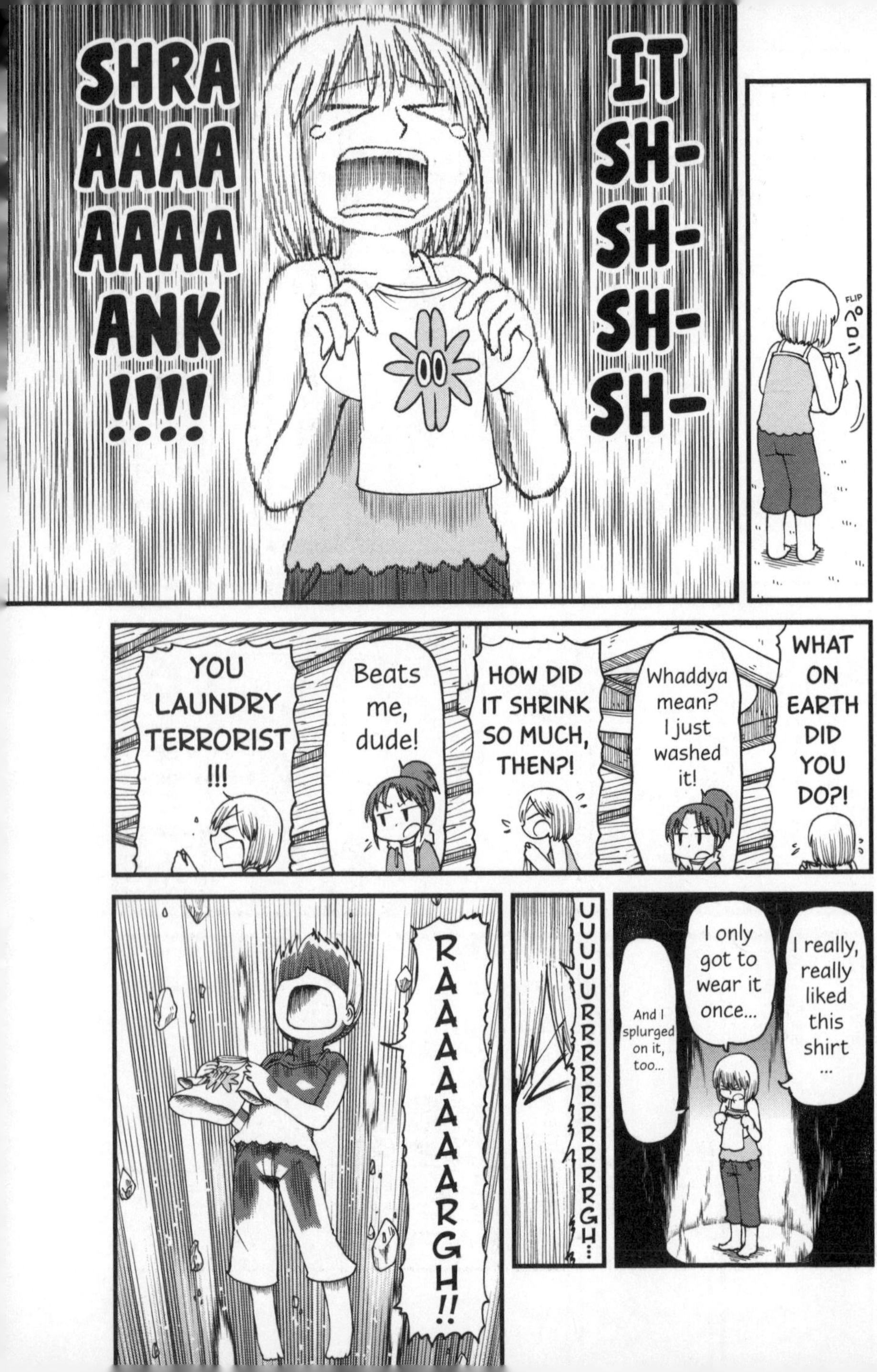
FLIP
ぺロ
IT SH-SH-SH-SH-
SHRAAAAAAAAAAANK!!!!
WHAT ON EARTH DID YOU DO?!
Whaddya mean? I just washed it!
HOW DID IT SHRINK SO MUCH, THEN?!
Beats me, dude!
YOU LAUNDRY TERRORIST!!!
I really, really liked this shirt...
I only got to wear it once...
And I splurged on it, too...
UUUUURRRRRRRRRGH...
RAAAAAAARGH!!

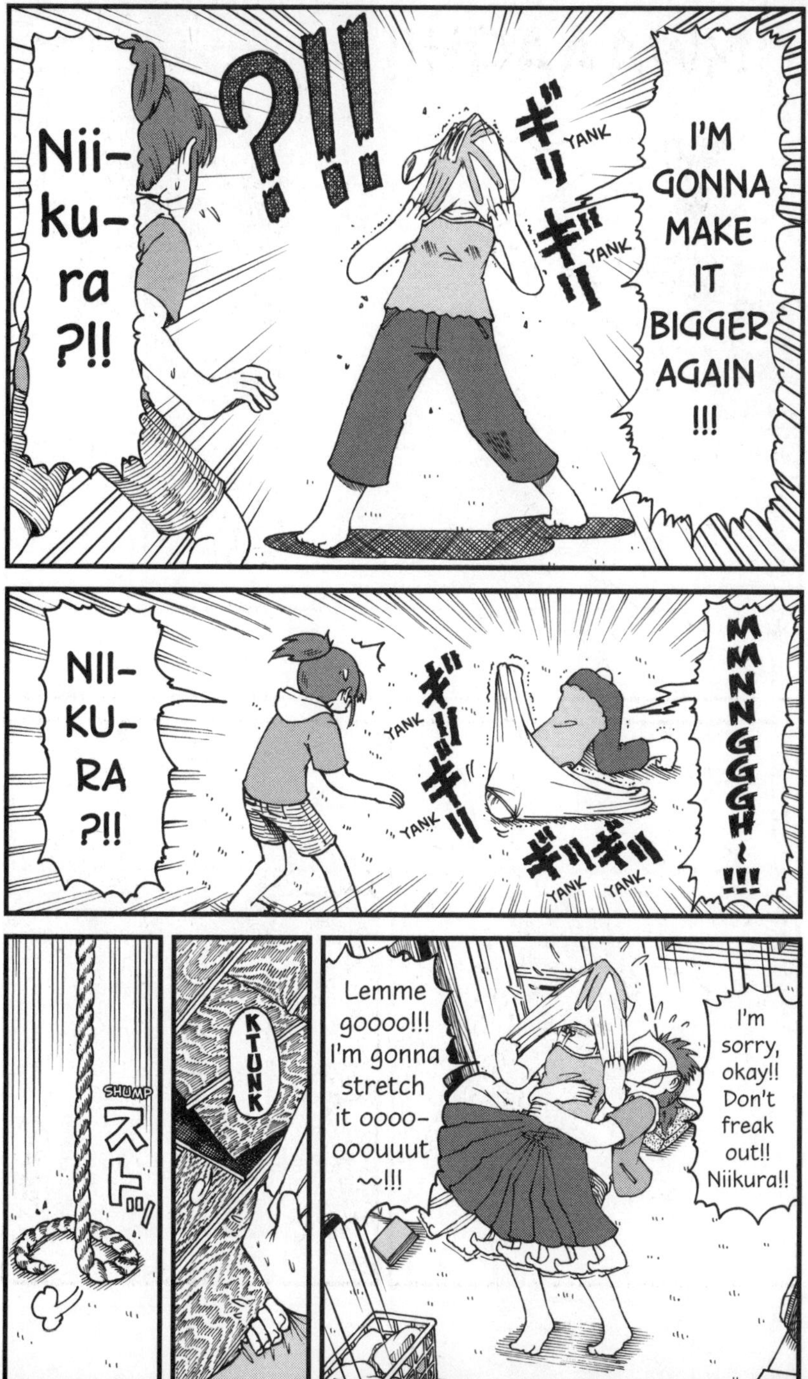

I'M GONNA MAKE IT BIGGER AGAIN!!!
ギリ YANK
ギリ YANK
?!!
Niikura?!!
MMNNGGGH~!!!
ギリ YANK
ギリ YANK
ギリギリ YANK YANK
NII-KURA?!!
I'm sorry, okay!! Don't freak out!! Niikura!!
Lemme goooo!!! I'm gonna stretch it oooo-oooouuut~!!!
KTUNK
SHUMP
ストッ

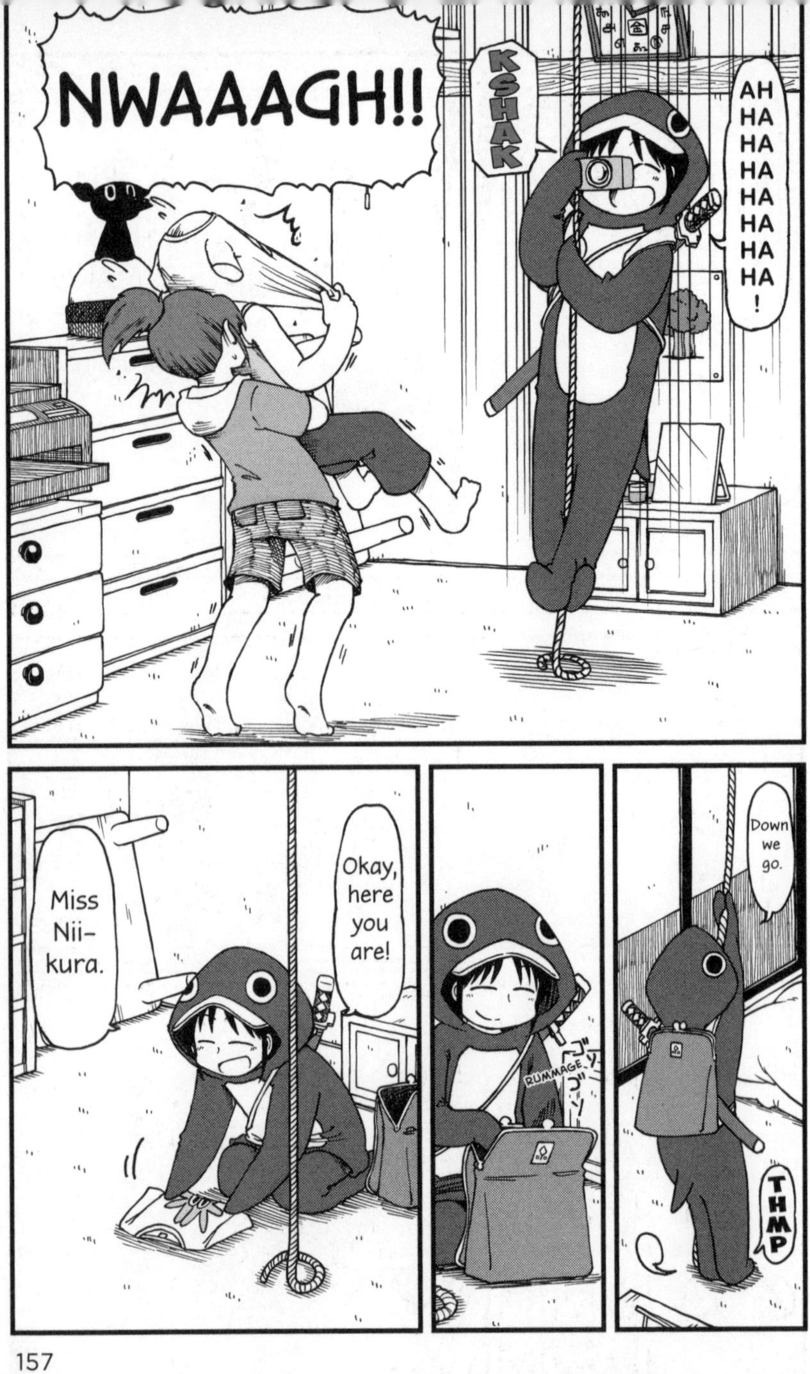
AH HA HA HA HA HA HA HA!
KSHAK
NWAAAGH!!
Down we go.
THMP
RUMMAGE
Okay, here you are!
Miss Nii-kura.

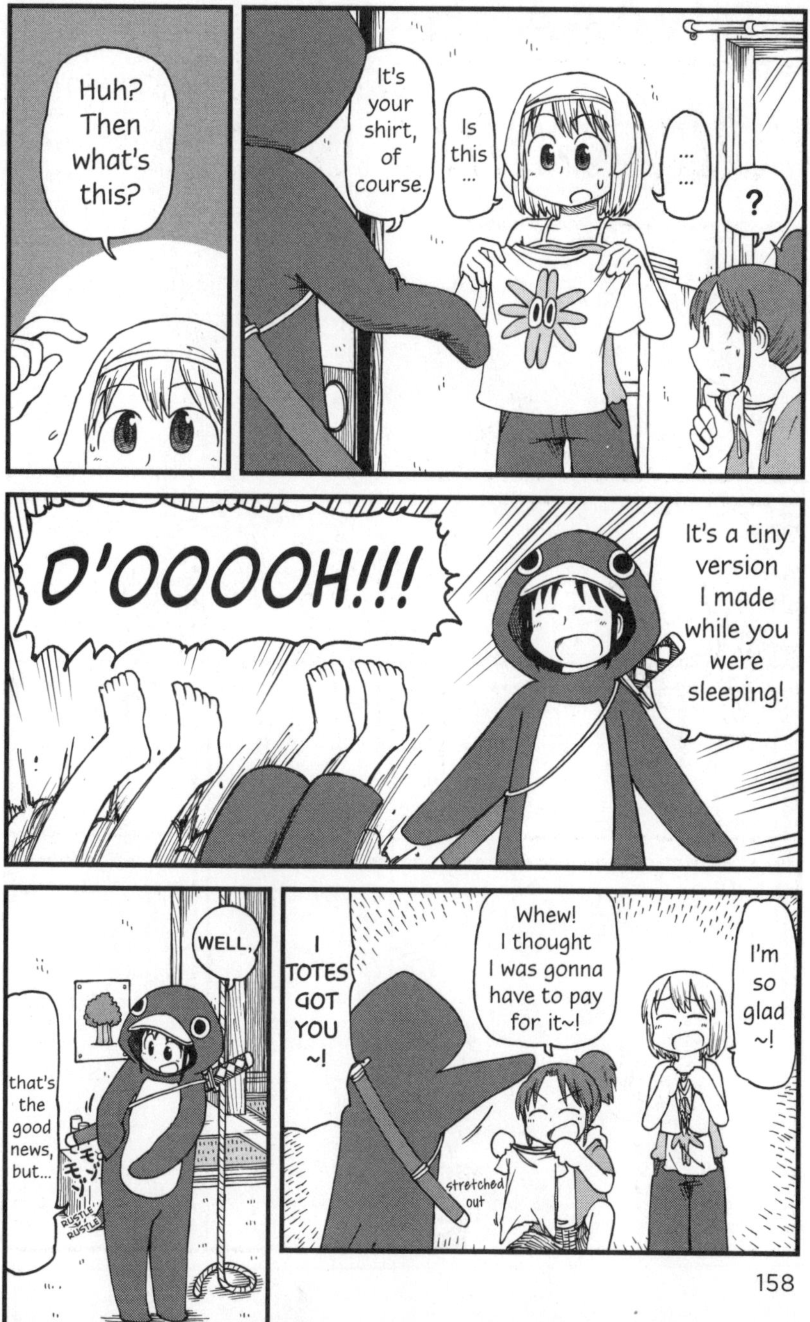
?
…
…
Is this …
It's your shirt, of course.
Huh? Then what's this?
It's a tiny version I made while you were sleeping!
D'OOOOH!!!
I'm so glad ~!
Whew! I thought I was gonna have to pay for it~!
I TOTES GOT YOU ~!
stretched out
WELL,
that's the good news, but...
モゾモゾ
RUSTLE RUSTLE

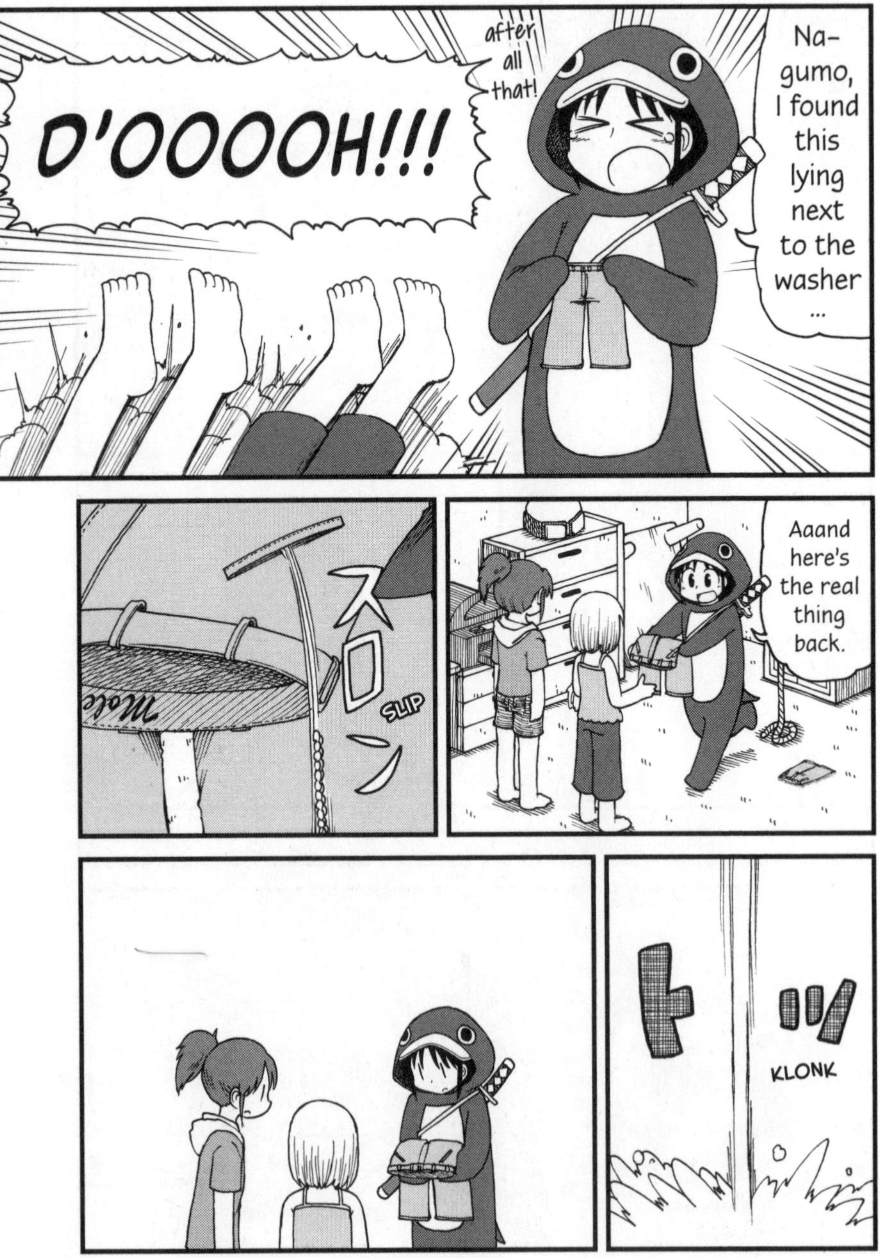
Na-
gumo,
I found
this
lying
next
to the
washer
...
after
all
that!
D'OOOOH!!!
Aaand
here's
the real
thing
back.
スロン
SLIP
トッ
KLONK

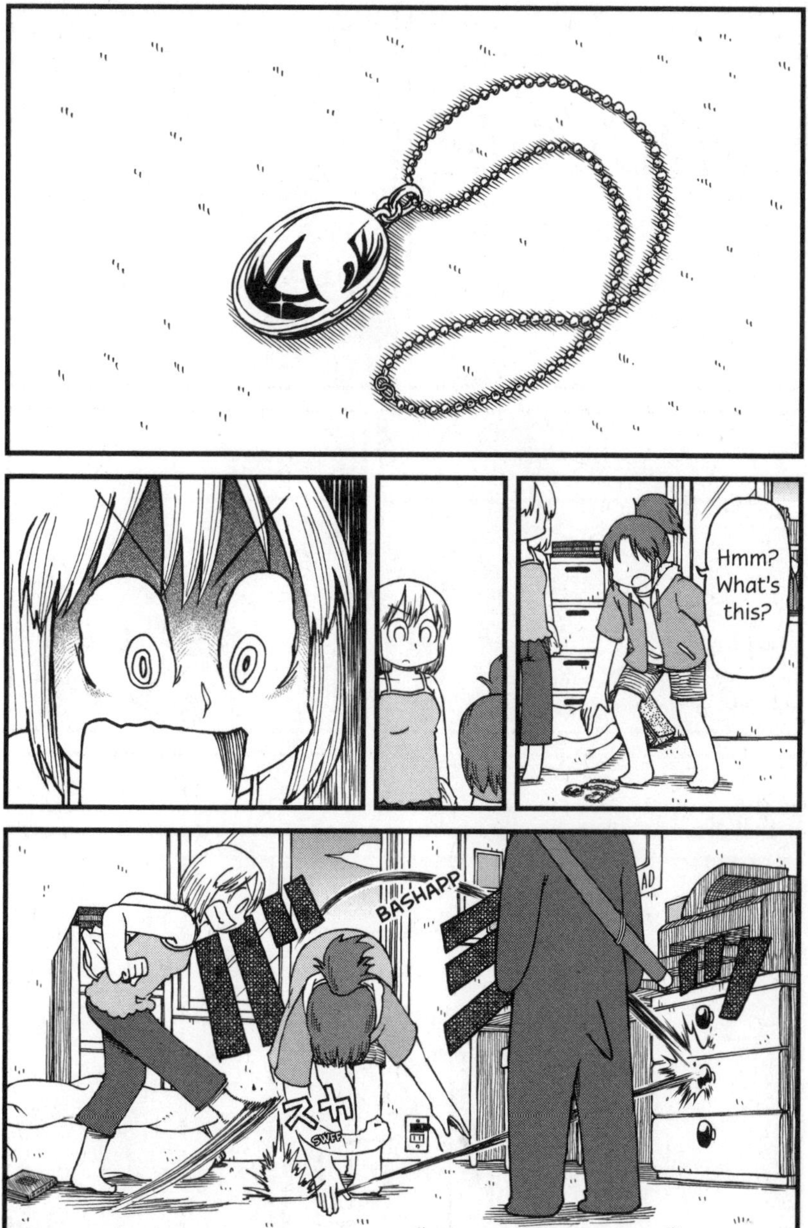
Hmm? What's this?
BASHAPP
スカ
SWFF

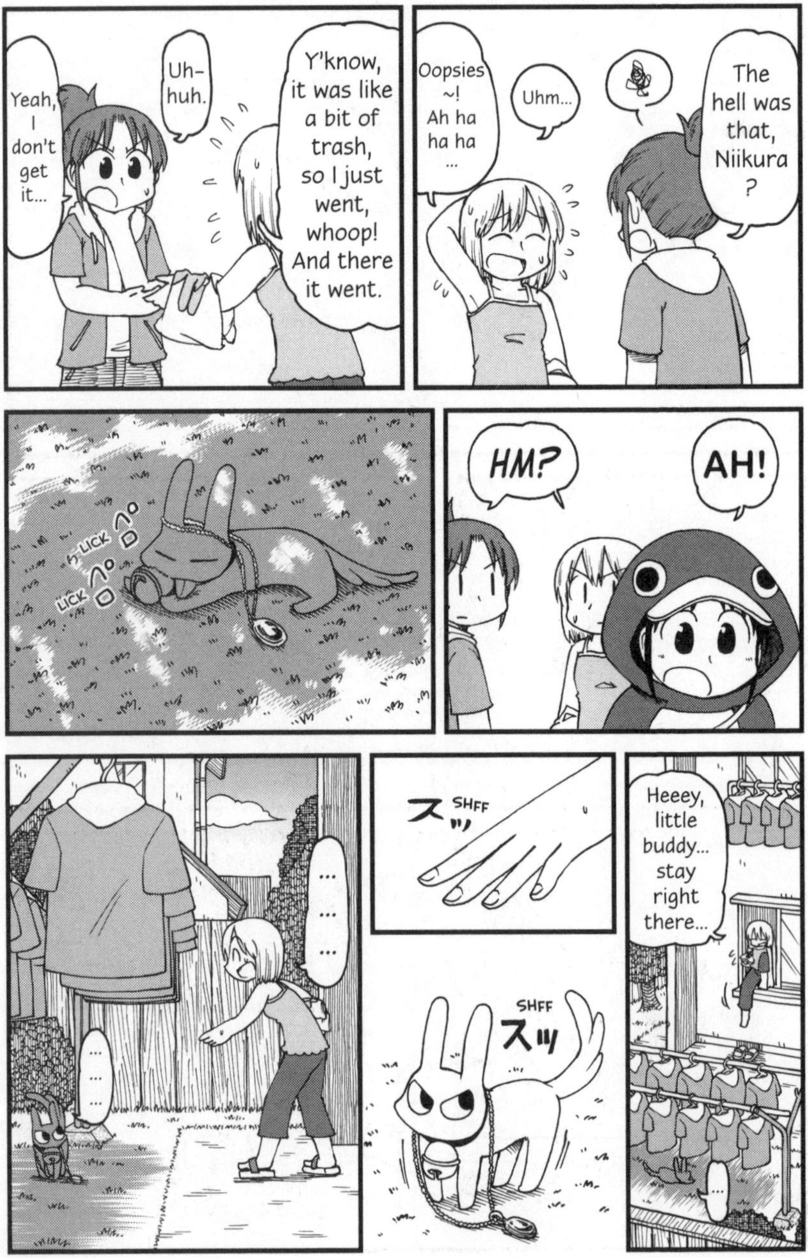

The hell was that, Niikura?
Uhm...
Oopsies~! Ah ha ha ha...
Y'know, it was like a bit of trash, so I just went, whoop! And there it went.
Uh-huh.
Yeah, I don't get it...
AH!
HM?
ペロ LICK
ペロ LICK
Heeey, little buddy... stay right there...
...
スッ SHFF
スッ SHFF
... ...
... ...

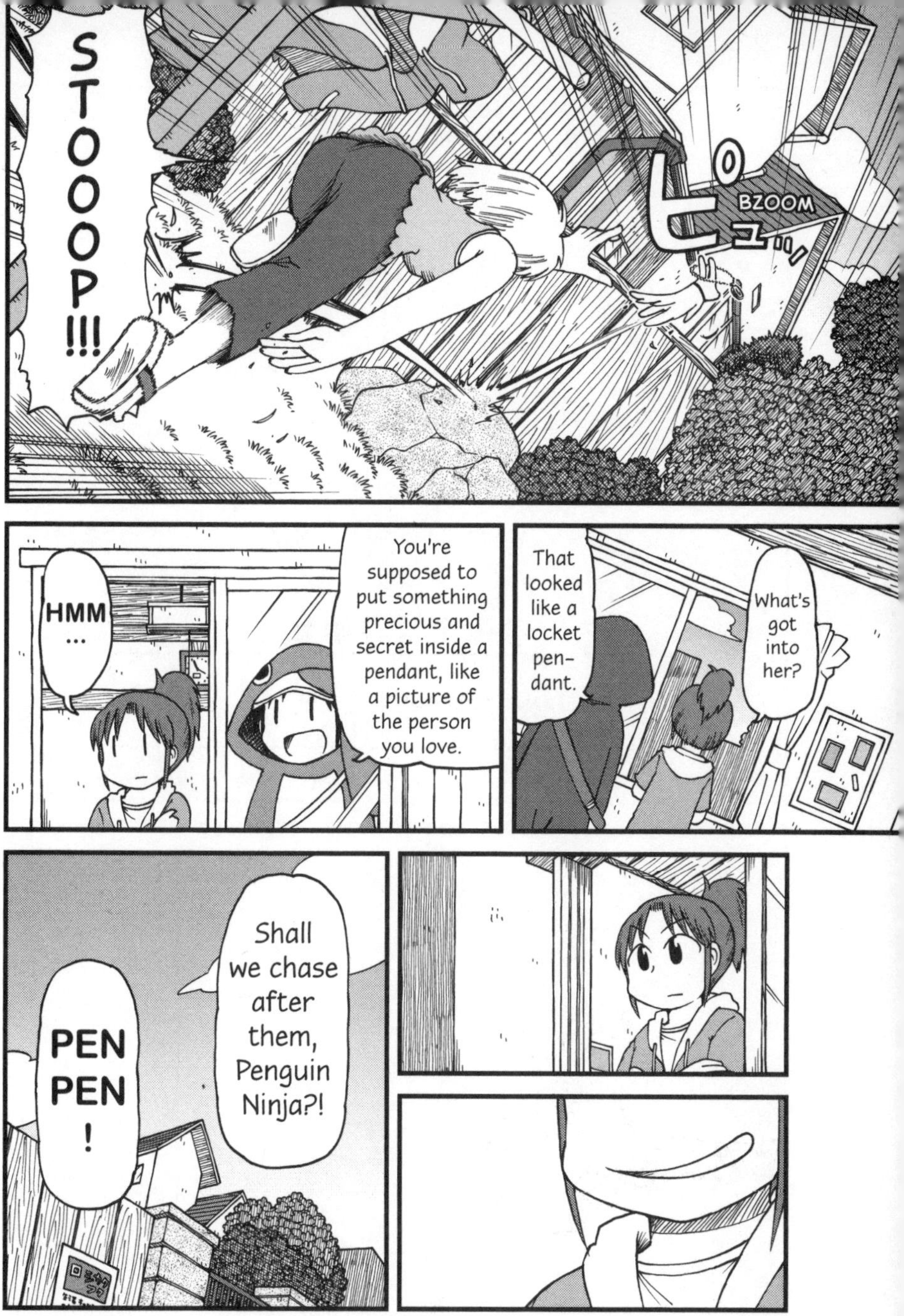
BZOOM
STOOOP!!!
What's got into her?
That looked like a locket pen-dant.
You're supposed to put something precious and secret inside a pendant, like a picture of the person you love.
HMM...
Shall we chase after them, Penguin Ninja?!
PEN PEN!

CONTENTS

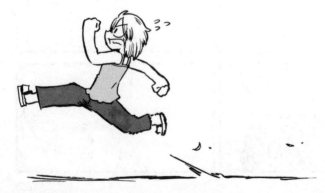

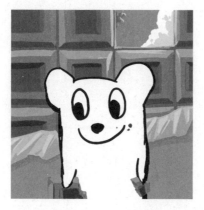

Recent Author Photo

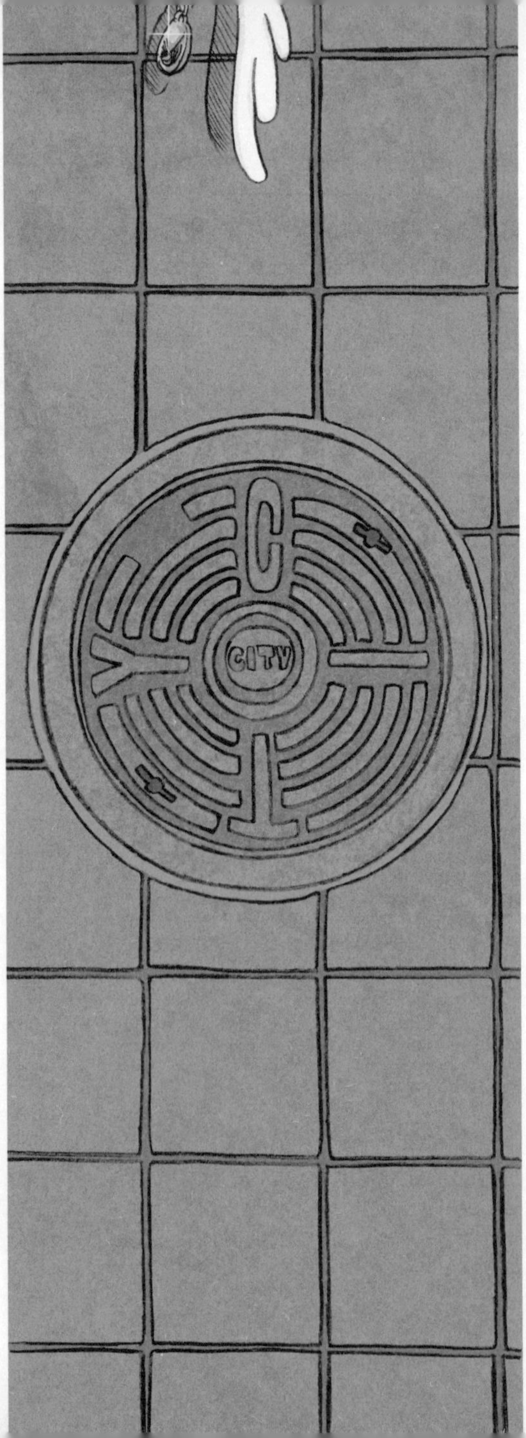
CITY

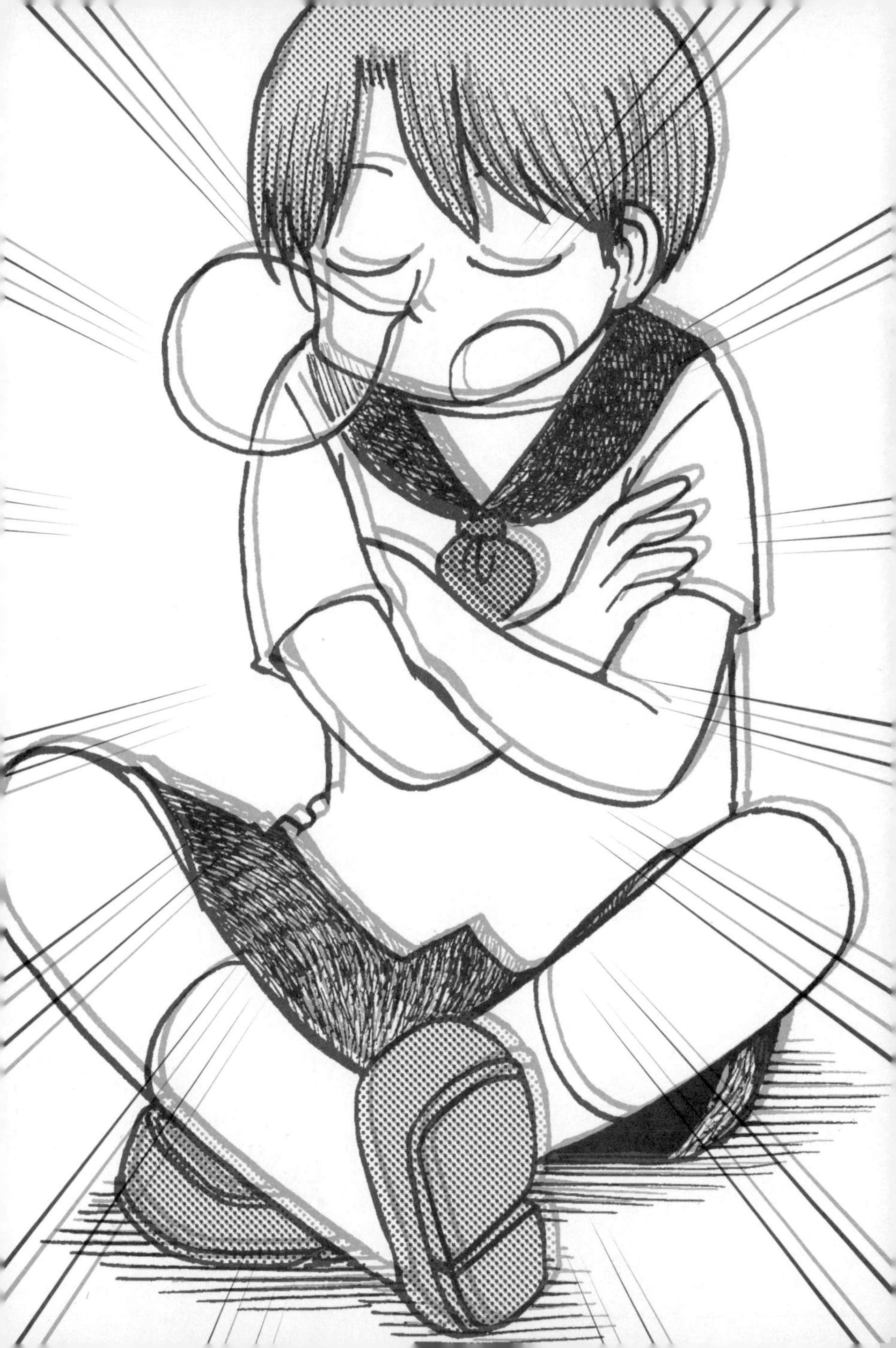

CITY

3

RE A CH
MAH JONGG
TANIGAWA

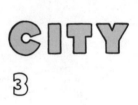

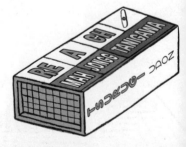

define "ordinary"

in this just-surreal-enough take on the "school genre" of manga, a group of friends (which includes a robot built by a child professor) grapples with all sorts of unexpected situations in their daily lives as high schoolers.

the gags, jokes, puns and random haiku keep this series off-kilter even as the characters grow and change. check out this new take on a storied genre and meet the new ordinary.

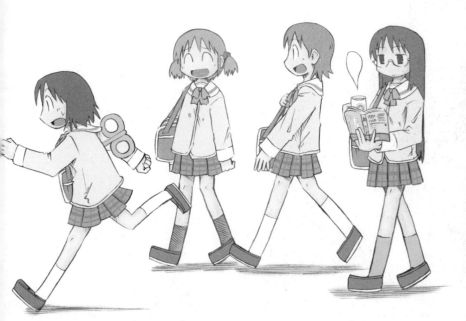

all volumes
available now!

nichijou

my ordinary life

keiichi
arawi

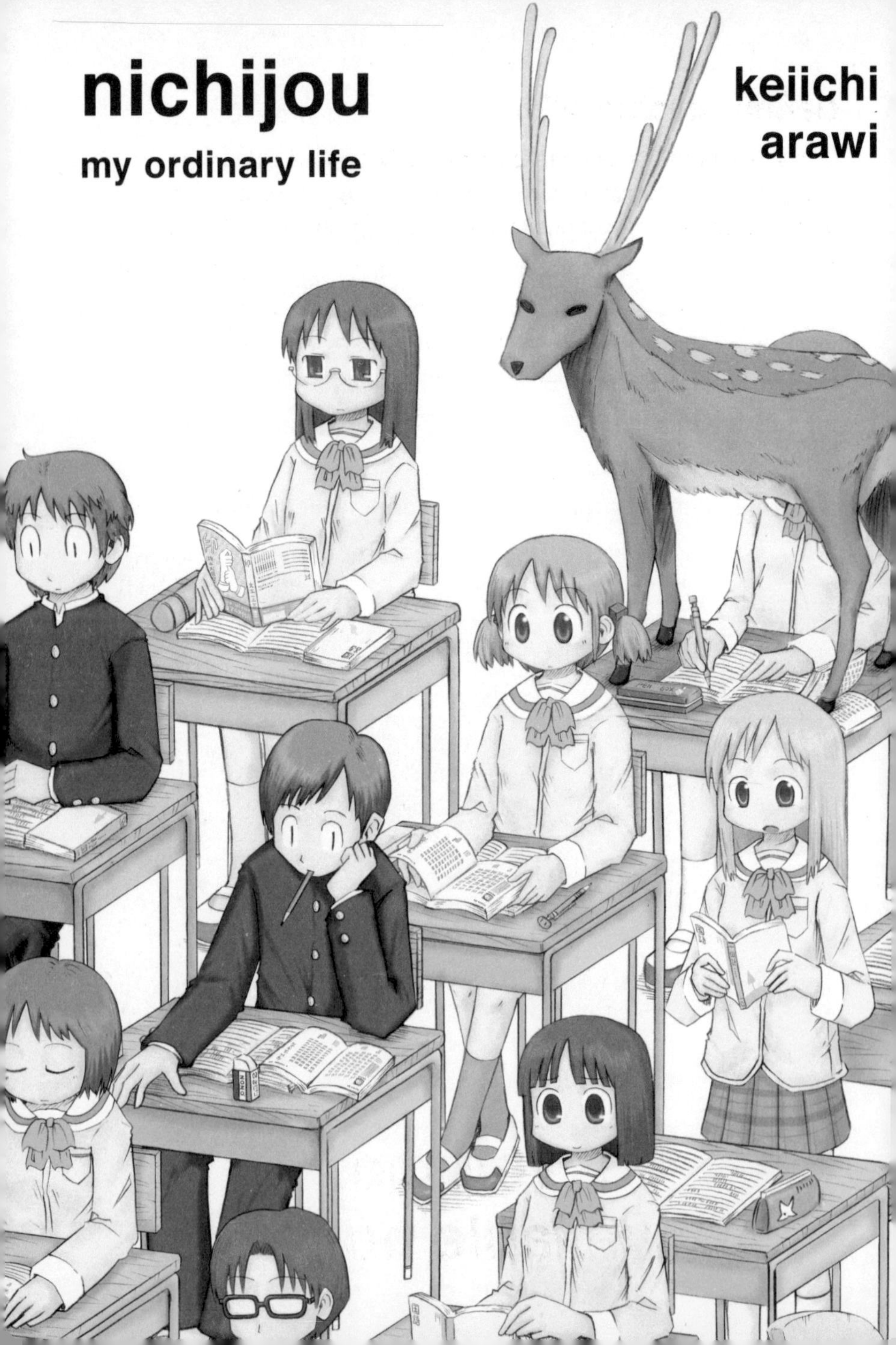

The follow up to the hit manga series ***nichijou***, ***Helvetica Standard*** is a full-color anthology of Keiichi Arawi's comic art and design work. Funny and heartwarming, ***Helvetica Standard*** is a humorous look at modern day Japanese design in comic form.

Helvetica Standard is a deep dive into the artistic and creative world of Keiichi Arawi. Part comic, part diary, part art and design book, ***Helvetica Standard*** is a deconstruction of the world of ***nichijou***.

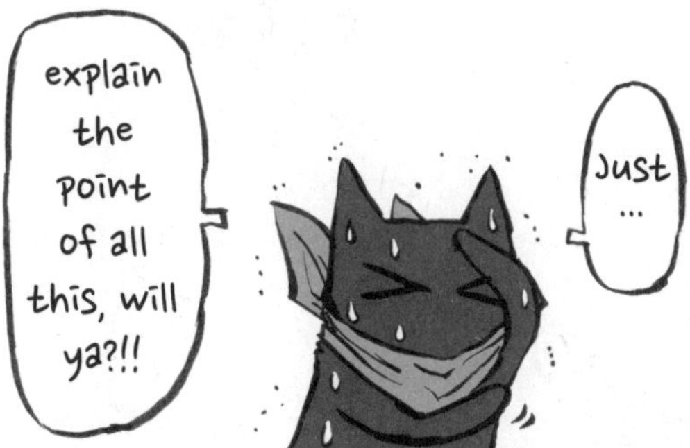

explain the point of all this, will ya?!!
Just ...

Helvetica Standard
Bold

Helvetica Standard
Italic

Both Parts Available Now!

Keiichi Arawi

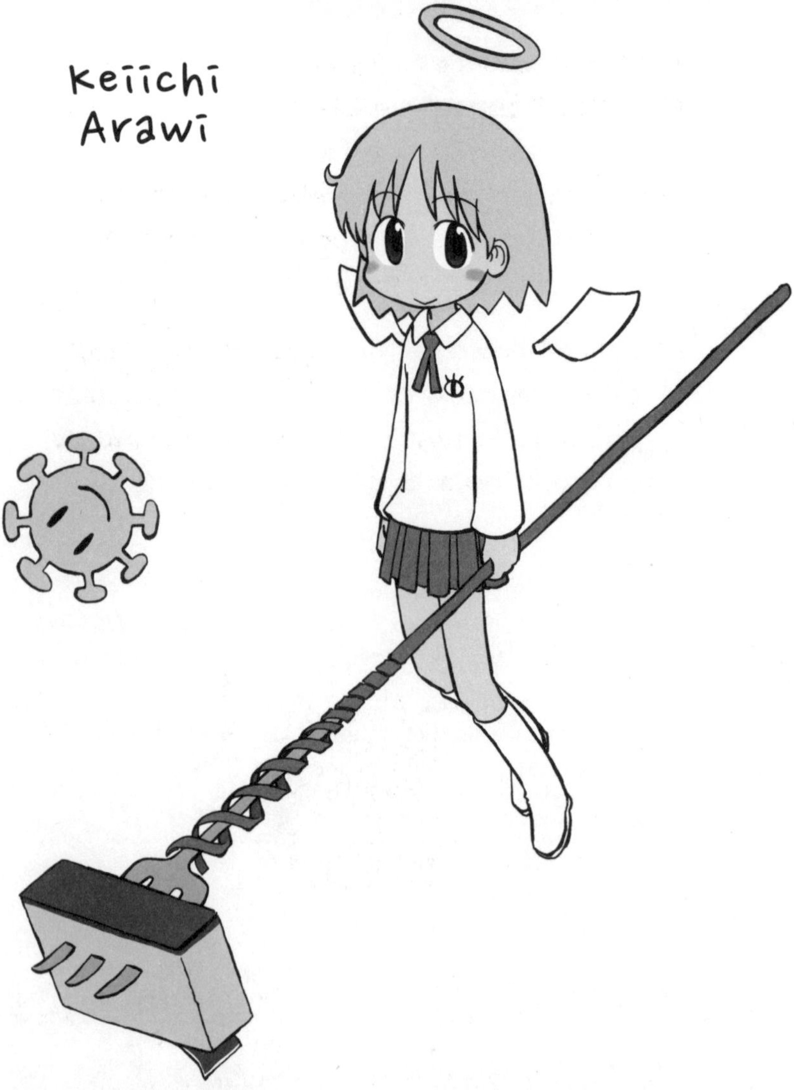

Helvetica Standard

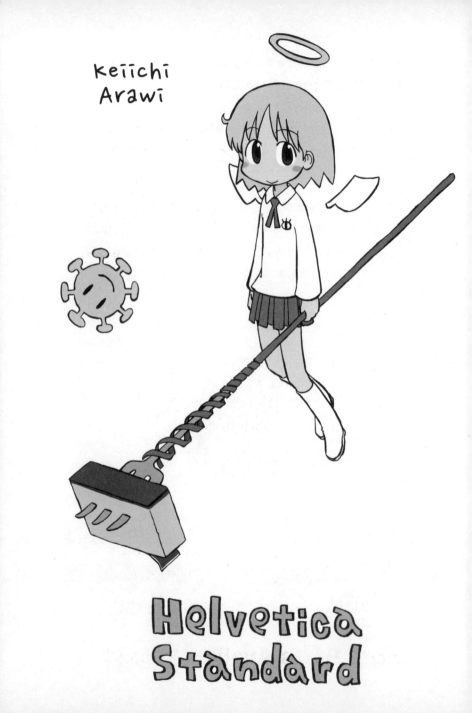

CITY 3

A Vertical Comics Edition

Translation: Jenny McKeon
Production: Grace Lu
          Hiroko Mizuno

© Keiichi ARAWI 2017
First published in Japan in 2017 by Kodansha, Ltd., Tokyo
Publication rights for this English edition arranged through Kodansha, Ltd., Tokyo
English language version produced by Vertical, Inc.

Translation provided by Vertical Comics, 2018
Published by Vertical Comics, an imprint of Vertical, Inc., New York

Originally published in Japanese as *CITY 3* by Kodansha, Ltd.
CITY first serialized in *Morning,* Kodansha, Ltd., 2016-

This is a work of fiction.

ISBN: 978-1-947194-18-2

Manufactured in Canada

First Edition

Vertical, Inc.
451 Park Avenue South
7th Floor
New York, NY 10016
www.vertical-comics.com

Vertical books are distributed through Penguin-Random House Publisher Services.